I MUST BE
A MERMAID

I MUST BE A MERMAID

Deep Fear of Shallow Living

CHARLENE HICKEY

'I Must be a mermaid, Rango. I have no fear of depths and a great fear of shallow living'
- Anaïs Nin (1903 – 1977)

The stories in this book reflect the author's recollection of events. Some names have been changed to protect the privacy of those depicted.

For Tony, my Merman.

*Thank you, in advance, to my family who I know will
forgive my excessively free-spirited story
and sharing of it!*

Contents

CHAPTER I

Little Red

1983

Sitting poolside in her gold triangle bikini, Mum looked to me like an angel with her slender sun-kissed body and bleach blonde hair. Dipping her feet in the water, she watched me on a towel nearby. I was easily pleased, always a quiet child. It was normal for me to sit in silence, playing with my toys or scribbling on paper. She smiled, closed her eyes and tilted her face towards the bright Ibizan sun, all the tension slipping away from her body in the healing warmth. A mere second passed before she heard a small *plop.* Knowing instantly, as only mothers can, that the 'plop' had a deadly ring to it, her head spun to the towel where I had been. Empty. Her eyes darted back, searching the surface of the

1

pool. Nothing. Panicking, when I was nowhere to be seen, her heart suddenly sank. As had I.

Glaring into the water, she saw an unusual sight. There I was, sitting on the pool floor as if it was the most normal thing in the world. Immediately, she jumped in, scooped me up and held me up in the air, looking in shock at my blinking wet eyes.

"You ok poppet? You alright?" she stammered frantically. I was fine. Unlike my poor mum who was petrified. The flicker of time I had taken to get into the water was inconceivable. I didn't hear this story until I was much older. She was, understandably, reluctant to tell it. Apparently, when she caught sight of me on the blue tiled floor, I looked as calm as if I was simply watching TV in the living room. Maybe I slipped and was in shock. Maybe it wasn't an accident at all. Maybe I remembered the sensation of floating during Mum's pregnancy and I wanted to be back in the comfort and security of the womb. Maybe I felt safe under the water. Maybe I felt at home. If truth be told, for years—decades—after I was pulled from the bottom of that pool, I struggled to ever feel at home again.

2015

"Need directions?" I said to him quietly with a smile, before heading towards the lounge area. I'd always been confident with men, totally comfortable flirting and making the first move. It never occurred to me to wait for them to approach me first. What was there to lose? I mean, who *doesn't* like being chatted up? It's flattering. It's a bit of harmless fun. I'd check for the white tan line or indent of a missing wedding ring, of course.

I first saw Will in the Spring, standing in reception, looking lost in a West London hotel. As I left my room on the top floor and walked from the lift, I quickly deduced that he was young, good-looking, clean shaven and athletic. Casually dressed in leisure wear, yet immaculate, peering from beneath heavy eyebrows in that typically cute, bad boy way. His eyes darted towards the Receptionist who glanced up at us, then to a group of lads at the bar who were revving up for a night out.

"Just meeting the boys for a stag do," he said and flashed a cheeky grin.

"Well, I won't keep you then." I lowered my eyes in mock disappointment and turned to walk away.

"I'm Will," he said quickly in a less cocky tone, and followed me to the leather sofas like a puppy. The predictable flirty chat began. Soon enough, we were in my room.

"I can tell you're in the military. Very well trained, soldier!" I laughed, as he took his perfectly clean shoes off and placed them neatly under the desk.

"Ha! Yeah …old habits…" he said.

I sat on the bed, leaning back on my arms. He looked right into me as he came closer. His eyes were dark brown, they looked kind but solemn. At just twenty-eight years old he had an even younger face, and with a small dimple in his chin and freshly barbered hair, he could have stepped out of a 1950s film.

He was full of passion, full of energy. I'd forgotten what twenty-something boys were like. I was thirty-four. Not a huge age gap but there is a noticeable difference between men in their twenties and men forty-plus. I think I'd call it *eagerness*. They may sometimes lack knowledge of the complexities of women, which usually comes with the more mature or worldly man, but they made up for it with sheer stamina. In the moments when we were catching our breath, he'd stare deeply into my eyes again. I couldn't believe it was so intense. I couldn't believe my luck that he was so gorgeous.

Exhausted, we laid on the bed talking. My visions kicked in immediately, although this time they were out of focus. I couldn't 'see' him; I couldn't read his 'story.' But there was sadness beneath the smiles. I could tell he concealed heavy emotions, so I kept the conversation light. I told him about my life, the way I lived, well, most of it; and what I wanted to achieve. I told him more than I ever told guys I'd just met. When I asked him about the Army, in true squaddie style, he gave short answers and then reverted back to me.

"You're perfect," he said suddenly.

"No, I'm NOT!" I shrieked. "Far from it!" I glanced to the bedside drawer, remembering how, just moments before I met him, I'd been reading a book on how to heal from eating disorders. I'd stashed it away before leaving the room. Bulimia wasn't very sexy.

"You are," he said, dressing back in his clothes which hung over the chair. "I've gotta go already. I don't want to, but I have to, I'm really sorry."

"It's fine," I shrugged. "You don't have to apologise." We were both adults, we knew what this was about. I would be lying, though, if I said I didn't hope to see him again. I hadn't felt this strongly about anyone in a long time. Exchanging numbers, he promised to come and see me again when he next got time off.

"I can't always use my phone," he said. "I'll message you, soon as I can."

I didn't know anything about army life. This was my first experience with a military man. I guessed that communication could be tricky, which added to the excitement. My heart thumped as soon as he left. *A soldier? What was I getting myself into?* A mixture of anxiety and joy rolled around my body as I lay there watching my imagination spin. It didn't matter how detached I tried to be, the same old film-roll of what might be always played out in my mind whenever I met someone new.

Through Summer and Autumn, we only reunited a handful of times. We'd cocoon ourselves in hotel rooms for precious hours until the minute he had to leave again. It was intoxicating waiting for him to arrive, euphoric when we finally let loose on each other.

"Do you believe in destiny?" I asked him while nestled in his arms.

"I don't know," he said seriously. "I mean, your actions determine your life's outcome, don't they?" He stared at the painting of a black swan hanging on the hotel wall.

"Or maybe we all have a fate, no matter what we do?" I said, stroking his fingers.

"Maybe you're destined to be a beautiful swan, even if you're an ugly fucker!!" I cackled.

Will burst into laughter. "You always see the bright side, don't you? You're so positive." He squeezed me tight. I wondered if I should tell him that it hadn't always been like that, that I used to suffer with depression, that it was meditation, magic and prayer that saved me. But I always hesitated. He seemed such a realist. I couldn't very well say, *all you need is love,* when he was preparing for war.

Once again, the part we dreaded came too soon and my tummy tightened, watching Will pick up his coat to leave. "Let me know when you're back at the barracks" I said.

"Sure. Remember though babe, I can't always use my phone," he sighed. I had become used to this conversation. I still wasn't entirely sure what he did when he was away, but I knew his current work was some sort of security out in Iraq. He said he wasn't in too much danger but I still worried.

"Yeah, I know, I know," I whined with a sad pout.

"God, you're so hot!" He said, grabbing my waist which was synched in with a black basque, pulling me towards him. "How the hell am I going to be able to stop thinking about you in those stockings? I wish I could be with you every day," he said, bowing his head into my chest. He told me that he'd never met anyone like me. He told me with melancholy eyes that I melted his heart. Each time he'd say things which plunged me deeper into a dream-like state.

Once he left, I'd wonder around town in a haze, visiting galleries, New-Age shops, erotic boutiques and bookstores, soaking up every minute of city life while I could. With all the entrepreneurs and creatives and young minds buzzing around, you could almost taste the diversity and hear the hum of new ideas in the air. Before I met Will I had been flitting back and forth between the island and the UK quite frequently. I was bored in Jersey, restless with small-town living, fed up with bumping into people left, right and centre, who knew me, knew my business or wanted to know my business. I'm not being rude, that's just the way it is in a tiny place. It's a microcosm, a beautiful miniature world in which One can forget that the Universe exists beyond the seawater mote. A thirty-minute flight over to the mainland brought me space, open minds and, most importantly, anonymity. I'd pick an area of London and book a room or short-stay apartment, using it as a base to explore for a day or two. The city excited me, it made me feel alive and reminded me of my teenage years back home when I'd sneak off to sweaty clubs to dance all night with beautiful strangers.

Back on the island, everything felt slower and so far-removed from the things I'd done in London. I threw myself into my artwork and counted the days until I'd go back. I was noticeably different. At a Summer music festival by the sea, my girlfriends nudged me as cute guys looked my way, but I had no interest. Contrary to my usual frisky behaviour, all I could think about was him. It was such a relief to feel free from the pursuit of attention. As far as I was concerned, I was saving myself a whole lot of wasted time, energy and disappointment by staying away from other men while I waited for my soldier. These boys didn't know the meaning of romance; they were too busy playing the field, or PlayStation, to understand what I longed for.

Six months later

Sitting in the pub toilet cubicle, I read the text messages which had just come through on my phone, over and over again. I tried to absorb all the words and stop the sentences from jumping around like sand-flies, but my head spun, heart raced, and everything swirled around me. I had known something dark was on the horizon, the Tarot had told me. The *Death* card had plagued my readings for months now. I knew deep down what was coming, but I wouldn't let the thoughts penetrate my brain.

Will was not in the Army. He wasn't a soldier at all. He was, in fact, a builder. And he had a girlfriend. And he was a father to a young child. The Tarot image on the *Death* card — the Grim Reaper riding the horse — very rarely meant actual physical death. More commonly, it was some sort of ending or big transformation. He and his girlfriend had been 'going through a rough patch' apparently. That's when he met me and we started the so-called, long-distance relationship: me in the English Channel, him in the 'barracks' or 'deployed overseas'. He told me all of this over text. He couldn't speak to me because he was 'so ashamed'. He didn't seem to feel much shame while his cock was in my mouth.

I felt like the biggest idiot that ever existed. I wanted to cry. I wanted to laugh. I wanted to punch his face. I wanted to punch *my* face. Why ON EARTH had I expected him to be different? Why was I shocked? Why *would* he tell me the truth? We had met in totally promiscuous circumstances and, as usual, I got carried away and dived straight in the deep end.

It was all so obvious now. My friends had sceptically quizzed me about this new love of mine who rarely made contact outside the hotel rooms. I had been so blissfully, romantically enfurled in my dream, and my life had become so enchanted since I met him. My creativity flourished, unique opportunities floated my way, I was focused and driven with my art and design work more than ever before. I had been craving romance in my life when I met Will and the soldier story did the trick.

It was as if, in having this person in my life — who was never actually really there — created a big gap. A vast space. A deep well. For love and positivity to come pouring in. Love is such potent fuel for motivation, even when it is all a fantasy. But the dream was shattered and my well was empty again.

"Why Will? I just don't understand," I poured out in my replies to his texts. It was a futile question; he was quite simply, just another bad boy. But our connection had seemed so real.

"Why did you need to do that?... tell all those lies? Why didn't you just break up with your girlfriend? Why couldn't you just be yourself with me?"

How could I possibly be with a girl like you...just being me? I'm nothing, he wrote back.

Will had been feeling depressed for the best part of the year when I met him that afternoon in London. He had not been looking for a new relationship and definitely hadn't expected to meet someone who would fall for him. When I showed genuine interest, he didn't want to be himself. He wanted to be someone purposeful, someone worthy. He remembered his good friend in the Army, the way he always got so much attention and admiration. Without thinking twice, he adopted a new persona. Who was I kidding anyway? I was basically leading a double life too; my stays in the city were an escape. I felt like someone else, I even *looked* like someone else. My London self was unwaveringly confident, sexy and assured. My Jersey self, showed every flaw, every weakness, and never truly fit in with the islanders, despite my yearning to. Maybe I deserved the deception. Maybe it was karma.

Maybe he was just a dick.

I should have known there was trouble when I saw nothing but grey mist and shadows as I looked for his *story*.

I felt numb as I read his messages over and over again. How many times could I get this wrong? I had been so naïve again. The last guy I'd dated had used me for a plaything and here I was once more, a discarded toy. I used to laugh at the naked photo requests from men at midnight and the ex-wives calling during sex. I got a kick out of being the bad girl and prided myself for always being ready for action. I was never one of those girls who needed hours to prepare for a night out. I thought pampering and pruning was over-rated. Shoe-string budgets and backpacking had taught me a lot about simple beauty and spontaneous fun. At the drop of a hat, my long hair was dry shampooed, my eyes were lined with black kohl and the important areas of my body were washed and shaved in record time. But now it all felt so hollow. I wanted to believe in the good in men. But why did they keep letting me down? Why did I keep letting *myself* down by choosing the wrong ones? Why did I keep walking into their traps like Little Red Riding Hood to the wolf?

Will was now just one percent of the hefty proportion of messed-up relationships I'd had — and I'd had enough. Drowning my sorrows in wine with friends after every break-up wasn't funny anymore, it was worrying. My love-life was a whirlpool which was swiftly plummeting me to the ocean floor. I didn't want to drown. I wanted freedom.

I'd been soul-searching for years. Why wasn't I fixed? I'd tried holistic therapies and workshops and retreats and spiritual practices. I'd read a million self-help books. Things changed in other areas of my life, but nothing changed when it came to my dating habits. Was I *attracting* these men? Was I in-fact calling them to me? Did I, on some unconscious level, *want* these men? How did Little Red Riding Hood learn her lesson? Back in University I wrote my final year dissertation on the origins of the Grimm fairy tales, and in some early versions, Little Red was tricked into taking her clothes off and climbing into bed with the wolf. He then ate her alive. *Please don't let me become like her,* I thought. I looked up to the roof of the toilet cubicle for some sort of divine confirmation of my plea being heard.

Pulling myself to my feet, still feeling nauseous, I pushed the door open with my head and wobbled over to the sinks. I stood in front of the mirror, staring into my own red eyes, searching for answers. I heard strange, quiet echoing voices. *It's a message,* I thought. *What's it saying?* I closed my eyes to better concentrate on the sound, as I normally did when receiving words from Spirit, but it was getting louder by the second. Suddenly, a tornado of heels, mini-skirts and big hair fell into the room and snapped me from my trance. Like a weird, abstract music video, two drunk women were now strutting before me, singing an animated rendition of Freddie Mercury's *I Want to Break Free.*

CHAPTER 2

Young, Free and Sexual

I got engaged on my sixteenth birthday. I had been with my boyfriend who was eighteen, for one whole year, an eternity as it felt then. Despite being young, I still maintain that it was actually true love. In fact, I believe that perhaps you can feel the complexities of love even more when you are of a tender age. Life hasn't gotten in the way, or tarnished the purity of your feelings, or made you question something which is so simple.

I was still at school, he was a first year at college. We met while working as sales assistants in a shoe shop in Woking. Our shared hatred for measuring screaming children's toes and the constant search for the left foot among piles of unsteady boxes in the warehouse, created a playful friendship which quickly led to girlfriend-boyfriend status. He'd pick me up from the school gates in his first car and drive us back to his house. Laughing, talking, and trying out 'Position of the Fortnight' from *More Magazine*, we'd make the most of our time alone before his mum got home.

The heavens opened as we walked hand-in-hand back from town, during the gloriously long summer holidays. Torrential rain poured down through the humid sky like a tap, soaking us through. We ran under an oak tree and clutched on to one another, his strong body shielding mine and *Lynx* body spray tingling in my nose. Pressed together, kissing passionately while water ran down our faces, I was infused with ecstasy and a whirlwind tore through my whole being. My heart pounded and I hoped that this was how life would always be from then on. Every spare minute we'd spend in each other's company, and it was with him that I had my first orgasm—with an actual person, not just by myself—which added some substantial weight to my rapturous feelings for him.

We woke up early, squashed together in my single bed on the morning of my sixteenth birthday, Dad still believing that I actually slept on the sofa in the living room when he stayed over. They guessed, of course, that we were having sex, but no one talked about it.

"Mum. I'm going on the pill," I told her suddenly at fifteen years old, while in the passenger seat of the car. And that was that.

He pulled out a gift-wrapped box and I had no idea of what he had planned. A pretty gold ring with a wishbone of chip diamond. Neither gold or diamond were particularly my style back then, I was more of a silver and crystal-wearing hippy girl, but I loved it all the same because of what it meant, because it felt extremely grown up, and that he had saved his hard-earned cash to buy it. Our engagement would be a secret from everyone, except our friends as we knew we'd get ridiculed by the adults and we didn't need their blessing; we knew it was *real*. When he asked me the question, I had no hesitation in answering. This was it. I loved him more than I could imagine loving anyone. He was the one. We would be together forever.

Together forever, that is, until we got bored of each other, and started arguing, and I became miserable, and he flirted with other girls and I broke up with him. I had told him that I hoped to go travelling once I'd finished Art College. He said I was "acting above my station." I was stunned. I didn't know what he meant or where it had come from, but I wasn't going to stick around to find out. All I knew was that it felt horribly crippling, controlling and like something that someone from

Downton Abbey would say. At sixteen years old, before I really knew anything about feminism and the power of the patriarch, even the Spice Girls had taught me that this didn't seem very *Girl Power*. His words scared the hell out of me. They threatened my freedom. They made me flee like a fox and I didn't stop running for another five years.

I'd always had a knowing during my teens that I must educate myself about the world, to learn more than what my immediate surroundings and peers were showing me. I knew there were different ways to live and feel, and something in me was desperate to experience them. After finishing Art school, contrary to what my *ex-fiancée* had told me, I went backpacking with my best friend Lara to South East Asia, New Zealand, Malaysia and Australia. Lara and I met at school when we were thirteen and became soul sisters at first sight. We bonded over the Bunsen Burner in science class and spent a dreamy first summer together, cycling along the leafy Basingstoke canal to and from each other's homes. Our days were spent hanging out at the skateboard ramp ogling boys, smoking badly-rolled weak spliffs and drinking pouches of strawberry daiquiri on sun loungers when our parents were out. We were always looking for excitement, plotting adventures and planning how to see the world. A few years down the line and we'd carry out our biggest mission: 'Escape Woking'.

Jetting off for a year with my partner in crime with nothing but a backpack and less than a thousand pounds in the bank, was the most awesome thing ever and I revelled in the freedom that I felt at last. I was exploring other cultures, other climates, other landscapes. I was also exploring my body. Back home, sex had been limited to the local lads: a mixture of public-school boys, Liam Gallagher wannabees, happy-hardcore ravers; and then there was the Italian community — who did at least have some passion — even if they did tend to have at least three girls on the go at any one time. But moving though countries like Thailand and Indonesia on the shoestring budget routes and hippie trails, where bright young things flocked from all over the world to find a different kind of fun and unusual flavours, we were inundated with advances from far more exotic men. And women.

Being with people who were way more uninhibited or enlightened than I was, pulled me out of my teenage tunnel and pushed me into a much more open-minded world. Beautiful Brazilians danced with me in reggae clubs and made love to me fervidly under moonlight, encouraging me to show off my shape and embrace my curves. My new sexual experiences were proving to me that rounded bellies and jiggly bits and imperfect bodies were all ok. In fact, more than ok. They were real, and real was raw, and raw was wild, and wild was sexy. I felt like the real me had landed.

Travel showed me expansiveness and beauty, spirituality and ritual, divinity and endless possibility. We took long haul flights, island-hopping boats, tin-can tuc-tucs and sleeper trains. We stayed in tents, beach huts, rented apartments and camped out in airports. We visited temples, markets, ceremonies and cities. We saw the brightest textile colours worn by Hindus and smelt the aromas of incense and spices filling the streets. In the tropics I bathed in waterfalls, kayaked in turquoise seas, snorkelled next to huge turtles and skinny-dipped at midnight. In the Subtropics I sunk into natural steaming hot springs and cooled off in the fresh ocean. We walked with backpacks in monsoon storms, blistering heat and freezing cold. We went to bars, clubs and full-moon parties. We made new friends from all over the globe, of all ages and backgrounds. We orienteered ourselves when we were lost. We learnt to hold our own as young female travellers. By nineteen years old, we were unrecognisable as the eighteen-year-olds who had left Heathrow Airport in spotless matching hiking gear.

We headed to Sydney after flying into Brisbane, working our way down the Gold coast on the Greyhound bus via Surfer's Paradise, and based ourselves in Bondi Beach to look for work. Our puny travel budget had dwindled fast since leaving home and we needed some income, or we'd be on our return flight to London before our folks could say, *Spare Room for Rent.* Lara managed to get a great junior role at fashion PR agency in the city. Meanwhile, I found a nanny position with a lovely family and a part time sales assistant job at a small clothing boutique in Bondi. It was a pocket-sized shop unit on the beach strip, run by lively Israelis who liked to play hangover-inducing club music from 9am. The owner gave me the benefit of the doubt when I first walked in with my CV, wearing tatty yoga pants and beaded vest from a month of sweating in Thailand. '*SOME FLIRTING*' read the name across the shop front (the Hebrew-English concept not quite translating as perhaps they imagined it did).

In complete contrast to my younger self who saw Lycra as the devil, soon enough I owned a new wardrobe of clothes including neon print bodycon dresses and skin-tight jeans. I had lost some weight, that was true, but it hadn't come from strict diets, laxatives or crazy exercising, like it always did before. Now, was the result of my life being full of things which excited me. I didn't need food to fill the void anymore. I didn't need food to calm the nerves. I didn't need food to feel better. Travel was my new distraction…my new comfort…my new obsession.

There's something about being on the opposite side of the planet — almost as far away from home as possible — that gives you a feeling of utter freedom. It suddenly dawned on us that we had a chance to live a completely new life, whatever life we desired, and not just for a few holiday weeks but for as long as we wished; well, at least for one whole gorgeous gap year anyway.

No one knew us. We had no one to answer to. We could be who we wanted to be and do whatever we wanted to do. Everything about Sydney felt alive. The sun shone all year and the weather was warm for most of it. Life was lived out in the open; everyone was outside walking, running, playing with their kids, driving their drop-tops, having BBQ's, doing yoga in parks and dining alfresco. Different corners of the city had its own style, from harbour-side glamour to surfy beach babes. We could pick and choose our identity on a day-to-day basis if we so wished. In the morning I might be a hippie chick wearing flip-flops, tie-dye threads and Indian beads, hanging out with other backpackers. In the evening, I could be a city girl in a tailored jacket and heels, going to a new cocktail bar in town.

I was anonymous and I loved it. No one knew us, no one could judge us. We were so far away geographically, yet we were still in a safe, English-speaking country. It was effortless to step into a new character and create a new version of ourselves. Between us, we made an eclectic group of friends which landed us at parties with bohemians, in nightclubs with models, and on yachts with entrepreneurs. I felt totally free and my sexuality begged to be explored further and further. In a heady mix of sunshine, champagne and recreational cocaine, I floated into an otherworldly state where male or female became irrelevant and all that mattered was pleasure. No one was there to tell me otherwise.

One year into our trip, with countless libidinous escapades already under my belt, it suddenly occurred to me that maybe I was a lesbian. On a trip to Darwin in the Northern Territory of Australia, where the air was the temperature of a sauna and I thought I might choke on the heat, we joined a tour guide and some fellow nomads for a five-day trek through the Outback. I was pushed to the parameters of my strength and endurance on the hike and put under a spell with the beauty of it all. It was unlike anything I had ever experienced in my life. We climbed rocks in torrid weather, flies swarming our faces continuously. We camped in the bush where Hunter spiders loomed nearby. We walked through wet jungle with leeches attaching themselves to our limbs, sucking our blood. And we swam in bright emerald lagoons where the world felt like heaven on earth. My physical body was breaking new personal limits. My mind was entering new realms.

As we wearily bumped along in the back of a pick-up, driving back to camp after a day of visiting Aboriginal caves, I caught myself watching one of the girls. A German in her early twenties and travelling alone. She was quiet but often smiling with shoulder-length dark brown hair, strong nose and pear-shaped body. She held on to the roof handle with one arm and gazed towards the front seats, tilting her head to see the road ahead. Something about her mesmerised me. My eyes wandered over her body. Her thighs were shapely and thick, her skin smooth and pale. I thought about kissing her and wondered what it would be like to lay beside her.

Sex with women wasn't new to me anymore; the parties I'd been to in Sydney had often led to late-night debauchery, but that was always just fun or drug-fuelled. This felt different. This was an alien thought for me at nineteen years old, but I felt like I could love this girl like I'd loved men. Perhaps more. Maybe it was because I was so close to nature, maybe because I was so stripped bare, so taken over by the elements, so undistracted by civilisation, that I was experiencing this indiscriminate feminine love— Mother Earth in all her glory. I thought back over my past boyfriends. Was it all a lie? I started to think about steamy afternoons spent in bed, the way their bodies locked so naturally in to mine. I glanced back to the tour guide and found myself eyeing up his big arms and strong hands as they grasped the steering wheel, keeping the truck as steady as possible on the rocky terrain. I noticed the sweat trickling down his bicep. I imagined him showering off and rubbing his body clean. I came to the, almost disappointing, realisation that I still liked men too. But something had changed in me. The yin-yang line had blurred, the rawness of nature had broken me down and made me redefine my own rules.

Flying over to nearby Bali with boundaries knocked down, a surge of power came over me. I felt more confident in myself and in my body than ever before. Lara too, was coming in to her own as she left the city and its fast pace behind, and fell in love with the colour, beauty, light and infectious charm of Indonesia.

"Maybe we could defer our places at Uni again and stay away another year?!" Lara said suddenly as she sat bolt upright in her hammock.

I looked at her with a smile. "There *are* still so many places we haven't been".

As we wandered further, and left our old selves further behind, our souls felt more alive each day and it must have shown. Everywhere we walked, eyes followed us. We must have been giving off an energy which oozed youthful ambition and lust. Life was in our hands and we were squeezing it for every drop.

CHAPTER 3

Shewolf

On the cusp of twenty-one I met Dan, a kind and intuitive Welsh boy in my Art class at University. I was fresh from my two gap years of travel and he had come back to school to pursue his natural talents after working in a job that stifled them. He had one serious girlfriend before me, who he met when he was barely a teenager. I had been 'sowing my seeds' far and wide since about the same age. One of four brothers, he was an independent young man. Losing his father when he was only a boy, he chose to make his own way in life which gave him a mature mind-set and I was drawn to his calm and wise, but rebellious, energy.

We were friends to begin with. A small group of us had galvanised instantly in the first semester. Whether sketching wrinkly naked models in the life-drawing studio or sitting in the back row during long seminars, we'd all chat continuously about nonsense, throwing around provocative questions to slowly reveal each other's true personalities. Teasing, flirting and sharing secrets, University was like one long slumber party. We were a unit, hanging out together every day and partying every night. Beer kegs down the beach and vodka shots lined up on the bar, alcohol worked its unique magic. Nightclubs were fertile ground for excited and horny students with family far away.

In a nightclub bathroom, my new friend Rachel and I hid ourselves from the dancefloor where we'd been edging closer and closer, and began kissing madly. Her lips were so soft, her tongue was so gentle, her hands pulled my top down and played with my breasts. Electricity shot up and down my body as we pushed harder against each other and her hand slipped under my skirt. With deep brown eyes and long wavy hair, it was like making love to myself; every touch in just the right place. The discreet rendezvous became a habit, and part of me wanted to take things further with her—make it more than just drunken fun which was never spoken of the next day. But she would never give in to her feelings; her childhood sweetheart waited back home for her. And even I, who secretly considered the possibility, didn't really have the guts to be open about my sexuality. While I was travelling, everything seemed so easy and undefined, but back on home turf, where people were put into boxes again, I worried about what others might say. In fact, back on home turf I wasn't even sure how I felt about it all.

It was a honeymoon period of friendship between all of us and I felt like I laughed more in those first few months of Uni than ever before in my life, erasing years of seriousness and anxiety that had built tombs of tension in my teenage years. I definitely didn't want to be one of those people who got tied up in a relationship during Uni, unable to enjoy the freedom of being a young, carefree student. I sowed a few more seeds with some fellow Freshers and tried to keep myself from falling into any obsessive infatuations—failing miserably. A beautiful boy called Joshua ruined my attempts to be wonderfully aloof and I spent many end-of-the-nights drunk sexting him back and forth before meeting him at his student digs where we'd shag frantically on the sofa, then wake up at 5am half dressed in his bed.

"I'll call you a taxi," he'd say, barely opening his eyes to reach for his mobile. Turned out he had a girlfriend back home.

But then there was Dan. Dan was one of our gang. Dan was gentle and thoughtful, funny and romantic, strong and protective. Our friendship crossed the boundary when I took him back to my dorm room after drinking a gallon of unidentified alco-pops, which came in four options at the student bar: red, yellow, green or blue. Within weeks we were in love. He had left his home in a small fishing town in South West Wales and moved to the city. It was a new start for him, a bit like it had been for me going to Australia, only on a Wales-sized scale. New things, new people, new opportunities, new lust for life. With our relationship speeding from 0-60 in one semester, I excitedly brought him home to Surrey at Christmas to meet my family and dragged him around London to all my favourite places. At a basement club on Oxford Street in the early hours, we danced in a little R'n'B bubble and vowed never to be apart.

Summer came early, the way it only does when you're deeply in love and we were living in a dream. With most of our art degree being practical work and no exams to study for, we took full advantage and bunked off half our classes. Days merged in to one long, warm, fuzzy haze. We'd lay for hours on the campus green, enveloped in a world of sunshine and happiness where nothing could touch us. I'd just passed my driving test and in my first car we packed blankets, swimmers and picnics. Driving along the beautiful rugged coastline we discovered secret beaches, hidden coves and had heart-to-heart chats to find out everything that went on inside each other's minds. At night we drank cheap wine, lit fires and spent sweat-drenched hours finding out everything about each other's bodies. Sex with him took me to places in my body that I'd never encountered before. Waves of pleasure, combined with a strong heart connection, and the thrill that our whole life still lay ahead of us, gave me sensations that ran so deep, it almost scared me. Our love was strong and intricate, we were entwined like vines on a tree, and sometimes I felt so intoxicated I thought I might be under a spell. The eating disorders I'd had in the past, remained absent and I felt blissfully free from them forever. I couldn't possibly, ever imagine being unhappy and unsatisfied again.

But the waves did eventually subside, like they always do, and life shifted back in to neutral. The intense pleasure waned and student loans ran out. My closest friend, Lara, moved to the South of France to pursue her dreams of a continental life. I was twenty-two and we were in our second year at University when I got a call from my sister to say that Dad was in Intensive Care. Two months later he was dead, aged just fifty-eight. I don't even remember the last time I spoke to him.

I couldn't begin to imagine what had happened to make him deteriorate so fast. He'd caught a virus that couldn't be identified. He'd been run down and working too hard. His lungs suffered, and when he couldn't catch his breath one night he was rushed to hospital, anesthetised and put on a ventilator. His body struggled to function by itself, resulting in a speedy decline of his organs and contraction of pneumonia. For a month, he was in the same state, being kept alive with medicine and machines while the doctors desperately tried to figure out what the virus was. Back from Uni, I would go in everyday to see him, looking at a motionless face which seemed so unfamiliar, talking to ears which didn't seem to hear me. I'd touch his hand and wonder if he felt me—or if he might in fact be watching me from a different place already. Unconsciousness confused me; where *was* he? *Where* had he gone?

Eventually they discovered it to be a rare infection. Being a hairdresser, he was in constant contact with people's hair—uniquely their hair follicles—which can carry all kinds of things. It's possible that one of his clients who was fresh back from their holidays, could have carried and passed on a virus. Of course, not all hairdressers end up in hospital after giving a shampoo and set to Mrs Smith from the village, who just returned from her all-inclusive to the Bahamas, hairdressing wouldn't be a very popular career path if that was the case. It was a very unusual situation.

At the time when he was in hospital and the doctors still spoke of his eventual return home—like it was a given—I reluctantly decided to leave my family temporarily while he was in a stable condition, to go back to University and try to piece together what I could of my coursework. I told my mum and my sister that if anything changed, I would come home immediately. However, coming back to my student room, looking at the happy drawings and light-hearted designs scattered on my desk, I sighed deeply and felt no certainty, let alone motivation, that I'd be able to finish my degree with the worry of Dad consuming my mind. My sister called not long after I'd settled back in and told me that he'd had taken a turn for the worse. The doctors predicted he had about three hours to live. I was a four-hour drive away. I sat at my desk and panicked.

"What am I going to do?" I breathlessly cried at Dan. "He's going to die...and I'm not there."

"We'll leave now," was his reassuring reply.

Dan calmed me down and with shaking hands I grabbed my things. Within minutes we were in the car. He drove us back to Surrey while I went through fits of tears and periods of staring blankly out the window. *What will I do if he dies while I'm on my way?* I kept saying in my head. I felt helpless. The entire journey was a blur. We arrived and dad was still alive, but the situation had got worse. The doctors discovered that he had contracted MRSA, a new highly contagious hospital superbug (which would soon become a devastating problem in the UK). Little did we know, his body had not been absorbing any of the antibiotics due to the bug and he was seriously undernourished from the all the fluids lost. The doctors were unnervingly quiet, and after a risky move to a London hospital to be quarantined, he stayed alive for a further three days.

We all slept in a small room in the hospital. On the second day, it was Mum's birthday. I remember stepping out of the main doors of the large sterile building on that cold February morning and walking down the road in the dull, grey area of London. I found a pharmacy and brought her some colourful, fluffy socks and a card, determined not to let her birthday go unacknowledged, despite the ordeal we were going through. The next day, as I sat holding onto Dan, the doctor explained that they must stop the medicine which was being pumped into his body continuously, to see if he would fight back. He then went on to say that, given his condition, it was unlikely that he *would* fight back, and we might want to say our goodbyes…just in case. At the moment the Doctor gently said those words—*just in case*— a sound came out of my mouth like I'd never heard myself make before; a kind of groan from within. Loud but muffled. Deep and guttural. My sister looked at me, as if in disbelief that it had come from her rarely outspoken sibling. Weirdly, I felt embarrassed of my outburst, wondering what everyone would think of me; and then ashamed; that I should still be so vain in the midst of death. I knew then, on a non-physical level of my being, that with the groan, something had been released from me which would never, ever go back inside.

I went into the room where he was laid out on the bed with tubes and machines all around. I looked at him; there was no life. He looked so different. His face was sunken and yellow, his eyelids were dark and deep. I knew his spirit had already left some time ago, regardless of the false rise and fall of his chest with the breathing apparatus. A nurse was busy in the room, adjusting and checking things, looking at the clipboard which hung at the end of his bed. *How was I supposed to say goodbye with her there?*

I'd thought of all kinds of things that I wanted to say to him while I was in the waiting room. But now, with the nurse overhearing everything, I said nothing. Without words, I told him that I would talk to him in my mind. It was very doubtful that he had any consciousness anyway, it seemed useless to speak out loud when he couldn't hear or reply. I don't remember what I tried to telepathically tell his soul, but I know it felt like nowhere near enough, and completely pointless. It was too late. I kissed his damp, cool forehead, trying not to wince. Intuitive I knew that this was not Dad. This was a body that had lost its life essence some time ago. The doctors stopped the treatment and waited. His body didn't fight back and he died within hours.

At the funeral the small church was packed with people from near and far, some I recognised, some I didn't. Strangers told me with tears streaming from their eyes, what an amazing man he was. Dad's best friend bravely stood at the altar and told us emotional, charming and funny stories of their mischievous past together. Hearing the room echo with gentle laughter was just what he would have wanted. My sister bravely did a beautiful reading and somehow held it together until the last word.

I sat on the wooden pew and silently drowned.

I'd been so strong throughout it all, but sitting in the old stone building, watching his body go past me in the hard coffin, watching my mother shake beside me. Life felt so horribly harsh.

The full impact of his death didn't really hit for some time. Over the next year I was too busy and too scared to grieve fully. We had to sort out Dad's possessions, we officially closed his business, we confirmed his bankruptcy and death to all the debtors; and we looked after Mum who was now on her own and couldn't pay the rent.

Standing in the middle of the council flat that I'd finally managed to organise for Mum, the smell of pee from the floor stung our noses and the dirty walls burnt our eyes. My heart wailed internally. I wanted to cave in and give up. Instead, in a millisecond of human time which felt like a whole lifetime in my head, I made the switch from daughter to friend.

"Don't worry," I told her, glancing at her weary face which now looked like a little girl's. "It's going to be fine. We'll make it lovely for you. New paint on the walls and new carpet will fix it up. At least you have a garden," I said, desperately grasping for a rope of positivity.

After two months at home I went back to Uni. With my nearly waist-length hair cropped short— which Mum reluctantly cut after I told her: *if you don't do it, I will*—I think my classmates assumed I'd gone mad from trauma. The truth was, I just needed a change. I needed to release and let go of something that was simple to release and let go of, and my hair was the easy sacrifice. Against the odds, I finished my art degree and posed for my graduation photo with just Mum at my side. Dan held my hand; his father a missing piece too. My tutors were lovely and had given me massive encouragement and extra time to complete my work over the Summer holidays. However, I was just about holding it all together on the outside, while everything on the inside of me began to crumble. The void I'd had when I was younger: the anxiety, insecurity and overwhelm that I'd felt so often, which had been patched over with travel and lust and laughter, tore open again.

As a child I was closest to my mum, but Dad had been the go-getter in the family, the one who told me to go for it when everyone else said I couldn't, the one who told me to do what made me happy, the one who always laughed, made everyone else laugh, and gave me my wicked sense of humour. The one who listened to music all day and inspired my love of jazz, soul and blues, the one who took risks, the one who would push a twenty pound note of his hard-earned cash in my hand just as I was heading out with friends and say, "Get yourself a few beers," even though I was only fifteen. The one who was full of child-like fun, the one who had overflowing generosity for his family — if not himself; the one who taught me how to swim, the one who spent hours with me in the sea. He was half Irish. His father was born in Union Hall, just west of Glandore Harbour in County Cork. There is a family crest which sits at the top of Dad's gravestone, reminding me that many of the Hickeys throughout the world who left Ireland and spread far and wide, all originate from a tiny fishing village. His father died before I was born—before his time too—but I know that Ireland was where I got my wild roots from.

I'd be lying, though, if I didn't also say that Dad had become grumpy with age. That he had a short temper, that he was very stressed; that a lot of the time my mum, sister and I were walking on eggshells, not knowing what mood he'd be in or when he would snap. He gave so much of his energy at work with his clients. He was the absolute life and soul of the salon and only showed his happy face to outsiders. But when he got home, often he had nothing left in the tank. The brown envelopes containing bills would be opened, the big bright smile would close, and it became clear to me, later in life, that he too suffered with the highs and lows I came to know in myself so well. He hated aging, even though he was only in his fifties. Renowned for being such a lively and good-looking young man, losing fitness and losing energy made him resent his ever-restrictive body. "Shoot me when I get old!" he'd say in half jest to us all the time. I'm sure that during those last hours when he knew he was leaving his body—though he knew he was leaving behind three women who depended on him—he also knew that we were extremely resilient and resourceful, even if *we* didn't yet know it. His death bought about trauma, deep sadness and brutal life lessons. But eventually, his death also made us more connected. It made us fiercer.

My relationship with Dan was deteriorating. Slowly but surely my spirit was disappearing. I was dealing with my loss, I was full of sorrow for my mum who was now left on her own, and I was resisting joy and lacking libido because I felt guilty for having any pleasure, especially sexual. Eventually, it took its toll on Dan who had been so supportive throughout, and he too, started to withdraw. Far removed from my original freewheeling self, I'd become horribly reliant on him. My independence had vanished. We were such a two-man team who did everything together, and now I didn't know how to be without him. I had lost Me, and wondered where the hell she was. He'd fallen in love with the fun, crazy, carefree, self-confident, sexually liberated and brave artist girl. I'd become a shadow of all those things. I wanted them back as much as he did. My soul was split in two with the part of me who adored him and couldn't bear to hurt or lose him, and the part that wanted to scream and howl and run for the hills, naked under the full moon.

CHAPTER 4

Angels, Fairies and Wise Bears

May 2005

I was twenty-four when Dan and I split up. Around the same time, I was contacted out of the blue by Susie. Susie was a holistic therapist and clairsentient. Gentle and kind, compassionate but direct, small but strong; she was a mother, masseuse and martial art expert. I had spoken to her a while back when I needed some help with my eating disorders, and I had found her techniques to be very loving yet powerful; penetrating straight to the core of my issues and initiating my journey into self-healing.

In the unexpected email she sent, she told me that "one of my angels" had contacted her, to pass a message on to me. I had never considered that I might have my *own* angels. I believed strongly in the spirit world and on many occasions, without really acknowledging that I was doing it, had sent a silent call for protection when I was in dangerous situations and always seemed to receive it, but I hadn't thought much about there being anyone out there who was specifically linked to me. I always felt I was quite a lucky person and that if I put my heart into my decisions, then things always worked out; maybe not I the way I *hoped* they would work out, but they worked out well, all the same. It never occurred to me that perhaps I had always subconsciously asked for help, and intuitively trusted that it would be somehow given. I suppose I was inherently optimistic, even when life felt bleak. My default reaction to unusual opportunities, meetings and experiences was to say 'yes' to them. Even just one glimmer of faith allowed divinity to creep in and do its work.

Susie told me that I had an angel who was watching over me and, although confused as to what it meant, she passed on the word 'fairy' which had been whispered in her ear when she asked who was making contact through her. It turned out that Fairy was the nickname of my maternal great grandmother. She died long before I was born, and I only discovered this information when asking my mum if the word meant anything to her. Mum knew little about her; only that she was the single survivor of a set of triplets (which accounted for all the sets of twins in our family), that she was very gentle and kind, and that she had French blood running through her veins from somewhere in the family tree. Mum had never heard her actual name spoken before, but she remembered her living in a house called *Fairy Glen* in Berkshire, which must have been why she adopted the affectionate name.

I looked at a single sepia photo that we had of her when she was a young woman and instantly saw a strong resemblance. Like many teens, in the midst of adolescent angst, I used to think I might be adopted. I would look at myself in the mirror next to my joyful, blonde-haired, blue-eyed mother and sister; me with my olive skin, green-brown eyes and moody temperament. Looking at Fairy in that picture, with a strong nose, dark hair, and determined eyes like mine, I felt a thread woven between myself and her which defied time and space. In an instant I knew she had been like me, and knew she'd been here with me all along. With my Grandad's wild Irish roots, and my Great Grandmother's quiet magic, I was some kind of hybrid who longed to stand on stage and perform...while wearing an invisible cloak.

Fairy told Susie that I had given up on something recently and that I should not stop; that success was just around the corner and that the only reason things hadn't worked out so far was because it hadn't been the right time. My immediate thoughts turned to Dan. *That must be it*, I thought. I'd given up on our relationship not long before Susie wrote to me. *Maybe I should have stuck it out?* I worried. But no, that wasn't it, Susie assured me. This was to do with my career, my life purpose. I was confused. I felt further away from any sort of 'success' than ever before. I was a graduate on the doll, with an art degree and a bank balance that hadn't seen plus figures for some time. It had been a year since Dan and I had finished University and we'd tried our best to run a small creative business, but with living and working together and me still trying to deal with dad's death, struggling for money put a further strain on us. Going separate ways felt like a bullet to both our hearts but it was a necessary sacrifice. Things couldn't go on as they were. Our love had seemed so natural, we slotted into each other like two jigsaw pieces. When we broke up I felt like an astronaut floating in space, my cable severed from the spacecraft. Every night I sobbed myself to sleep. Every morning there was a second of blissful unknowing, and then the realisation. My chest hurt deep inside and I felt sick constantly. For months I played sad songs over and over, in some hope that they would wrench the unbearable feeling out of me. Then, one day…no particular day…it stopped. The pain lessened. Just enough to carry on and just enough to remind me that there was future.

I gave up on all my art projects and took a full-time job as a waitress. There was a big Italian restaurant with a bar, gelateria and pizzeria which sat out on the headland in the little fishing village of Mumbles. It had one of the best outside seating areas overlooking the lighthouse and became extremely busy during the Summer. It appealed to everyone: tourists who wanted to take photos, hungry surfers who wanted chips and beer, salty kids wanting ice-cream and Welsh students looking for good coffee. Myself and a troop of other young girls and boys in all-black uniforms, continually marched like ants from the kitchen to the courtyard with full trays. Meanwhile, others worked like robots at their stations, scooping mounds of strawberry sundaes and squeezing espressos out by the dozen.

I moved out of the flat that Dan and I had lived in, and in to a house-share with no less than five guys. I was so scared and depressed since the break-up that I decided to surround myself with as many fun, young people as possible. Initially, they said there would be another new female housemate too, but apparently she changed her mind; I should have seen the sign. The house was huge, owned by one of the lads Tom, and kitted out with cool statement pieces from South East Asia, where he escaped every winter. I wasn't quite sure where he got the money to own such a place but seeing the comings and goings of people with blood-shot eyes from his room, made me not want to question it.

It was a perfect party pad. These five boys lived for the weekend and didn't know the meaning of *too far.* I began taking every shift going at the restaurant and when I finished each night, I'd either go out drinking with the work gang or come home and party with my housemates. Total distraction was my goal. Going to work with a hideous hangover became the norm, but the fun I was having, and the camaraderie and laughter at work, was precisely the remedy for my self-pity. I didn't forget what Fairy had said to me though. I printed out the email from Susie and kept it in my bag at all times, pulling it out and reading it when I was on the bus or walking to work or crying in my room. I had to keep looking at it to believe it had actually happened — that someone, somewhere was reaching out to me from beyond this world. I didn't care if it made sense or not; it comforted and excited me and I knew deep down that what she said was true. However, I was perplexed by what Fairy predicted. *How I was going to 'find success' in my art, when I was completely uninspired, continuously intoxicated with either vodka or caffeine, and had no spare time that wasn't spent in bed recovering?*

Meanwhile though, something *was* happening to me on some sort of level. Despite abusing my body with lack of sleep and alcohol, *something* inside me was coming alive again. It may not have been the healthiest transition, but with all the new friendship and partying and working myself to the bone, I felt like I was having some sort of life-overhaul. By using up every ounce of my energy, by fuelling myself with fun, by burning the candle at both ends, I was in fact igniting my soul. I was doing exactly what I wanted, when I wanted. I wasn't asking for permission. I wasn't putting anyone else first. I was listening to my heart again, like I used to when I was travelling. Being single meant I could come and go as I pleased. Fending for myself meant I had to ask for more help, and therefore talk to more people. Lying in bed alone made me think deeper thoughts. I had fallen in to a serious relationship very young and had kept quiet about my changing needs as the years passed. During my time with Dan I had changed from a girl in to a woman, I wasn't the same person. My adventurous spirit hungered for more. I was feeding it again.

It was true, that my creative side had been ignored. I hadn't painted anything for nearly a year and I knew I didn't want to be a waitress for the rest of my life, but in time I came to understand that when Fairy had said 'success was just around the corner,' that corner didn't have to be so close. That corner could be a week, a month, a year, five years. It would be when the time was right. I took pressure off myself to figure it all out right away and left the house with the five boys when the craziness got too much; it got to the point where I was locking my bedroom door to stop random people climbing in to bed with me. It all came to a head when I had to call the police to stop my *own* house party. I said farewell to non-stop revelry and moved in to a lovely cottage with two of my workmates, where life got a lot calmer.

I was fed up with being a waitress though; yelled at by the chefs, moaned at by customers and on a minimum wage income, but it served a purpose and kept me on track while I got myself together. The heartache from Dan subsided and I was getting on pretty well. My friends were the centre of my Universe and got me through each monotonous day. As I stood at the bar with my black round waiting tray on my hip, chatting to my friend Bear who was on the other side serving drinks, talking to him about feminism and porn or something to that usual effect,

I saw a hand go up at one of the tables in the cafe area. For a moment, my eyes sent daggers towards the diners. Customers beckoning me over to tend to their every whim had become the bane of my life. Being a waitress sucked, it wasn't for me, I didn't have the energy to kiss-ass for much longer. I strolled over, forcing a smile as I reached the table.

"Hi, how are you?" a young blonde man said to me, sitting with a couple.

"Yeah good thanks," I blandly replied. "What can I get you?"

"Three coffees please. How long have you been working here?"

"Ages," I replied, unbothered with small talk. I barely looked at him as I wiped the crumbs off the table with my cloth and left to get the drinks.

"You bitch!" Bear laughed as I came back to the bar and handed him the coffee order.

"What?" I said, puzzled by his outburst.

"That poor guy... he was really trying to get your attention and you totally blew him off! And he's cute".

"Really?" I asked, surprised. "I didn't notice".

"Isn't he the singer from the band the other night? The one who stuck his trombone in your face?" he added with a dead-pan stare.

Bear was one in a million. Four years my junior and nicknamed for his large frame, grizzly beard and fine covering of ginger fur, we hit loggerheads when we first met. I didn't quite understand him initially and immediately got on the defence when he casually dropped un-PC comments into conversation. But I soon came to understand and love his dry humour, provocative chat and social intelligence. He lived an unconventional life; he'd searched his deepest depths — he was still searching — and beneath his big bear suit was a beautiful soul. We became very close, very fast and shared all our darkest secrets.

"Really?" I asked for the second time and squinted over to where the blonde boy was sitting. He was now in animated conversation. "Oh yeah, it *is* him".

I'd been so preoccupied and completely disinterested in relationships, that I had become oblivious to anyone chatting me up. I had always been a big flirt before. I was renowned by old friends for my self-assured boldness with men and promiscuous behaviour, but all of that had been absent in those months since the break-up. Suddenly I remembered. He had been playing in a band at Coffee Cesso, a blues café-bar on the marina that I went to after work. He was charismatic, good-looking with bright blue eyes and golden curls, and played a range of instruments as well as being the lead singer. Most the girls in the audience were swooning. I was sat right in front of the stage having a deep and meaningful with my friend Tammy about her dream to run her own surf hostel, and failed to notice that he was trying to get my attention. After the performance, he tapped me on the shoulder and said, "Sorry for nearly hitting you with my trombone!" with a charming grin on his face.

"That's ok," I said, spinning back around to continue my conversation.

While talking to Bear, and realising how blind I'd come to the affections of men, I decided that it was time I climbed out of my pit and stepped in to my prowess again. I glanced over to the table where trombone boy was making moves to leave. *Shit!* I thought, *he's going.* Without giving it a second thought, I ran to the kitchen. Grabbing a pen and pad I jotted my name and number down, ripped the sheet off and folded it up. By the time I came back out he was walking towards the exit. I went straight up to him.

"Thanks for coming," I said, and discreetly pushed the little square into his palm to avoid embarrassment. Thank God, he understood and smiled without opening his hand to see what I'd given him.

"See you soon. My name's Jack". And with that he left. A sigh of relief came out of my mouth as I strolled back to the bar where Bear was watching with amusement. I looked down at my order pad, the blue carbon paper had made it's duplicate of my scrawl. At the top on the book stub, and repeated at the bottom, was the order number. Eleven. I stared at it for a moment and Bear peered over my shoulder.

"11,11," he snuffed a little laugh.

"What?"

"Never mind," he said, then looked down. "Here," he handed me a book, "I got this for you".

The Tao of Pooh and the Te of Piglet, read the sky-blue front cover. It was the most obscure book title I'd ever seen. It was Bear all over.

"Taoism," he said. "Chinese philosophy... explained with Winnie The Pooh. You'll like it". I took the book with Bear's hand-written note inside the cover:

To help you on your spiritual journey, it read. I felt, somehow, I was going to need it.

I didn't know much about spiritual journeys. However, I did know about boys, as I embarked on a steamy six-month journey of sex. I went into my relationship with Jack with the intention to let go of everything. I wanted to have fun. I wanted to feel like me again. The me before Dad died. The me before my heart broke.

It was a fresh start and I had nothing to lose. I started painting again. I was a waitress and an Artist, he was a barman and a musician. As long as we paid our rent and bills and turned up to work when we had to, we could do whatever the hell we wanted. Our goal wasn't money or possessions, it was free time. Every minute outside our jobs was spent making love or making art. Naked, in his studio flat above the pub, I'd sketch while he wrote songs, and he'd play guitar while I painted, the sun pouring in through the large windows which overlooked the bay. Utterly delicious slices of time which happened before selfies, Snapchat, Facebook or Instagram felt the need to freeze the flow or solidify the magic which had no captions, filters or borders. Just in-the-moment-ness. On stormy days, we'd slip briefly from the bedcovers to make coffee and within minutes we'd be back in a pile, wrestling, rolling and tumbling to the floor. The merging of our lust and creativity caused in me a kind of eruption, and my body was experiencing a different sexual energy that I had never before felt. A 'Kundalini Awakening' perhaps, as mentioned in an article I'd stumbled across while researching more on Taoism.

We couldn't keep our hands off each other. The chemistry was like combustion. It didn't matter where we were—a pub, a party, out walking—we'd sneak off and find somewhere to release that energy. However, I had a problem. He was falling fast in love, but I could not—even though I adored him. He did all the perfect things; he walked in the rain to the restaurant with flowers to cheer me up, he made me dinner, he left me poems, he wrote me love songs. And I came to all his gigs, I painted for him, I made friends with his friends, I even met his folks. I wanted to give him everything but my heart just wouldn't let me. Usually I would be the one to fall head-over-heels within weeks; it was so unlike me not to be the one running full speed into love, but I realised that my heart still pined for Dan. Reluctantly, I stopped trying to run full speed and instead, walked away.

Whenever I could get some quiet time and still my mind, I'd call to Fairy. I didn't know where she resided, but it felt like she was *in* me and all around me. I'd ask her to keep me strong, to show me what to do next, to soothe me when I felt scared and gather me when I felt scattered. I'd hear her replies in a version of my own inner voice which I somehow knew was hers; because no matter how upset or nervous or broken I felt when I called out, her voice was always calm and made me instantly feel that everything would be ok. When I couldn't hear her replies, I thanked her for listening anyway and thanked her in advance for the answers I knew she'd eventually send. Sometimes she spoke to me through songs, sometimes through strangers, sometimes through books, sometimes through films, sometimes through feelings. She always reassured me that my impulsive, intense and unusual ways of living were characteristics passed down to me through my strong and mystic female ancestors.

She explained in my dreams that the energy I felt with Jack was a necessary wake-up call to get me back on my passionate path. She explained in my thoughts that my young soulmate Dan had been an essential education in love. She explained through music that losing my father had been a lesson in loss. She urged me to be brave when I was surrounded by people who didn't understand me and to stay true to the requests of my heart. She told me that all the support I needed could be called upon at any time via my *Sisters* in the other realms.

CHAPTER 5

Burlesque Bravery

I hadn't forgotten what Fairy said about 'success being just around the corner,' and so I continued to paint after leaving Jack, determined to get back on my artistic track. It felt so good to be creating again, even if what I was creating wasn't all that good… or meaningful… or interesting. It simply seemed the right thing to do; to keep my hand in it, before my hands forgot what *it* actually was.

Dan and I decided to meet as friends. We missed each other terribly and decided that seeing one another on neutral ground, on a purely platonic basis, might help us to better understand what happened between us and move on. Obviously, it was a naïve idea, since we'd end each meeting in tears and in each other's arms. While in a café or in a pub we'd talk about our lives since separating, being mindful to avoid speak of any sexual partners, of course. This was somewhat of a challenge for me as I'd spent a fair bit of time in the sack since we'd parted.

"You look different," he said. My recent 'awakening' must have been showing.

"I feel different," I replied, honestly.

In a rush of adrenalin, I shot round to his work one day and flung myself onto him. "Let's get back together!" I cried. "Let's just do it…who cares what we *should* or *shouldn't* do? …let's just do it".

Once the emotions had subsided and the idea had sunk in, we agreed that this time things had to be different. We needed a change, we needed a new environment, we needed better job opportunities, and that meant leaving Wales. I moved back to Surrey, slept on my Mum's sofabed and looked for work while Dan tied up loose ends in Swansea.

Despite having no marketing experience, I managed to summon everything I'd ever learnt from previous jobs, to apply for a marketing position which was being advertised for a local theatre. I had filled out the form with the most grown-up answers I could think of. I poured over my personal statement, switching between a formal and friendly approach, unsure as to how I should come across. I'd never really had to apply for a *serious* job before. All my previous work was either while I was travelling or at college and University, or through a temp agency where your CV was suffice and the agent was the middle-man, making you sound amazing so that they could get their chunk of commission.

I wrote about my experience of working in a lingerie shop where the brand had an excellent reputation and customer service was strong. *Yes, that would impress them,* I assured myself. I looked at the first question:

GIVE AN EXAMPLE OF A TIME YOU DEALT WITH A CHALLENGING SITUATION IN THE WORKPLACE.

I filled out my answer:
'I once had a male customer come in to the store and ask me to measure him for stockings and a corset. This was slightly awkward as he was large man and it was obvious that none of our female garments would fit him. I believe I handled the situation very well by explaining respectfully to him that our shop had a women-only changing room policy and so I would be unable to measure him accurately. I also suggested that there might be other shops (perhaps in Soho) where they offer a far better range of the kind of things he was looking for'.

I looked back over my answer. No, I couldn't write that. DELETE, DELETE. *Why did I always end up bringing the conversation back to sex? Come on Char, focus, be professional,* I told myself and opened a bottle of wine. This was taking longer than expected. I reached the final question and just as I was about to hit *send* on the email, I had a last-minute change of heart on the 'About Me' section. It was late and I'd been working my way nicely through the bottle of Sauvignon Blanc. Reading back over my cringe-inducing words, I began to feel that I held little hope of receiving a positive reply. *Fuck it!* I thought. *I wasn't going to get this job.* I scrapped the bit about enjoying exercise and going to the cinema in my spare time, and hastily wrote in its place: *I mostly go out to pubs and clubs with my mates and get drunk.* I giggled to myself thinking that I may as well be honest. I didn't stand a chance in hell of getting an interview. I didn't even really know what marketing was.

Forty applications from Business and Marketing graduates got shortlisted. Six people were interviewed. I was one of them. How I actually I got an interview was beyond me, but realising that I'd somehow blagged it through the application stage, I was now freaking out about convincing them I knew what I was doing. The Head of Art and Leisure Marketing for the local Council sat behind a long desk with a young woman—the Theatre Marketing Manager—next to him. I sat in a chair opposite, pulling nervously at my slightly-too-tight blouse. He asked me what plan I would have for a marketing campaign to get the theatre some more interest and more revenue. I literally had no idea what he meant. I'd foolishly thought it wouldn't *really* be about marketing; more like a bit of admin help, possibly some flyer distribution.

I sat there silently mortified and actually had to answer 'I don't know' to half of the questions. I felt like a complete moron. They looked at me sympathetically, shifted in their seats and I think they actually felt more awkward than I did. But regardless of the shame, wherever possible and whenever I was asked something to do with customer service or anything remotely creative, I tried to my upmost to be as enthusiastic as possible.

By some kind of Christmas Panto miracle, I got the job.

I became more like a BFF than an ADMIN. ASS. to my manager Sally. The bond between us was sealed when she pulled me, by my feet, off the theatre stage floor at 3am after the staff Christmas do. She later told me that the part in my application about 'getting drunk on the weekends' had won me the interview. She couldn't stand hiring another boring assistant. More and more of my Sunday mornings were spent dying on Sally's sofa after out-of-control cast parties. I also negotiated working more hours over less days so that I could dedicate more time to my art.

However, when Dan came back to England, we moved to South East London and the commute to my job was too far. I was also having far too many close calls with *Josephs* under their *technicolour dream coats,* and far too many crushes on androgynous backing dancers. Besides, marketing was a great CV-filler but it wasn't my passion. I handed in my notice to a sad-faced Sally.

"Who am I going to fucking find to replace you now?!... Who's gonna be my shot-drinking sidekick?" Was her heart-felt reaction.

We moved into a house-share with friends of Dan's — a mate from school who'd become an actor, and his girlfriend who was also an actress. We were excited about living in London, we wanted to be in a creative hub surrounded by other creative people where we could really give our art careers a chance. I took on some temporary office jobs to pay the bills while I applied to Illustration Agencies. I worked as a receptionist in a school which had weapon detectors on the doors, and an administrator for Lewisham Council where I spent my lunch breaks in the grey carpark to get 'fresh air'. I was a PA to a pervy Executive who liked to tell me about his big cars and the exotic destinations that he was (reluctantly) taking his wife to. I hated it. Week by week I became miserable. My body was literally screaming at me to make a change. My back was always aching from sitting at a desk and I had an 'occasional' eating disorder—although I wouldn't admit to myself that's what it was—which was becoming more frequent by the day.

Bulimia was my subconscious way of trying to control my worries which were exploding inside my head, and my emotions which were overwhelming my heart once again. It was my little secret. Not a secret I was proud of, but a secret, nonetheless.

It didn't feel like a good secret when I binged until my stomach ached, nor did it feel like a good secret when I was forcing myself to throw-up. But there was something strangely good about the way I felt afterwards which made no sense. Somehow, I felt a little bit proud of myself—as if I had sorted out my own problem. In some weird, irrational way, I felt like I had taken matters into my own hands and taken care of myself, even though it was so utterly destructive. This was the one area in my life where I didn't have to depend on anyone else. When all was chaos, bulimia made me feel self-reliant. Sometimes I didn't even think what I was doing was anything unusual, it became so normal to me. I had always been a 'foodie' and filling my stomach with copious amounts of food that I craved—food which I usually tried to resist in order to stay slim—was a temporary high, a momentary comfort; then completely emptying it out felt cathartic, like a release. It was like my reset button, clearing out all the crap that was stored inside. But of course, it didn't clear it out, it simply pushed it deeper into the recesses of my mind. In Victorian times, some doctors who worked in *lunatic asylums* induced purging on their patients with rubber-gloved hands, to 'remove madness' or 'demons' from their bodies, or to calm a frenzy. Back then, I'd never even heard of this historical method, but perhaps somewhere in my subconscious, I thought I could do the same. Perhaps I was also trying to remove my demons.

I grew to despise the temp agency, flinching when I saw the phone number pop up on my phone, wincing as they told me about my next appointment which was: *Sorry…not quite up to your requested £10 hourly rate…but a good opportunity to get your WPM up to speed*. Meanwhile, despite the heart-to-hearts and the change of scene, my relationship with Dan was extremely turbulent again, as were my finances. My debts were turning into mountains and I couldn't see a way over them. Added on top of that, I was still quietly suffering with the grief of dad's death which I hadn't fully given in to. I had needed to be strong for mum, who was now on her own, and there had been so many practicalities to take care of when it happened. There wasn't much time for lying about, sobbing.

A few years down the line I was far from being in a good place, but the one thing I knew and constantly fell back on, was that I was always happy when was drawing or painting.

2007

Thank God, my ardent friend Lucy took me to the LBF (London Burlesque Festival) when I was having a serious Artist's block. Nothing was moving me creatively when I first went back to Surrey. I didn't know what to paint anymore. At Uni I had specialised in children's book illustration but I should have known that wasn't really my thing; my mind was far too rude for kids' stories.

At that time, Lucy was working as a costume designer and I was staring at my empty sketchbook mournfully. She thought the festival in Shepherd's Bush would be good way for us to get inspired (and basically be an excuse for a night out dressed like slappers). That night inspired me more than I could have imagined.

In sublime outfits and stage props to match, we watched girl after girl stride on to the stage at the aptly named *Bush Hall*. We saw young women, mature women, women with big curves and cellulite, women with athletic straight-up-and-down bodies, women with muscles, women with flat chests, women with massive boobs. We gazed at them in awe while they were dancing, shaking, jiggling, swooshing and grinding. In their unusual acts they laughed, joked, sang, whispered, moaned and purred. Some were loud, some were silent, some were animated, some poker-faced. Their styles were comedic, dominating, light-hearted, submissive, dark, melancholic and artistic. They seduced, provoked, lured, tricked and teased. They wore nipple tassels, high heels, slippers, bikinis, leathers, horse tails, night gowns, alien costumes, bear suits and hula skirts. They used fire sticks, whips, feather fans, fake blood, giant tea-cups, balloons and disco balls. Lucy and I loved every single minute of the magic and madness. We got completely lost in crowds of corsets and tuxedos, dancing our stockings off to electro-swing music. Each and every one of the performers showed us what their mummas gave them and proudly paraded their unique bodies. I bubbled over with joy. I was overcome by excitement. I was flooded with feminist pride. That night I went to sleep with champagne in my blood and sequin-clad bottoms shimmying in my eyes. Somehow, I would express how I felt about this wonderful thing I had witnessed.

Between the desperation of my day jobs and the sadness of my sinking relationship I spent my spare time trying to capture, with paint, what I had seen at the show. It became a brilliant way for me to channel my feelings and release my emotions. I would paint as soon as I woke up, cramming an hour or just thirty minutes in before work, and late in to the night, paying the price the next day when my eyes begged to close in front of the glaring computer screen. I'd cry while working on some pictures and feel ecstatic while painting others. I'd pour my heart's longing in to detailed portraits and throw my anger in to fast, charcoal sketches. Still unsatisfied though—that my paintings weren't telling the whole story—I decided they needed tangible texture to make the viewer want to reach out and touch them, just like the audience wanted with the girls on stage.

I began to scour charity shops, antique fairs, markets and haberdasheries in South London for fabrics, beads, costume jewellery, vintage lace and silks that I could incorporate into my pictures. I contorted my body around the large artwork, stitching individual sequins onto painted lingerie and cut my fingers trying to puncture PVC with thick needles to attach it to the canvas. I was obsessed with finding the right adornments and my collection of brooches, dismantles necklaces and torn-apart clothing was growing by the day, all in some attempt to bring the female subjects and their backdrops to life. It was like therapy for me. I drew girls with sexy curves and big confidence. They wore exquisite garments, they oozed sex appeal. I wanted to *be* those burlesque beauties. I wanted to live in their dreamy worlds. Despite the chaos in the rest of my life, I channelled any energy I could in to the one thing that felt positive: my flowing creativity.

Before I knew it, my canvases were taking over the flat and I needed somewhere to put them. In between the mind-numbing data-entry and filing that I did in my day jobs, I made the most of my time sat in front of the computer and emailed as many bars, clubs and restaurants as possible. I eventually found a new sexy little cocktail lounge on the outskirts of London who were keen to hang my artwork. I started to sell my paintings, making some much-needed extra cash. The bar owners gained original art for their empty walls and received a cut of any sales; it was a win-win for all of us.

Next, I organised a regular weekend stall at Greenwich Market. I'd pack up my car on Saturday nights, get up at 5am Sunday morning and head for the River Thames. The famous undercover market was situated near to the 19th century dry-docked Cutty Sark ship and the Maritime Museum, making it a tourist hot-spot. In the surrounding area were quirky pubs, kitsch second-hand shops and an arthouse cinema, drawing in thrifty and alternative types too.

The huge Old Royal Naval College was a spectacular World Heritage building with the river on one side and Greenwich Park on the other. With large grassy banks and tree-lined walkways, the park, along with the college, was a popular set for big budget films like *Four Weddings and a Funeral, The Kings Speech* and James Bond's *Skyfall.* Then there's the Millennium Dome, looking like it's just landed from another planet, which hosted some of the biggest modern musicians. In this London borough where Mean-Solar-Time (GMT) is calculated — setting the clocks for the whole of the UK — ironically, Greenwich itself felt like a time warp that zipped from one era to the next at every street corner. Old and new, regal and bohemian, students and Hollywood stars; somehow, they all sat side by side comfortably.

Renowned for being a launchpad for new designers and entrepreneurs, traders of the market were expected to make their little space attractive and unique. Working alone, I'd have no choice but to ask the most honest-looking person near me to watch over my possessions while I parked my car and emptied its contents. In four or five runs, I carried my paintings, frames, stall fixtures and decorations from the loading zone outside, to my stand. When I came back I'd decorate my allocated unit with flocked wall coverings, retro lamps and sensual trimmings to transform the stark metal grid in to some sort of Art Deco boudoir. I'd then man the stall until 5pm, chatting to anyone who showed interest in my work. Finally, I'd pay the £50 seller's fee — prizing it out of my wallet on days when I'd made zero sales — then pack up all my stuff again and go home. It was hard work and depressing when I ended up even more out of pocket, but I knew I had to do it. Something in me needed to reach out. Something told me I had to share my creativity. Something kept reminding me that I had skills and talents that couldn't be wasted. Somewhere inside of me was a girl who knew she could do more; and be more.

In addition to hanging my art in the bar and at the market, I also contacted Burlesque show organisers and drove across London alone at night, normally getting lost on the way, to hold small stands in clubs where I could showcase my work and network with the performers. I figured that if I mixed in the right circles then my work might be appreciated. Even when they were in dodgy basement bars, the shows were all about glitz and glamour. It was good to be in the company of such outgoing and colourful people, while things elsewhere in my life were fading to grey.

Eventually, I got to know faces on the Burlesque circuit and made some good friends. We'd all rock up with our large bags and boxes, me with my easels and paintings, the dancers with their costumes and props. There was a kinship between us; we understood the courage it took to work hard on your art form, carry it across the city with you and put it out to the world, not knowing if you'd be applauded or laughed at, acknowledged or shunned. Not knowing if you'd make any money at the end of it. We all recognised in each other, a gutsy woman beneath the soft feathers, and strength within the steel-boned corsets.

Diamonds and Pearls was a regular event specifically for girls…who like girls. I'd been invited along by the host when she saw my artwork at a show one night. At the small club tucked away in Clerkenwell, I popped backstage to see one of the performers I knew. Chatting to my friend Coco with a glass of cheap white wine, while she pulled fishnets over her voluptuous thighs, I looked to my left. A cute-faced, tiny figure was applying glitter to her lips and hairspray to her peroxide hair. She wore a diamante thong and matching nipple pasties, leaving sweet F.A to the imagination. Her waist was tiny, her boobs were full and pert, her butt was round and firm. She was the kind of girl that men crashed their cars while craning their necks to see.

"You look lovely," I said to the her, feeling horribly inferior in my over-washed black dress which hung from under the bust to distract from my belly. "I hope you don't mind me asking," I said to her, "But how do you look like that? … I promise this isn't a chat-up line but...like...do you work-out?!" I prayed that she'd tell me she spent all day in the gym and ate nothing but cabbage soup, giving me good reason not to envy her.

"Thank you, sweetie," she replied with straight, glowing white teeth. "Well, I work-out at home occasionally, but not much else. I don't really have time...I'm studying and working too. I eat what I want mostly but try not to over-do it. I dunno, I guess I'm just quite lucky".

I smiled at her and wished her well with the show, spinning back around and slumping in my chair. Deflated, I downed the remains of my wine. Coco and I exchanged glances and she shrugged, shoe-horning her curves into a gold corset, spilling out from all edges. *I guess I'm just quite lucky*. Her words went around in my head. I suppose she was making the most of her luck. I knew how much these girls put into their shows; they didn't merely take their clothes off, they worked damn hard on their performances, bookings and complicated logistics of their schedules. Most of them had day-jobs to hold down. 'Lucky' was choosing to use her beautiful body to better her life. I guess that's what we should all do with whatever has been God-given to us. I hadn't been gifted with the face or measurements of a Barbie doll, or — more importantly — the talent and sheer guts to go on stage, but I *had* been gifted with art in my veins. I would better my life with that.

I started to sell more paintings and prints each month and I was being asked to do large commissioned pieces for private clients. Women began approaching me for burlesque style self-portraits. They loved having such empowering images of themselves to look at. I received emotional letters of thanks from ladies across the country for helping them to embrace their sexuality; it seemed I had a knack for bringing out the goddess in girls.

I got invited to very interesting after-parties where cocaine was passed round like canapes and quirky people without kids owned labyrinthine, *Grand Design* type homes. Gilded gold mirrors turned in to secret doorways, which opened up into places called 'The White Room' or 'The Cellar'. Men wore make-up. Women wore top hats. Naked bodies ran across hallways. On one hand, it was exhilarating. On the other hand, I was still with Dan and refrained from staying out too late or going to too many parties, in fear of being kidnapped by temptation.

My insecurities and feelings of being 'lost' still resided in my home life. In 2010, it all came to a head. My art was popular but still not popular enough to make ends meet. Painting sales were unpredictable and unreliable. My food addictions were out of control. I was in financial debt and I couldn't see the light. I had never told Dan about my bulimia. He knew I struggled with my fluctuating weight and anxieties around my body if it wasn't 'the right size' in my mind, but he had no idea of the scale it had secretly reached. I felt way too ashamed and embarrassed to tell him. The girl who binged and threw up her food was a stranger; if I let her out and introduced her to the world, who knew what would happen? On no particular day, for no particular reason, I finally gave in. I was weak, I couldn't pretend anymore, I knew I needed to reach out. I knew I needed help and only he would understand. Only he'd seen me at my worse. The truth came out as he knelt at the edge of the bath and I sat with my arms wrapped around my knees in hot water. I felt a rush of relief but it was short-lived.

"Oh Char," he said with a sad eyes, moving to sit on the toilet lid. "That's not good babe".

"I know, I know… but …" I couldn't think what to say. I assumed that if I could just get the words out then he would take it all away. I just wanted him to rescue me.

"Why?" He paused. "Please don't do this to yourself". I could see his face searching his brain for answers. This was unknown territory. "Look, it'll be ok, we'll work it out, just stop ok babe? I'm gonna put the kettle on".

I felt the big empty hole inside of me grow bigger. *Just stop.* Why didn't I think of that? I said under my breath as he left.

My mind turned to ESCAPE mode. Fight-or-flight kicked in and 'flight' was dominating my thoughts. It was always my answer: leave. Move on. Run away. Start again. But I loved Dan so much, I couldn't go...and where would I go? What would I do?... and then what? My head was full of confusion. Every time I got in my car alone it was like a switch flicked. In this little metal capsule, safely contained, not needing to talk or interact with anyone, my head had a field day. As I drove around London in traffic, ring-roads and roundabouts, my brain was also spinning and thoughts bottle-necked. Ideas of leaving and the possible consequences, would continuously spring back and forth until the moment I reached my destination, when I'd have to act normal again.

Before sleep I'd read *Paulo Coelho* books, clinging on to every word as if my life depended on absorbing them into my blood like a transfusion. Every sentence called me to somewhere or something. I had to find out where or what that was. On days off I went walking and running to try and gain clarity. I missed the sea. I desperately needed to be in the calmness of nature but finding quiet, natural spaces close to home in London was tricky. We lived in a place called Honor Oak Park which— as the name suggests—did have a small green at top of the hill road our flat was on, but I always found it to be too busy. I needed to be able to cry without people staring. The tears were coming thick and fast. Crystal Palace Park was one of my go-tos for running; it was big enough to leave a decent gap between myself and others, so as not to gain attention with my panda eyes.

More often though, I found myself in graveyards and cemeteries. If I could manage to stumble across a church, I could usually find a burial ground. Far from being sombre or morbid, I actually found it unbelievably soothing. It was quiet. There was grass, trees and birds, and no one bothered me if I was crying. I felt comforted by the angel monuments and cherub statues. I imagined that the names etched on the stones and plaques were my ancestors who were sending me messages of wisdom and hope. I spoke to Fairy openly. As I walked, surrounded by death, I knew something was coming to an end. In the last week of Summer, I went away to see an old friend. To my own shock, I cheated on Dan.

CHAPTER 6

A Recipe For Change

Ingredients:
1 small island
1 sun-ripened beach party
½ litre of vodka
1 steamy campervan
A generous amount of shagging
Plenty of salt water

Desperate for a change of scene and respite from the stress I was feeling, I made plans to spend a weekend in Jersey. I'd never been to the Channel Islands, I didn't really see any point in going. What was *there* anyway, besides cows and old people? But it was an easy getaway for a break from fast-paced living, and a chance to see an old girlfriend who could always reduce me to laughing snorts. Gemma grew up in Jersey, and since we became besties on our travels nine years before, she had made regular visits to London so that we could catch up and she could get a taste of 'The Big Smoke'.

"Come to the island in the Summer," she said over email. "You'll love it". I wasn't sure that I'd love it, but I did need *something* to look forward to.

Gemma, Lara and I became friends in New Zealand on a glacier hike, which became fondly known to us as *Fat Camp*. When signing up for the trek there were three options: Slow, medium or fast. We had chosen the more leisurely walk up the icy track, not wanting to exert ourselves too much, especially with hostel hangovers from absurd drinking games the night before. Our lovely Kiwi guide, Rob, didn't know what he'd let himself in for. With regular snack breaks, pausing for photo sessions and moaning about aching muscles, we ended up taking a full four hours longer than the fast group. When we finally arrived back at base we were excited to pick up our completion certificates. Rob speedily signed the pieces of paper, threw them into our hands and then legged it, like a boy who'd been forced to take the ugly girl to the school dance, dumping us as soon as he reached the gates.

Jersey is the largest (if you can call nine by five miles 'large') of seven inhabited islands in an archipelago off the North French coast, and you can drive around its perimeter in about forty-five minutes. I always wondered why on earth Gemma stayed in such a small and quiet place on the planet when she was a globetrotter at heart. I didn't get why she didn't just come and live in London or move to Australia where she had family. Surely there were more exciting and opportune places to live? However, as soon as she picked me up from the airport and drove us to a surf club for a drink, all became clear. I looked out to the sea; the waves crashing on the sand; the seagulls calling. The sun was bright, the horizon was clear, people were smiling and laughing, wearing board shorts, bikini tops and *Billabong* T-shirts. During the scenic route Gemma took us on, out of the car window I saw old farms, sweeping bays, tiny coves, small country lanes with French names and rows of rhododendron bushes in pinks, purples and blues.

"I had no idea it was like this here," I said to Gemma while swigging a bottle of Bud. "It's dreamy. I feel so relaxed. I feel like I can breathe again".

"Yeh, it's cool, huh? We're pretty lucky to live here," she said, gazing at a surfer carrying his board under one arm, wetsuit rolled halfway down his toned body.

"I think I want to live here," I said seriously.

"HA HA!" Gemma nearly chocked on her beer. "Of course you do! Everyone says that at first. It's just because you're on holiday. It's a novelty for you. You'd get bored in no time, Char".

I laughed with her and nodded in agreement. But secretly, inside, I really *did* feel it. Weirdly, I felt like this was *home*. It was strange because I never particularly felt that anywhere was home, let alone a place where I'd only just arrived; and I had stayed in far more exotic and appealing places, which definitely *didn't* feel like home.

We went to the supermarket to stock up on booze and snacks. A friend of Gemma's was having a party at St Ouens Bay, a long, rugged beach on the west of the island which had the best surf and caught the last of the sun. We planned to go along and sleep in her campervan for the night. The day had been warm and everyone displayed glowing tanned skin as the sky turned orange. I was introduced to various people, all smiling widely and hugging me like they'd been my friends for years. I couldn't help but be in awe, and also a bit jealous; is this how life *always* was here? I wanted *my* life to be like this; beach parties, sea air, healthy, good-looking faces, far enough away from the mainland to forget about all the depressing stuff that was going on there.

Sipping vodka and orange from a plastic cup, my eyes moved to a guy laughing animatedly in the distance. I watched him secretly, behind the group I was with. Curly brown hair, long but not too long, just long enough to be hot. An athletic and strong-looking body beneath surf shorts and t shirt. A big white smile and a gorgeous face. I couldn't help but keep watching him. I scolded myself for being so superficial, but before I had time to affirm Sarah Jessica Parker's wisdom in my head: '*Men who are too good looking are never good in bed because they never had to be*' — and before I had time to remind myself that I was not single and therefore should not even be working out who *is* and *is not* good in bed anyway — he looked over at me. I immediately diverted my glare in an uncharacteristically shy way. He was so stunning that it was too uncomfortable for me to look at him. But of course, I did eventually look back, and we continued to catch each other's glances. *Why was he not already with a girl? Why weren't girls swarming around him?* I wondered. *Was I seeing something they weren't?* Then the unthinkable happened, he started walking towards me. I shifted from one foot to the other three times before he arrived at our group. Instantly I felt like I was twelve years old again. I flashed back to nights at the *RollerDrome* in Woking, watching the cool older boy skate over with style and confidence. I'd soon realise he wasn't skating towards me but instead, heading to the snack machine behind me. But this guy *was* coming towards me. He stopped next to Gemma and put his arms out.

"GEM!" He cried, "How's it going babe?" Gemma got pulled in to his squeeze and stood there with her arms pinned to her sides, for what seemed like half an hour.

"Hi Ryan, good thanks. You ok?" She replied, once freed of his grip and laughing at his enthusiasm.

"Yeh, brilliant!" Ryan beamed. "And you...how are you doing?" He asked a second time, his eyes flicking over to me.

"Yup.... I'm... good," Gemma replied again, looking at me and back to him. "Good to see you, it's been a while".

"Yeh, yeh, I knoooow, mad isn't it?... time flies and all that. So... er... how's business going? Busy?" Ryan persisted. "Got loads of clients? How's the new salon?" He asked, turning to me intermittently.

"G r e a t   t h a n k s   R y a n," she said slowly, obviously feeling like her answer was futile. She rolled her eyes before introducing me. "This is my friend Char, she's visiting from the UK".

"Oh, hi!" he said, as if he hadn't noticed me there before.

"Hi," I smiled, trying to hide my giddiness.

Everything outside the immediate foreground faded out of view while we talked and Gemma moved away. I was mesmerised by his big, brown twinkling eyes which lit up when he spoke, and his wolf-like canine teeth which I found insanely sexy. He was so interested in me; a slow rolling wave of questions came from his mouth which I answered wilfully — subconsciously eliminating all the things I didn't want him to know.

"So how do you know Gem? How long are you here for? Do you like the island? What do you do back home?" He listened to every word of my answers. Then, as we went to get a drink from the makeshift bar and moved to a quieter spot — and moved closer together — more questions in stronger waves.

"What's it like being an Artist? You must get a lot of attention? You have stunning eyes. Your eyelashes so long!" Feeling high with flattery, I noticed Gemma suddenly, on the other side of the fire, chatting to another group of people. *I should probably go back and talk to her*; the thought hung loosely in the air before I looked back to Ryan. I hesitated for a second, flashes entering my mind of Dan at home, waiting for me to return and tell him about my weekend. Without consideration I shut the thoughts down. I was enjoying myself at last and I couldn't stop. It felt good to flirt, to be free for a moment, for someone to look at me and find me curious and attractive, to know nothing of my dark moods and disorders. We topped our drinks up again and again. The surrounding buzz grew louder with more laughter, more talking, more Jack Johnson playing from speakers and the occasional call to someone down the beach, "MATE! ...GRAB SOME MORE BEER FROM MY VAN, WOULD YA?"

"And what about you?" I asked, realising I'd been talking about myself A LOT. "So, do you live with..."

"I live on my own". He interjected, intuitively noticing my subtle withdrawal as I assumed the unlikelihood of him being single. My warped rationale had somehow decided that if at least *one* of us was, then that made it ok. "I like my own space, y'know?"

"Yeh, I know what you mean," I said.

The sun sank in to the sea and the coral coloured sky, very quickly turned from dusk to dark, leaving light glowing only in patches from fires, candles and mobile phones. My head swam in a carefree way that it hadn't for a long time. Being on this island made me switch off from everything else and I allowed my mind to flow serenely, pretending to be in a different body, in a different life, in a different time. I told Ryan about myself as if I was the person I wanted to be.

"I mostly paint female nudes and burlesque performers, and exhibit them in bars and at shows," I said, like it was the easiest thing in the world and like I wasn't plunging to the depths of financial debt.

"I live with some actors in a houseshare in South East London. It's pretty colourful!" I informed him, missing out details like the fact that I sometimes did coke on the weekends to feel more alive, and that I had to work day jobs, staring at a computer, spending lunch breaks surrounded by grey cement, my evenings often ending in tears. And that other detail… that I had a boyfriend.

"I'd love to live by the sea". That part was true. I couldn't imagine needing drugs to make the pink horizon — or the moon, which was creeping in on the sea — more interesting.

"Wow, cool!" he'd respond to the tales I told of my life, brushing his curls aside. "You're a real free-spirit, aren't you?"

I couldn't have felt further away from that description if I tried. He told me that he was a carpenter. He had learnt the trade from his father and loved what he did. He was from the mainland too but had moved here after visiting a friend and loved the easy way of life. He oozed happiness, confidence, contentment… and sex. Our conversation paused and then suddenly we kissed. His lips were every bit as nice as I'd imagined. He kissed perfectly; not too much so that people would shout 'GET A ROOM!' but enough to make my thighs tingle, and to feel like the entire world had turned to watercolour around me. "Do you fancy a stroll?" he asked, taking my hand.

We walked along the path above the beach, the noise of the revellers eventually muffling as we went further in to the darkness. The waves were loud, despite the tide being far out. The rolling and crashing water carried though the breeze, reminding me that She—the ocean—was there even when you couldn't see her. My heart thumped at the thrill of being by the sea in the middle of the night, holding hands with a stranger, not knowing what would happen. Life at home had become so predictable. I loved Dan dearly, but our passion had hit a wall. I knew there was *more* inside of me, *more* that I craved, but I was too afraid or embarrassed to show it…or give it… or ask for it. As soon as the lights from fires and parked vans diminished and we were completely alone, my passion hit a new wall—the *sea* wall.

With the water lapping behind us, the white noise of the waves switched off my chattering brain, and with vodka flowing through my veins I pressed him against the stone, kissing him hard. He pulled at the buttons on my jeans and within seconds I could feel his hands on me. Electricity shot through my body. "My van is further down," he paused to whisper. We pulled apart and carried on walking but only managed a few metres before stopping again.

This time he lifted me and sat me on the wall. By now we were in near blackness as he pulled my jeans down. Burying his head between my thighs I was dizzy with both the thrill and the fear of it all. It was so surreal. *How could this be happening?* It took us an eternity to reach his van, stopping every minute to taste each other again. In his camper, on my knees, I stripped off. Suddenly I saw myself as if I was floating above my own body. *Was I really doing this? Why was I letting this happen? I won't be able to take this back,* I thought, before quickly dismissing it.

As we had sex, I didn't feel like it was me. I felt like I was spying on another couple, a couple who were free and reckless and hopelessly in love. This couldn't be me. I had a boyfriend back home; I was depressed, scared and stuck in my life. But it was too late now to tell him I wasn't single. Far too late. Ryan wasn't there to listen to me cry about my problems. Instead, he held me in impossible positions, pulled back my hair, pushed my legs apart and pulled me on top of him, sweat dripping down our backs.

I went into denial. My continually questionable logic — which momentarily crept in while I gazed at the male figure moving in front of me — told me this: *Well, you've done it now, Char. It's too late. There's no point stopping.* Like when you cheat your diet and you say to yourself, *it's already ruined, I may as well eat the whole pizza now… and the crisps…and the chocolate… and the ice-cream.* With each new position I felt a release of pent-up frustration. I took out my anger on him; I forgot about my body issues; I fucked every last cell of sadness out of my body.

"You're wild," he said, seemingly surprised by my inhibition and sexual experience. I suppose I'd been fairly subdued at the party; I was kind of out of practice with the whole 'fun' thing. When we finally fell asleep it was light outside.

I woke soon after. Ryan lay like a beautiful Adonis on a pile of covers, his mane of curls scattered around his face, his body a bronzed landscape. God, he looked good. I stared at him from the corner of my eyes. *Had I really done that? Did that actually happen? Was I really selfish enough to do this to Dan for one night of escapism?* I couldn't bear to think about it. I closed my eyes, blocked it out and re-enacted the last few hours in my mind until my tired limbs took me into a heavy slumber. The sun was high in the sky by the time we woke, made love once more and eventually opened the sliding doors of the van. We squinted and looked out to the glistening sea. I breathed in deeply and smelt salty fresh air. People were already swimming and surfing. "Let's go in!" I beamed, the thrill of being near the beach still a complete novelty and still enough to distract my thoughts from reality.

"It'll be freezing," he said, yawning and stretching out his beautiful torso. He looked so calm and relaxed. I bet this was normal for him, nothing all that unusual, just another girl he'd pulled. He must have pulled millions, looking the way he did.

"I don't care," I said with mock bravery. "I just needed to get in that water". With me in just my bra and thong, him in his boardies, we ran down to the beach and dived in. The water immediately sent cold daggers into our skin. "SHIT! Shit! It's fucking freezing!" I screamed.

"I TOLD YOU!" He laughed, hopping up and down and holding his chest. I reached over and clung onto him.

Eventually our muscles stopped tensing against the cold and our grasp on each other softened. I swept my hands up and down his body under the water, still in disbelief. We kissed and I tasted the salty water on his lips. Swinging my legs up to wrap around his waist, from nowhere, warmth rushed back into my skin and he pushed himself against me, making my head spin once again. The heat between us was insane, but not even fire was enough to keep the chill of the English Channel from working its way back in. We shivered and laughed, easing out of each other's grip and into the low waves to move around. Swimming away from Ryan, I let the water wash away all the sweat, the salt, the cum. I floated on my back and stared at the sun. *What now*?

CHAPTER 7

No Man's Land

Employing my previous tactic of simply denying reality, thoughts of life back home got heavy-handedly shoved to the back of the queue in my mind, joining a crowd of fears and shame which resided there, desperately trying to make their way to the front and tell tales on me like a teacher's pet: *Miss…Miss…Charlene cheated on her boyfriend …she did…she had sex with a stranger… and she doesn't even regret it…she told me…Miss…I think you should punish her.*

SHUT IT GOBBY! I told the annoying brat in my head.

Getting dressed in front of Ryan as if he was my boyfriend, I temporarily revelled in this alter ego I seemed to have adopted, who happily chatted about simple things like the tides and laughed at the weird screeches coming from seagulls. Gemma and her friends, one by one also crawled out from vans nearby like spiders from under rocks. We meandered along the beach to a nearby café, everyone groaning about their raging hangovers and giggling over stories from the night before. I wondered what they were thinking about me. It was obvious what had happened as Ryan and I walked hand in hand, but no one made comment. They were either really polite or – and I prayed this wasn't the case – so disgusted by my blatant promiscuity that they couldn't bring themselves to acknowledge it. Perhaps these friendly islanders were far more sophisticated; perhaps they found my kind of behaviour crude; maybe I'd been in London too long, the place where anything and everything happened.

"Where did Nikki go so early then?" One of the girls asked the group just as we reached the café doors.

"I think she shagged that Aussie barman," someone replied.

"Oh yeah. Nice one! Wanna sit by the window?" She asked the group, pointing to a bench which gazed over the long stretch of cream coloured sand. Thank God, it seemed these people were unjudgmental when it came to slutty behaviour. Eating saucer-sized plates of eggs, bacon, mushrooms, hash browns and beans, I looked around the table at the happy faces. "How do you guys know each other?" I asked while mopping up yolk with my toast.

"We went to school together," said Gemma, nodding towards a girl wearing a Roxy halter-neck dress and an oversized hoodie. She smiled with cheeks full of food.

"I've known James since nursery," said one of the lads.

"Yeh, and he still pisses his pants!" replied a red-haired boy in a Kaiser Chiefs T-shirt.

"We kinda all grew up together, but didn't all know each other...if you know what I mean?" said Libby, who I vaguely remembered talking to early in the evening about her love of interior design. She worked in finance but wanted to go into property development and was interested in my paintings. "Everyone knows everyone here".

"That must be so nice," I sighed, feeling envious of such solid foundations and being part of a comforting community.

"Hmmm..." Libby laughed under her breath and raised an eyebrow, while the others made similar grunts and sniggers. "I guess it's nice... *sometimes*. "So anyway," Libby changed the subject, "Who's up for crashing at my place and lounging in the garden with Bloody Marys to nurse our hangovers...maybe a BBQ later?"

This was *so* fun. It felt so different to my life. I felt so at ease here. It felt like an alternative life — one I *could* have had — in a parallel universe or something. I could have grown up by the beach. These could have been my friends. I didn't want to go home. Why would I live in the city when I could be doing this? Chilling with lovely people, having breakfast by the sea at the weekends. I didn't have many friends in London. I met new people all the time, but the kind of characters I was drawn to were usually adventurers or radicals and therefore always transient. Just as a connected to a fellow artist or wild-hearted colleague, they'd be preparing to move on — just as I used to when I was backpacking. My good friends were either in other countries or scattered around the UK; getting in and out of town was a mission. I'd have to organise in advance to see anyone or do anything, and half the day would be written off by train journeys or traffic; there were no *just popping around for a cuppa* scenarios. Here, on this little island everyone was so close. The longest possible commute was the length of one TEDx talk; spontaneous hang-outs were far more frequent. It highlighted to me even more, the things that were missing in my life and I felt the sadness start to creep back in.

"What about you Char?" One of the girls asked. I loved that she already called me by my abbreviated name, it sounded so sweet and familiar. "What's it like in London? Must be wicked, hey? I went to Uni on the mainland, I miss it sometimes".

"Yeah, it's great, I love it," I lied. "Full of creativity…festivals and exhibitions on all through Summer". Ryan looked at me with excited eyes, like he was proud to have bedded such a cultural chick. Truth was, I was so skint I couldn't afford to go to most of the events happening just a few tubes-stops away from my flat. "New Year's Eve is pretty cool too," I continued, feeling a bit better that this was actually truth. "Everyone just piles into the city to watch the fireworks for free. They're amazing, I saw them last year…" I paused for a second, "…with my flatmates," remembering I had watched them with Dan, and that I had started having a panic attack in the middle of the heaving mass of people because I'd taken some drugs which were having a bad effect, and that he had saved me, pulling me out of the crowd, holding me and calming me down, unbothered that we ended up missing the whole display.

He was such a good guy. My belly churned and I could feel my full-English rising. I put my knife and fork down and sipped tea slowly to calm my nerves and settle my stomach. Everything about this weekend had me acting out of character. It was unheard of for me to not clear my plate — a trait I'd had since childhood and probably half the reason I ended up becoming bulimic. I never knew when to stop. I always wanted more.

It suddenly dawned on me that still, no one was acknowledging the fact that Ryan and I had hooked up. Not that I expected a fanfare or interview of course; it would have been a bit awkward if they had stood outside the campervan cheering and applauding, going on to quiz us in the cafe about the intricacies of our night together: *So Char, did Ryan satisfy you? And Ryan, did she do reverse-cowgirl?* No, that would have been a tad uncomfortable. But it was starting to feel like an elephant in the middle of the room. Did they even know I had a boyfriend? I suppose Gemma wouldn't have told them. At that time, Facebook had not long been in existence and social media was in its infancy, let alone accessible on your mobile. I had just about set up a profile which consisted of little more than a pouty selfie and old grainy scanned photos from school, so it was unlikely that I had been stalked by these guys yet. *Oh God,* I thought, *I know what's going on.* The reason no one was batting an eyelid was because this wasn't unusual. This had happened before—possibly many times.

I looked at Ryan who was sitting opposite me, in conversation with James. He was so gorgeous without even trying. The waitress came to our table, sticking her chest out, desperate to get his attention and he offered a polite 'hello' as she collected empties. *Fuck!* I thought. It suddenly became very clear: *he has them falling at his feet.* The only reason he hadn't been inundated at the party was because 'everyone knows everyone'. Any single girls last night had probably already been with him, or their best friend was one of his ex's. I was just another one of his conquests. I was his latest fling. How utterly embarrassing. This lot were probably looking at me and feeling sorry; *poor girl, here he goes again, another one who will come and go, another holiday maker gets her heart broken.* Why was I even worried? This wasn't going anywhere. I had a boyfriend, I lived in London, I was just a bit of fun for him. He had a good time and that was that. End of. Everything would go back to normal and the island would be a nice dream to remember once in a while.

~~~

Libby owned a beautiful house on the east coast. Standing in her brand-new monochrome kitchen with marble-effect worktops, I was in awe at what she had achieved. Just one year older than me, she had married young, worked hard in finance, gained promotions and bought her first home which was a new build but still in-keeping with original local architecture. Granite had been quarried in Jersey for centuries and it was used everywhere on the island. From garden walls to fortifications, to defences built during the German occupation in the second World War. Large pale slabs of stone with flecks of pink framed Libby's house and featured in the fireplaces and doorways. The interior was immaculate with an elegantly muted palette throughout.

"You see, I could do with something on the walls," she said as she gave me a tour. "We need some colour, some character... maybe something a bit more *sensual* for the bedroom," She added, flashing a cheeky grin. "I've kept a budget aside for art, but I just haven't seen anything I want yet that doesn't cost an arm and a leg".

As I peered into each sparse room with hessian-coloured furniture and expensive-looking linen, I wondered how many other young women like her owned their own homes and had such disposable income. I didn't know anyone back home who wasn't up to their eyeballs in debt or still living in slightly grotty house-shares. My head flooded with alien thoughts: *Perhaps I could sell my paintings here. Maybe I could hold exhibitions. I wonder if I could rent a little art studio?*

Whooa! Hang on there, sister! What on Earth are you thinking? My Left Brain butted in. I quickly told myself not to be so stupid. But something inside of me wanted to dwell in the fantasy. Fragments of long-lost wishes began to float around and form stories in my mind: Living by the sea. Being a successful artist. Freedom.

The reality of home drifted further and further away as I joined the gang outside who were making a blanket camp on the grass and listening to Ben Harper. I looked at Ryan who was lying on his front, leaning on his elbows and gesticulating while talking—something which I already recognised as one of his cute mannerisms. He was so *physical.* Everything he did came from his body. My eyes followed the line of his strong back down to his rounded butt. I remembered how it looked naked, perfectly shaped with a tan line. He turned towards me and smiled a bashful smile, surprising me with his show of shyness. Suddenly he didn't seem so confident.

"Right, who want's Bloody Marys?" Libby called.

The music came to an end and paused briefly before the next track, and I could hear birds singing in the magnolia trees above us. The sun was hot and everyone basked, taking off layers and hitching up skirts to get some colour on their shoulders and thighs. Ryan rolled onto his side and patted the blanket next to him, opening his arm to invite me in. *May as well enjoy it while it lasts,* I thought. I didn't know if I'd ever feel so welcome again. I laid with my head resting on his bicep while his other arm pulled me in close. His hand rested on my belly — the epicentre of so much of my past pain and everyday anxiety — the warmth from him melting it all away. Ryan seemed genuinely affectionate; it was different to most one-night stands. Memories from the night before breezed in and out of my mind and I surrendered to the moment, feeling weightless, floating in happiness while the sun projected peachy orange illuminations through my closed eyelids.

Coolness in the air pulled me out of sleep and dark shadows over my eyes finally woke me; the sun had disappeared behind large clouds. We had all been snoozing and chatting for the last four hours, and now, as the hair of the dog wore off, the grogginess set in.

"Ok folks, I'm off. I'm cream-crackered and gotta be at work early tomorrow," one of the lads said in a long-drawn-out yawn. "It's been great, thanks Libby. When's the next bus?" She hugged him goodbye and flopped back onto the floor.

"Me too babe," said one of the girls and gathered the contents of her bag which had somehow scattered between the kitchen, garden table and under people's sleeping bodies. Ryan ran his hand through his hair, "You can come back with me if you want". My whole Being wanted to scream, "YEEEEEEESSSSSS!" I wanted him to sweep me up and take me to his home and tell me that I could stay there forever. I wanted to lie in his bed and forget about what I'd done. I wanted us to make love for hours-on-end and fall asleep in each other's arms again.

"I can't," was my real reply.

We spent the next half an hour saying goodbye, until Gemma had to intervene. "Call me when you're home ok," he said sincerely. "And we'll work out when to see each other again".

"Ok," I replied, knowing full-well I wouldn't.

Back at Gemma's flat, the sun went down, the evening drew in and everything turned from pink to grey. The impact of what I had done began to sink in and my euphoria turned to terror as the postponed hangover finally kicked in. "Gemma, what will I do?" I ask her, tears instantly welling up in my eyes. I didn't need to explain what I meant. She understood.

"I don't know babe," she said, crying with me — her hangover also taking control. In the morning I would be flying back to London and back to Dan. Thinking about what I was going to say, was too much to bear. We resolved to eating pizza and laying either ends of the couch with a duvet while watching chick-flicks. Gemma patted my feet each time she caught me weeping as the emotional scenes worked their cheesy power. "Don't worry babe," was all she could say. I had fucked up royally; worrying was all I could do.

I got the train back home from Gatwick, my head spinning throughout the entire journey. When I reached the station, Dan was waiting there. I hadn't expected him to meet me. As usual, being his kind self, he had thought it a nice thing to do. He hugged me and kissed me and asked how my weekend was. I felt like a monster. Despite having the whole morning to think, I still didn't know what I would say. It wasn't until I saw his sweet face that I decided, in an instant, that I would say nothing.

That evening we made dinner at home and chatted about ordinary things. I told him that Gemma and I had visited beaches and landmarks and that Jersey was surprisingly nice. Everything seemed normal and happy and I looked the way I always did — except, I felt like an evil clone of myself that had kidnapped the old Char and left her on the island. I felt like I was made of thin glass and it would only take one wrong question to make me shatter into a million pieces. I wondered how I could possibly sustain this front. We went to bed that night and made love. I laid there while he went down on me, astonished by my own audacity. *What* was I? *Who* was I? *How* could I be so cruel, so cold, so deceiving? Could I really just act like the weekend never happened?

The next day rolled around and Dan went off early to catch his train into the city centre, looking smart and sexy as always in his slim-fit shirt and chinos. Once he had left, I sat on the bed and looked around our room. A simple canvas I had painted of him, hung on the wall. It was from a photo that I adored; a time when we were first falling in love. I cried hard without warning. Usually you know the tears are coming but these were fast and fierce. My hands shot up to my face as if to try and stop them or push them back in. I reached for my phone; I needed to tell someone — someone who knew me well and knew Dan too.

Hi babe…can you talk? I really need to talk, I text Lucy, my burlesque-loving friend. She called back immediately, always intuitively knowing when something was important and not just an outfit dilemma. I filled her in on all the details and she reacted as only a best friend does: un-shocked and unquestioning.

"I think I'm just gonna come out with it, Lucy…and tell him what I did," I whispered down the line, not wanting my flatmates to overhear. I never knew if they were in or not with their irregular acting work schedules. "I don't know if I can contain it much longer babe".

"Bloody hell. Ok. Right. Listen babe, I don't think you should tell him — not just yet anyway," Her voice was more serious than I'd heard it in a long time.

"But...."

"Hear me out," she persisted.

"You need to think Char; about what's going to happen *after* you tell him".

"I can't," I said, starting to cry again. "I can't think that far. All I can think is that with every single second that goes by, I am lying more and more to someone I love".

Lucy tried her best to suggest breaking it to Dan gently and trying to work things out with him; she explained to me the possible consequences of blurting out the truth and told me, once more, to think hard about what my plan might be if I did. Her voice sounded like there was a time delay, my brain not quite taking it in. "I just want to make sure you're ok. It's quite a big deal babe. Who knows how he'll react," she said in a way that I could imagine her saddened, sympathetic face on the other end of the phone. She really liked Dan and I knew, that despite being my loyal friend, she was upset for both of us. Eventually I hung up, refusing to promise that I wouldn't do anything hasty. I took her thoughts on board but I couldn't be sure what I'd say or do, and I wasn't prepared to lie to another person I cared about by taking a vow of silence which I'd most likely break. I sat back on the edge of the bed. I needed another opinion.

Lara popped immediately to mind. Lara knew what I was like and she knew Dan well. We'd seen each other at our best and worst on our travels together. From drunken one-night-stands with unsavoury characters to falling in love with natives from far-off lands. *Perhaps she'll feel differently about my predicament,* I hoped. I text her, knowing she wouldn't be able to talk. It was one hour ahead in France and she'd already be at work, knee-deep in phone calls, emails and admin at her high profile job on the Cote d'Azure.

Bonjour! I typed, oddly light-heartedly. *Er…ok…I have a dilemma….*

I waited, staring at the phone for three long minutes.

Shoot. She wrote back.

So…I kinda cheated on Dan on the weekend…well, not kinda…I seriously cheated on him…. badly cheated actually….and…I think I have to tell him.

FUCKETY FUCK. She replied.

Yeah…it's pretty fucked up. I wrote as the tears came again and I froze, waiting for her words of wisdom.

Maybe wait a little bit, sweetie. You don't have to do anything crazy. I mean, I know he probably needs to know…but…have you considered what he'll say? Or what you'll do? And there it was. The same response. The response I didn't want to hear. Why didn't I want to hear it? Why couldn't I just wait and work things out in my head and find a time when it wouldn't be so devastating for Dan? He'd just started a great new job. Things were just starting to look up for him. He was putting so much energy into bettering his life…OUR life. I looked at my bedside table, at the tiny mirrored picture frame with a photo of Dad in it. I didn't deal with loss well. If it was going to be over between us then I wanted it to be like ripping a plaster. I couldn't bear the agony of prolonging it. I couldn't deal with the guilt. Maybe that was selfish. I was the one who'd caused the pain yet I was the one who wanted the quick relief. "What would you do, Dad?" I said out loud, as I often did in times of confusion. And as always, nothing. I picked up the small picture. *Why doesn't he ever talk to me?*

By the time Dan got home from work I was a nervous wreck. I did my best to busy myself with laundry and cooking and then diverting attention by watching TV with our housemates in the living room. I was dreading going to bed. I couldn't be intimate with him again. As we turned in and turned out the lights I was relieved when he told me he was exhausted and fell asleep within minutes. I stared at the ceiling which was just visible from the street lights that crept through the gap in the curtains. My heart started to thump. Minute by minute it got faster and faster. I couldn't control it; every time I tried to relax, it just beat harder. Aware that I was now panting, I was worried Dan might hear me in the quiet room. I rolled onto my side but my lungs felt stifled and I rolled back. Despite having shared the same bed with him every night, I now had that bizarre sensation of sleeping uncomfortably close to someone for the first time, when your most natural reflex — breathing — becomes the hardest thing in the world. Inhales and exhales are elongated and shortened; you alternate between open mouth and closed mouth, unable to remember how you usually do it. Eventually my breaths became so irregular that I panicked. Oxygen was failing to make it in.

Dan jumped awake as I gasped loudly. "What's wrong babe?" He asked, quickly turning to face me. "What's the matter?" He placed his hand on me. "Shit! Your heart is pounding out of your chest". My head was exploding and words pushed their way towards my mouth. I thought about Lucy and Lara telling me to wait but the words pushed past. Before I knew it, I was saying them:

"I-slept-with-someone". I whispered at full speed. The words fell out and air rushed in to replace them.

"What?" I could just about see his brow dip in the orange light.

"I...slept with someone...in Jersey". The first time I said it out loud was immediate relief. The second time, it sounded foreign and my feelings turned back to terror.

"I can't believe you're saying this, Char. What the fuck? Why?...What are y'...Are you serious? He shook his head, frowning like it wasn't really happening.

But we had sex last ni'.... Oh my God." He sounded disgusted.

The next two hours were a sea storm and I was on a small raft. Thrashing, tumbling, plunging and drowning. Shivering, crying, clinging on for dear life. Still in a state of shock, he told me to tell him everything.

"You don't need to know the details...."

"TELL ME". He insisted. My limbs felt tired and heavy, my brain pounded. He wanted to know who the other man was, his name, his job. He asked me what I did with him—exactly what I did—and what he did to me. I shamefully answered, feeling like the lowest of the low. He asked me if I enjoyed it; if he made me come. I hung my head and cried. "Stop," I begged.

I watched him, hunched over on the bed; he looked broken. Even in his anger he wasn't aggressive towards me. I could see he was hurting bad. Lifting his head, the painting of him was is in his eyeline. Reaching over to it he hooked it off the wall. My legs went weak as he snapped it in two, before throwing it to the floor and crying. Simultaneously I felt a visceral rip in my heart.

The storm finally passed. An eerie quiet filled the room. We sat in silence with sore, puffy faces, the space between us, a vast ocean.

The stillness broke hours later with his softened and tired voice. "I dunno...I mean, maybe we could get over this... I understand that it *can* happen in relationships...I know you haven't been happy..."

I looked up, dumbfounded by his response. I hadn't imagined that he might consider forgiving me. I didn't want him to forgive me. How could he ever trust me again? How could I ever make up for the betrayal?

"I can't Dan".

His face changed. "Oh, I get it. You did it on purpose, didn't you?" He replied with a pained expression and a harsh tone. "You assumed I wouldn't take you back. You don't even *want* to work things out, do you?" He laughed stiffly. "You just want out. That is bullshit Char; you did it so you could have an excuse to break up. That's such a cowardly way to do it. Why didn't you just leave me? It would have been so much easier. Why did you have to do *this*?"

"No Dan, it's not like that." My plea sounded so weak.

"Whatever". His eyes turned vacant. "You got what you wanted".

In strange unison we climbed back under the duvet and lay there stiff as planks. We were like rival soldiers on ceasefire; the bed, No Man's Land; both needing rest, despite the bloody and brutal war that had just taken place. In that moment, I remembered my father's cold body laid out in hospital. The sadness I felt ran just as deep.

In the unknown hours of the early morning, while it was still just about dark, without words, we moved towards the middle of the bed and embraced each other's worn-out, trembling bodies and wept. Then slowly, as light crept in, we moved away again.

"Don't be here when I get back". Dan said, swallowing tears as he grabbed his coat and left to go to work the following morning.

CHAPTER 8

Villains in the Night

My world sunk into a cold, dark hole. A solemn, single chime rang slowly over and over in my head like a funeral toll; and yet this had been all my doing. It was *me* who had bludgeoned the bond. Only *I* had killed our relationship. Dan and I had been together almost six years. Of course, six years isn't a lifetime and we weren't husband and wife, nor did we have children, but it felt as good as a marriage. We had a closeness which tied the knot between us without any certificates. Every single one of our future plans were made with each other in mind, without a second thought. In stereotypical art-student nonconformist fashion, we agreed that a wedding was a waste of time, that we didn't need gold rings or papers to pledge our love; that we should be free, and *choose* to stay. For some reason—

which I was yet to define—I didn't feel free, and I inadvertently, *chose* to leave.

I could have just not told him. It was one night and he would never have known, but despite my infidelity I still loved him dearly. It would be a lie and I couldn't stand a relationship with lies. I would be kidding myself if I thought I could go on as if nothing had happened. Maybe those two words can never go together: 'infidelity' and 'love'. However, I knew there was a deeper reason for my actions. Cheating was the catalyst of change for me— admittedly not a noble one. A change that had been brewing inside of me for some time; one I had been denying. Everything in life had been shouting at me to do things differently but I was so scared. However, there comes a point where the fear of nothing changing is far more frightening. There comes a point when your soul does a deal with you and says, "This could all end in disaster… but at least it will be *different*". Dan wasn't the problem, I was.

I decided to call Lucy again. She was the only other girl I knew who was as resourceful as me. The only other chick who didn't need men or money to get what she wanted out of life. We had met on the first day of art college where I soon discovered how ridiculously creative with textiles, and mean with a pair or fabric scissors, she was. Driving like a

Parisian with a mouth like a sailor, Lucy was funny, feisty and somewhere between Denise Van Outen and Kirsty Allsopp. We would dance all night at clubs in Kingston upon Thames until our feet begged for mercy. Men who dared take up our dance space were kicked to the curb.

"Oh, come on Char," she'd say when I told her I had college work to do on a Friday night, "Just come out you idiot!"

"No, I can't, really," I'd say. "I've got half a sketchbook to fill before Monday".

"I'll pick you up at eight," was always her reply.

Crying down the phone once again, I filled Lucy in on the latest. "I've got to get out of the flat today Lucy…how am I going to do that?" I sobbed, "I've got loads of stuff here. I don't want to go to Mum's, she's gonna be so upset, I can't deal with her sadness as well".

"Ok. Look," Lucy said sternly. "We'll sort it. I'm coming over. Just gimme a few mins to do something ok? I'll call you right back".

I nodded in agreement silently, as if she could see me through the phone. The phone rang twenty minutes later.

"Okay!" Lucy's voice was enthusiastic. "I've got a van, it's a bit dodgy, but it's the best I could do. I'll be about half an hour…urgh…there'll be fucking traffic at this time, won't there? ….I'll be about an hour, ok babes?" I wanted to ask her where she'd got the van and tell her how much I appreciated her and say sorry for involving her in my mess but I couldn't speak. The tears kept on streaming. Just about managing a squeaky "Thank you," I continued with my futile nodding down the phone while she reassured me and told me to start putting things in bags, before hanging up.

Standing in the lounge, looking at the large paintings I had on the wall and wondering what on Earth I was going to do with them, I peered out of the curtains as a loud engine revved. From the window of a dicey-looking white van I spotted Lucy's signature wide, straight-toothed smile as she made a *Tah-Dah!* gesture; and despite the ordeal, I couldn't help but laugh. "How did you get your hands on that?!" I asked her as she came through the front door with her arms open and pulling me in for a bear hug. Her warmth sent me over the edge again.

"Why do I do these things?" I burst out onto her shoulder, leaving wet marks on her Breton stripe T-shirt. "But seriously," I continued, wiping my eyes, "Where the hell did you get that van?"

"You know that young, cute Italian in my neighbourhood? Well... just flashed the old eyelashes a bit, didn't I?...told him there was a damsel in distress, *et Voila!* ...had to convince him not to come with me though". She said, rolling her eyes.

"You're amazing," I stammered, "I don't know what I would do wi…"

"Ok, Ok," she butted in, "You can thank me later with wine. We've got work to do. This is the plan: throw stuff in bin bags, put bin bags in van, drive van to your mum's garage, say hello to your mum—keep it short and sweet or else you'll bloody meltdown again—get back in the van and come stay at my place. Ok?" The *Ok?* Wasn't really a question but I was more than happy for her to take charge.

"So, how much have you packed already?" Lucy asked with her hands on her hips. I stood with a roll of black bags in hand, feeling like a failed contestant on *Cash in the Attic*.

"I've put some clothes in a backpack," I answered feebly.

"Riiiiight, we're gonna need a bit more than that babes". Lucy looked around the room and sighed. "OK, give that here," she reached for roll and started ripping bags off. "You do the chest of drawers first and I'll empty the wardrobe". Working fast, she piled clothes, still on hangers, into the sacks. Meanwhile, I opened drawers and started picking things out and looking at them.

"Don't stop!" She called, "Just throw it all in".

"It's so hard," I said, welling up again, "He gave me this for my last birthday". I held in the air, a handmade card with loving words inside.

" J u s t   p u t   i t   i n   t h e   b a g, " Lucy said slowly and gently. She came over to where I was sitting on the floor and put her arms around me. "Listen, *everything* is going to have memories… and it's gonna be painful…and you can go through it all another time, but right now we just need to get it all out of here, ok?" I nodded, knowing she was right but wanting to just run to Dan and say sorry, and for him to forgive me, and forget this ever happened, and go back to normal — even if 'normal' was in pieces.

Bin bag by bin bag, room by room, we emptied the flat of my existence. Occasionally I stopped and folded in despair as I stumbled across yet another photo or love note; or when I discovered yet another cupboard filled with our shared possessions. Each time, Lucy would give me a proverbial slap around the face and tell me to keep packing. We needed to be out by the time Dan came home and it was already late afternoon.

In a two-woman bucket-brigade, we loaded the van up with heavy overflowing bags. "Blimey Char! How many clothes do you have?!" Lucy huffed, looking over her shoulder nervously every minute in case Dan came home early. She was friends with him too, the last thing she wanted was to be awkwardly caught in the middle of what was looking more and more like a heist on his home. My personal effects seemed to have been breeding in the flat and doubling in size; we finally hit the road about three hours later than expected.

Driving back out of London through rush hour traffic, in a vehicle which sounded like we might lose the back-end on Tooting Bec Road, by the time we reached Mum's and I gave her the gloomy news, it was pitch black outside. Mum had limited space in her allocated garage from the housing association. I promised her it wouldn't be for long and that I'd be at Lucy's for the time being, keeping it quick so as not to hear the inevitable question: *What are you going to do?* I had no clue what I was going to do.

"Ok let's get this done," Lucy continued to be my motivator. "The sooner we're done, the sooner we can go home and drink vodka". Unloading the bags into the cold garage with lowlight torches, I felt ashamed of the situation I'd put myself in.

"I'm such a loser," I announced as I held a painting of a curvaceous female nude in front of me and began to cry for the hundredth time that day. A car pulled into the estate. Like villains caught in the night, we stood ridged as blinding lights lit up the scene of two girls hauling goods from a white van into a secret store. The driver eyeballed me suspiciously with painted boobs flashing back at his headlamps, before moving to a space further down the carpark. We erupted into much needed laughter.

$$\sim\!\!\sim$$

"You can stay here as long as you like," Lucy said kindly. She knew what it was to need a bolthole when things got tough. She'd been through it too.

"Thanks babe". I was so grateful. "But I need a plan. I'll get one, I promise".

"Alright, but there's no rush". We sat on the sofa with goldfish bowls of vodka and cranberry. Finally resting after a full day of panic and hard labour, my head began to catch up with the reality. The uncontrollable tears returned. I cried and told her everything I felt, over and over again, torturing every detail of what had happened and how it had got to this point. Lucy sat quietly with me while I wept and jabbered incoherent words, because that's what friends do; they don't try to give you all the answers, they just listen to your questions. They don't try to fix it, they just rest with you while you're broken.

I stayed in the spare bedroom which had naturally turned into a haberdashery. Any plans Lucy's husband might have to turn the room into a shared space would be in vain. Her couture creations had a life of their own. Flopping onto the futon which had been pulled out between a dressmaking dummy and a cutting table, piled high with scraps of fabrics, tubs of vintage buttons and reels of lace trim. I stared at my unusual surroundings through beer goggles. How strange and sad it felt to suddenly be exiled from own bed, out of my home, out of the arms of my boyfriend and now taking refuge in a room with other detached, discarded and waiting-to-be-used things. I looked at Lucy's sewing machine and wished she could simply stitch my life back together, making it all glittery and beautiful again.

In the morning, with puffy eyes and a soggy pillow I reached for my phone. Nothing. I heard Lucy getting ready for work and instantly felt guilty. I couldn't loll around all day, I needed to gather my thoughts. I needed to get things sorted. I needed to keep focused or I'd end up being *that* friend who never leaves the sofabed. I suddenly remembered that I had been halfway through a commissioned painting for a client up until 22 hours ago when my life came to a screeching halt. I was already late delivering it to her after the last-minute trip to Jersey. Whatever happened, I had to finish it. God knows I needed the money.

"You alright babes?" Lucy's head popped around the door. "I'm shooting off but help yourself to anything ok and just chill. It's gonna be ok".

I nodded. "Thank you so much for all of this".

"No problemo!" she sang cheerfully as she turned to leave.

"Oh…Lucy?" I called quickly, hoping to catch her.

"Yeah?"

"Is it ok if I paint in here?"

"Of course," she shouted from the stairs, "My junk room is your junk room!"

Immediately, I felt a spring of relief. Throughout my life, whatever was going on, painting was always something I knew how to do. It was the only way I knew how to be ok when other things weren't. It was an external force which lived outside of the mundane. It didn't matter if I was rich or poor, single or attached, settled or on the move, happy or sad. Working on a painting was like going to a temple, praying and feeling the presence of the divine; it was my salvation from disappointment. That said—as with religion—it was also sometimes the cause of much frustration and confusion. If my artwork didn't turn out as I'd imagined or colours didn't feel harmonious or faces looked devilish instead of angelic, it was easy to lose faith. At those times I had to dig even deeper, paint harder and believe in myself even more. I decided in that moment, at a time when I had no direction at all, painting would be my holy grail.

Sitting on the floor with a large picture propped up against the wall, I felt calm wash over me as my hands automatically went to work in the way they knew well. The image I'd created for my client who was a burlesque performer, was of her, wearing a beautiful mermaid tail as she did in her shows. It was almost complete, all it needed was adornments. I found stitching embellishments onto canvas, deeply therapeutic. With my eyes fixed on the needle and thread as they meticulously fastened sequins, beads and jewels to the taut surface, I would drift off, thinking, staring, switching into Right Brain and going into some sort of meditation for hours on end. My mind floated around my predicament, although not quite as emotionally attached to the whole thing as before. I watched it like a movie of someone else's story. I saw London with its busyness and crowds. I saw me, the protagonist, crying, stressed, abusing my body. I saw myself on the short flight to the Jersey, looking out of the small window at the sea below. And then my vision burst into sunlight. Flashes of that weekend whizzed past my eyes like a speed train; beaches, bonfires, sand dunes, fields, seagulls calling, faces smiling, country lanes, salty sea air, waves crashing, small villages, French street names and harbours filled with sailing yachts and fishing boats. Most of all, the feeling of joy. As I sewed aqua marine sequins one by one, my eyes dazzled with the rows of tiny metallic discs and the mermaid's tail began to move. An idea—clear as day—dropped into my mind like a pebble into a glassy lake. It was the clearest idea that I've ever had; clarity had never been so vivid. A decision had never been so solid.

I would move to the island. No question.

I felt both excited and petrified all at once by this oracular message. I definitely knew I *wanted* it; but how on earth could I pull it off? Within minutes I was already doubting my crystal-clear choice. Doubts crept in like cockroaches. *You can't just leave. Where will you live? You can't afford it. How will you earn money? Your home is here. Your family are here. Is it even legal to work there? Don't you need a visa or something? What about all your stuff? Where will you go while you work all this out? You can't stay on Lucy's futon for the next two months. What will people think? They'll say you're running away. Be realistic Char.* That last subconscious comment halted the thought trail; in fact, it properly pissed me off. People were always telling me to 'be realistic'. What the hell did that even mean? Who decides what is *realistic* anyway? Why *couldn't* I do what my heart desired?

Just then, a small white feather floated onto my painting. I stared at it, scared to move, as though if I did I would break a spell. Even though Lucy's dressing room was full of props and costumes with large rainbow coloured ostrich feathers, this one was different. It was tiny and pure white. I looked around for proof of its origin. I couldn't see anything with white feathers anywhere. I had read somewhere that they were a symbol of angels being near and I immediately thought of Fairy; I hadn't thought of her for some time.

I could easily argue that the feather came from one of the many creations in Lucy's spare room, but I choose to embrace the sign and the *knowing* feeling that came with it. This, to me, was further evidence that I should dismiss the 'be realistic' attitude. It was up to *me* what I did and did not believe, and it was up to *me* what I did with my life. I knew that Fairy was confirming my decision and telling me not to be fearful. In a kind of trance, I put my needle and thread down and reached for a pen from a pot on the table. On a clean page in my sketchbook I wrote at the top:

To Do List
Under the title I scribbled:

1. *Find out cost of ferry to Jersey.*

CHAPTER 9

Lighthouse

Determined to follow through on my vision, I made a plan of what I needed to do in order to make my move to the island. I took the plunge and booked a place on the Portsmouth to Jersey slow ferry for me and my car, giving myself a three-week deadline to work through each item on my To-Do list. The crossing would be overnight, taking ten hours. I couldn't afford a cabin so I'd be making do, sleeping on a seat. Most people would take the much shorter ferry which takes less than half the time, but the traditional cargo boat was cheaper and I needed to save every penny I could. Plus, I liked the idea of having time to switch off. Staring out to water for hours on end with little sleep, was just what I needed. I had things to think about. I was in no hurry. Being *all at sea* was where I was right now.

Sitting with a cappuccino at a coffee shop in Richmond Upon Thames, feelings of peace cut through the fear as I researched Jersey residency laws, rules for employment, rooms for rent, cost of living, job vacancies and carparking permits. I was always relaxed while organising long trips or relocations; getting back on the move or going somewhere new was soothing to my gypsy-rooted heart—a positive distraction from the reason for it all.

Movement kept things flowing, stopped the stagnation and helped me to look forward, instead of backwards. Contrary to what I knew most people would be thinking, I didn't feel like I was 'running away'. I wasn't running from a mistake, I wasn't running from guilt, I wasn't running from responsibility. To me, I was *diving* into a new life, where things would be better all round—for everyone involved. What good was I to anyone, moping and crying about my circumstances? What good was I, being a burden on someone's sofa or a drain on someone's wallet? What good would it do me to be in the same city as an ex-boyfriend who didn't want to see my face? … or ex-flatmates and friends whose loyalties lay with him? I wasn't running away. I was diving into a chance to do things differently. I was diving into *new* responsibilities. I was diving into a fresh start. Like holding a blank canvas, paintbrush in hand.

There is nothing like a crisp white canvas, waiting for a new vision to be made manifest on it. I'd often worked over old paintings when I couldn't afford to spend any more money at the art shop or when I ran out of room for my creations, or when the picture just wasn't working out the way I'd planned. Sometimes I'd paint over artwork again and again until evidence of the old brushstrokes below, began to show in blemishes, bumps and lines. Reworking old, tired paintings limited what I could put on top. Dark colours and shapes often came through like shadows and flaws; the surface would be an uneven and unreliable foundation; occasionally cracks would form from piling on one-too-many layers; from trying too many times to get it right. There was nothing like a fresh new canvas. Unlimited. Untarnished. Bright and clean. No history. Anything was possible.

With the help of Gemma back in Jersey I arranged to rent an attic room in the same building as her. I didn't have much money to get started but she knew the landlord well and they were happy for me to pay my rent a month in arrears until I found a job. I didn't even know if I'd find a job that soon, but I had no alternative but to trust that something would work out. Somehow, things always worked out when I was away from home. I put it down to that gypsy-spirit again. Comfort and faith in the unknown.

~~~

October 2009

I left England with very little to my name. What I *did* have though, was a room to stay in, a car full of paintings and a will for things to be different. My only guide was my longing to feel happy and free. Driving onto the ferry, that old feeling of excitement entered my heart again; it was always there, lying dormant until the next adventure. Leaving my car in the bow of the boat, I headed upstairs and stopped outside on the deck before finding my seat. The air was cold but the freshness was welcome. As we trudged along, I watched the white-water trail from the stern and I contemplated my past and my future. My dad had essentially died from stress, I had been suffering from stress too, and I was seeing stress affect so many people in my life — and in the western world at large. Something had to change. *I* had to change.

Watching the south coast drift into the distance, I vowed that I would do whatever it took to decrease the anxiety in my life. I would not repeat familial or societal patterns of being governed by money; I would not be threatened by media ideals about what job I should have or how successful I should be, or what I should own by a certain age. I would not worry about getting married or having babies just because my peers were. I would not simply mirror the way everyone else was living around me.

I found my seat on the top deck and settled in for the long journey. Rummaging through my bag for one of the many supermarket snacks I'd piled in (the thrifty traveller in me knowing how easily I could lose cash buying food onboard), I found a book which I'd forgotten I'd even packed. Come to think of it, I couldn't actually remember where I got it in first place; someone must have given it to me.

YES MAN, read the title.

by Danny Wallace

'One little word can change your life,' read the subtitle.

'Now a major film starring Jim Carey'.

I'd found myself saying 'no' more and more lately. *No* to going for jobs because I didn't think I'd get them. *No* to nights out because I was so broke and too ashamed to let friends keep buying me drinks. *No* to food because I felt fat. *No* to my inner voice which was crying: *LISTEN TO ME!*

I had already come to learn that books often find you when you'll most benefit from reading them. I'd had a few novels and biographies 'jump out' at me from libraries and charity shops before, offering insight or inspiration when I needed it. Just as I was getting tired of saying 'No', this *Yes Man* book had landed in my hands. Without questioning its origin any further, I opened to the first page, and while making the crossing over the English Channel, I read it through to the end. It was very rare for me to finish a book in one sitting but the message spoke so strongly to me. I knew I had to start saying 'Yes' to my life again. I decided, the moment I stepped off the ferry I would be a *Yes Girl*. From that day on I would introduce myself as an 'Artist,' rather than someone who "does a bit of art on the side of jobs I hate". I would be open to new things, new ideas and new people.

Deciding to be a *Yes Girl* took effect immediately. In fact, it seemed that as soon as I booked that ferry ticket, things began shifting and falling into place; I literally saw my life changing before my eyes in a matter of weeks. Gemma let me help her by covering reception and cleaning on Saturdays in her beauty therapy studio. I also found a part-time position as a nanny for a lovely family through one of her clients. Plus, I landed a one-day-a-week job as a sales assistant where I was left to my own devices in a cute little boutique in town. In no time at all I had three perfect jobs. Despite juggling my days between employers and doing roles which were not so creative, I was much happier. The work was fun, simple, relaxed and encouraged me to meet new people and see different parts of the island. I loved the variety. I loved that I wasn't just in the same environment, doing the same thing every day.

Keeping my promise to myself, I told every person I met that I was an Artist, and I worked on paintings in my attic room every spare moment. I became super pro-active in the local artist community—joining group exhibitions, holding stands at various events and organising small solo displays of my art in bars and cafes. I went out with new friends and danced more than I had done for years.

I felt like a new person already. As I went for a run along the water's edge one day, out of nowhere, I became overwhelmed with feelings of happiness, relief and gratitude. Sitting on the sand, I looked out to the dormant lighthouse which waited for dusk to resume its warning light. It suddenly struck me: I was almost in disbelief that just a couple of months ago I was going for a run in a city and could only dream of living by a beach. I realised: *I had made all this happen.* And it had all happened so fast. I was somehow living a life that I loved, simply by saying 'Yes' to opportunities that came my way. Life was fitting around *me*, instead of *me* trying so hard to fit around life. I was using the *Law of Attraction* before I even knew what it was.

I got up, turned around and started to run home. Something made me look back momentarily. Although it was still a bright day with clear blue skies, I could have sworn I saw the lighthouse flash.

While doing all this positive activity, I was also going through a period of some serious letting-off steam. I wanted to somehow shake off the sadness and guilt that still resided in my bones, in spite of my new-found optimism. I worked hard all week but on Saturday nights I let my hair down, and it became more and more excessive as the weekends passed. Before long I was going off the rails. Drinking, partying and sex took over once again, and with the highs came the lows. The nights were wild but my hangovers were heavy and so was my heart. Each time I met a new guy and become infatuated, I'd go downstairs to see Gemma in her flat and tell her all about him.

"Do you think he's… you know… 'T.O?" she would ask, meaning 'The One'.

"Yes," I'd reply sincerely, "He is definitely T.O."

As winter got colder, I sat in my attic room watching *Sex and the City* boxsets with a bottomless glass of wine to delay the impending meltdown.

Bulimia kicked back in as I denied the struggle to deal with my emotions, which even positive thinking couldn't penetrate. Although *I* was the one who cheated and *I* was the one who left, deep down I felt total despair. My sadness was as strong as when I'd lost Dad and I realised then, that broken hearts and bereavement lived in the same dark shadows.

A wet wind blew outside and rattled my loft window, while a fat baby seagull screamed continuously for its mother. Lying on my bed in the dark, I pictured myself from a bird's-eye view. I was living on a tiny rock which felt like an invisible speck on the map of Europe. Even though it hadn't initially seemed like I was running away, it now appeared that I had banished myself to a tower surrounded by sea so that no one from my past could get to me. I was heading in to some sort of self-induced emotional rehab where I needed distance from my old life in order to look back.

Ryan and I were still in regular contact since that weekend I visited Jersey for the first time. He was beautiful. He was manly. He was self-sufficient. He was skilled with his hands. He was everything I wanted in a guy. But I couldn't handle the memories that came flooding back every time I saw his face; and I definitely didn't want it to look to others, like I'd left London to be with him. I hadn't. But I couldn't resist him though, and we had a magnetic attraction. We were both passionate, sexual and spontaneous. We were like animals chasing one another, pulling and running away each time one of us got caught; each time the tear in my heart getting torn a bit further down. It was only a matter of time before it ripped completely.

We both attended a mutual friend's birthday at a hotel, winding up at the end of the night in a room. I was crazy about him and lost control in his presence. So far we'd been caught on camera on a poker table in the back room of a bar, we'd ended up naked in a field under the full moon on the bonnet of his Jeep, and that night—at the hotel—I found myself being lashed with a leather horse whip; the pain, by far, outweighing the pleasure. It was supposed to be a bit of fun. He thought I was enjoying it of course, judging by my squeals. In my typical, always-wanting-to-please-others-way, I didn't let on that he was doing it all wrong and it was, in fact, excruciating. In the morning, everyone met in the dining room for breakfast and we barely spoke a word. I wanted the Earth to rise up around me and pull me down in to her core.

I got home and undressed. Turning to look in the mirror I stared at the huge, angry red welts on my backside and thighs. I stared and stared while my eyes filled up with painful saltwater until I couldn't see anymore. Falling on to the bed I lay quiet for a moment and the world spun around me, my heartbeat loud in my ears. I thought I'd been as low as I could go but this was a new level. I took one large breath in, and on the outbreath my soul screamed like never before.

I cried all afternoon and all night, my head pounding with crippling shame. Shame was what had brought me to this point. I'd kept it tucked down deep inside of me ever since cheating on Dan and now, subconsciously I had found a way to be punished. I'd already punished myself as much as I could by abusing my own body; now I was finding others to do it for me. It had to stop. I'd hit rock. This had to be a turning point or I'd end up in hospital.

How was I getting it so wrong again? I asked myself as I ran my fingers over the welts. I'd come here to start afresh. *How was it already so sour? I was supposed to be doing things better, making better choices, saying YES to my heart. What was I missing?*

CHAPTER 10

Aladdin's Cave

That night I allowed myself to cry until I had nothing more to shed. It was futile trying to stop the flood once the barriers had given way. I slept sporadically, waking at least once an hour and feeling the tension thump in my head before rolling back over again and again. Finally, I stepped out from the covers in a haze with no idea of the time. I knew it must be Sunday, but glancing to the window the sky looked dull. I couldn't tell if it was morning or evening. *How long had I been in bed?*

A single church bell rang in the distance and my first thought was my friend Lottie, a beautiful blonde ray of sunshine whose energy bounded off the walls. Our enthusiasm multiplied whenever we were together, and normal days out down the beach or sitting in the garden always turned into a mass of laughter and adventure. She had recently devoted herself to Christianity and we often talked about the big questions of life. It didn't matter that our beliefs weren't the same, we always agreed on the common truth: that all of life was mysteriously — albeit sometimes painfully — magical. I didn't feel like that anymore though.

I wasn't a church-goer at all but something pushed me. I picked up my phone and text her, saying simply that I was in a bad way, that I didn't want to talk about it but I needed support. I told her that I wanted to go to church and asked her where I could go. The words were weird to say: *I want to go to church.* I'd definitely never said that line in my life before. I had no idea about these things; could I just turn up to any church? Were there particular times? Would the doors be locked out of hours? Would they ask me if I was a Christian? Did I need to be a member? Would everyone look at me if I was crying? Like a guardian angel she replied in a flash, telling me to get in my car straight away and head down to St Pauls in town where, luckily for me, they were holding a *New Wine* evening.

"What time is it?" I asked her, slightly confused, also wondering how much wine was involved exactly. I'd had my fair share on Friday night, I wasn't sure that 'hair of the dog' was the best move.

"Coming up for eight 'o'clock," she answered.

"In the morning?" I scratched my head.

'No hun, in the evening,' she said gently, "Come down, it's about to start".

"Bloody hell!" I yelped, I'd been in bed for an entire day.

Contrary to my first guess, *New Wine* was not a piss-up in a church. It was, in fact, a kind of conference and celebration for churches from different towns, cities or countries to connect with each other. This was especially important for Jersey to keep up to speed with progression within modern Christianity, since they were cut off from the mainland. Lottie assured me that I would be welcome, that I could stand near the back and that she would look after me. Tip-toeing into the large, cold stone building filled with candles, I spotted her big smile. With prayer sheet in one hand and without words, she put out her free arm and pulled me in to her side where I silently wept throughout most of the service with its thought-provoking readings and emotive songs. I didn't need to tell her anything.

I was a little sceptical of Christianity I suppose, but a lot of what was being said made sense. The words I heard which broke through my own repetitive thoughts, were things about forgiveness; forgiving yourself as well as others, and the freedom that it brings. I always forgave others—I wasn't an angry or bitter person — but I'd never been very good at forgiving the one person who beat herself up all the time for such little things: Me. I wondered why I was so hard on myself.

"Are you gonna be ok honey? Why don't you start coming to church with me?" she gently suggested at the end of the night. I wasn't sure about it, but there was no reason I felt strong enough to say no. I needed *something.* I was at a loss with myself. I had no resistance left, no filters I could put on my fatigued face. What did I have to lose?

"Ok…I will," I said meekly.

Just as we were heading out of the nave I looked up at the gallery above us where more people were gathering their things and moving around. I did a double-take as I spotted a clock mounted on the mahogany balcony — eleven minutes past eleven. We stepped out into the entrance area and a small framed man came up to us. Lottie beamed.

"Ah! Peter…Hi!" She gave him a hug.

"Did you enjoy the conference?" he asked. He had an unbelievably kind face and the brightest blue eyes.

"Yes, it was brilliant!" Lottie replied excitedly. "Did you?"

"Wonderful" He said, and we all chatted for a while about the different speakers. I was happy to talk by then; the evening had really calmed me down and I felt quite comfortable among these people. It was obvious I had been crying but I didn't care. Everyone just offered me smiles and cups of tea.

"It was lovely to meet you Charlene," Peter said and headed to the refreshments table. As he left I turned to Lottie. "This is going to sound weird but, did you see his eyes?" I asked her under my breath. "They were insane! They looked like…I can't explain… like they were shining ridiculously… but no… not shining, as such…. they were incredible… like…." I hesitated while trying to think of the words.

"Like they were on fire… blue fire?" Lottie smiled.

"YES! Exactly," I squeaked, trying to keep my voice down. "You saw it too?"

"No, but I know what you mean."

"Oh," I was a bit confused, "That's strange. Maybe I just need more sleep." I rubbed my forehead.

"They say that if you see someone with blue flames in their eyes then you have seen the face of Jesus". I raised my eyebrows. "Just saying," She shrugged.

I committed to giving religious practice a go at least. In addition to the Sunday services, I began attending a weekly Christian club. I figured that if I was going to do this then I may as well get stuck right in. I never did anything half-heartedly; all or nothing, as always. I wanted to try to better understand the whole thing which was so new to me. Why was it that so much of the population followed Jesus? What was the deal? Had he REALLY existed...or was it just a legend? I never really thought that religion would be my path but I decided to explore it with curiosity and an open mind. The people I'd met so far—at a time when I was at my weakest—had shown me so much kindness and warmth, like a soothing balm on my heart.

I tried to embody everything that it taught me about compassion; there was no denying that compassion was the key to so many issues. It just made me wonder though, about Buddhism; wasn't that religion also based on compassion? I'd witnessed Buddhists in Thailand when I'd been backpacking there years ago. They seemed such gentle, helpful, content and peaceful people. I was confused. Buddhism looked so natural and made so much sense, but Christianity was teaching me that Jesus was the only true voice I should listen to. I tried hard to stay optimistic while endless questions played on my mind which couldn't be answered by the Bible alone. Unsurprisingly, the hardest question of all for me, was the one about no sex before marriage. I tried, I really did, but I couldn't quite get my head around it. What constituted as 'sex' anyway? I mean, aside from the *obvious.* But where was the line? What were the rules? Was it just penetration that was sinful out of wedlock? Was a blowjob ok?

I started dating a surfer and told him what I was doing. "We can do anything but sex," I tried to explain. I wasn't sure what I expected him to say, or whether he'd even stick around, but actually he was relaxed about it. By nature, surfers can be quite spiritual people in their own way. The connection they have with the sea, their awe and awareness of both its beauty and its immense strength, gives them a reverence and respect for its often-unseen power, and a humbleness for their small part in the grand scheme of nature. No, he didn't have a problem with the no-penetration rule. It was me who fell at the first hurdle and gave into his tanned washboard stomach.

∾

On a bright day in Autumn I followed my feet, meandering through town and onto St Aubins bay where I walked along the sand all the way down to the harbour, on the south west of the island. The small village was a favourite for tourists with its cute little shops, restaurants boasting fresh *moules et frites,* and a vintage fair where locals sold jewellery from the 1900s and shabby-chic furniture. With French gypsy-jazz spinning somewhere on an old record player, I browsed the tables which had no particular order. Nestled between 70s second-hand clothing rails and Art Deco poster prints, were green and blue glass fishing floats and old sea lanterns.

I'd been told by a friend to come and find Tamsyn, a girl who owned one of the boutiques. Potentially, she could be interested in selling my artwork. Walking past the boats in the harbour, the masts clanged gently in the breeze like a baby tinkering on a xylophone, I spotted the brightly coloured shop fascia.

Stepping into Tamsyn's shop was like stepping into Aladdin's cave; everywhere I looked I saw things I only dreamed about owning. In the middle of the room was a captivating tree, dried out and sprayed gold, branches reaching in all directions and bohemian jewellery hanging from every inch. I circled it in awe, running my hands through the Indian silk-covered beads, and silver chains with feathers and tassels in tropical sunset hues. On a table, a large wooden carving of an oversized hand held heaps of bracelets in its palm and stacks of rings with turquoise stones piled onto each finger. Along the walls were rails of clothes which looked like they were from Morocco, Mexico and Paris. *Hotel Costes* played on a stereo in the background and a Frankincense candle burnt in the air.

"The changing room's at the back if you want to try anything, darling," called a voice from the counter.

"Oh, hi!" I replied. "Are you Tamsyn? … I'm Charlene," I added as I walked over, assuming that she was. She looked cool and creative and like she was in charge.

"Yes," she answered with a smile, waiting for me to continue.

"Excellent! I mean, I was hoping to meet you. I'm an artist," I said in my now well-rehearsed, assertive way. My friend Lisa told me to pop down".

"Ah…yes," she said, her smile broadening. "Yes, she said you'd be down. I hear your art is amazing".

"Oh…well," I stuttered, a little uncomfortable. I was still working on taking compliments where my art was concerned. "So, I thought perhaps you might like to take some of my framed prints….to sell here in the boutique?" I got my phone out and started showing her pictures of my paintings.

There was a pause as she looked around.

"Look," I quickly broke the silence, "Don't worry if they're not suitable, it's fine, it was just an idea," I felt a bit embarrassed. Her stock was all so exquisite; my burlesque girls with their diamante thongs and small sequin bras were probably a touch untasteful for her chic interior.

"Oh no, no, not at all!" She sighed. "I love them, they're gorgeous, and I'm sure we can put one or two small ones out. But I don't really have much wall space". We both glanced around the shop; every space really had been utilised. Even windchimes hung from the ceiling and scarves from light fixtures.

"Of course, no worries, anything at all would be fantastic," I said happily, although feeling slightly deflated.

"Wait," Tamsyn went on. "There is something I would love you to do for me, but I feel a bit awkward asking. I'm not sure I could pay you what you'd need to charge. I'm on a bit of a budget here you see, I do all of this by myself".

"I know that feeling well!" I spouted, and she smiled, looking reassured. "Go ahead," I urged her.

She took me outside to the front of the shop and pointed to a wood-decked wall on the side of the building. "I want to do something with this," she said. "Something really special".

Tamsyn told me how she had always wanted to have a beautiful mural painted somewhere on the exterior, ever since she had moved into the premises. She had visions of a vivid, decorative design with a tactile surface which would reflect the boutique's style, and draw more customers in. I was excited by the idea and knew in an instant that I wanted to do it. I could already imagine what it would look like:

Indian henna shapes in Arabian colours with gold outlines; mosaic tiles, shells and beach glass attached with adhesive. It was going to take some time though. But the more we talked, the more we realised we had similar tastes and I liked the idea of spending time in her company, even if it meant losing out a bit, financially. The shop was empty of customers for a while, and our conversation flowed fast, whisking from art to travel to music; through to food, into relationships and back around to art.

"I better get back to work before it gets dark!" She joked, checking her watch.

"I'll do some designs for you and pop back then," I suggested.

"Listen, this is just an idea..." She looked a bit hesitant.

"Go for it," I asked eagerly, buzzing from our chat.

"There's this thing on next month...it's a dance weekend. It's quite expensive...and I really wanted to go...but I'm not sure who to go with. I was thinking maybe...you might like to come with me...I'd get your ticket, as part payment for the mural".

"Ooh! Sounds brilliant," I said, "I love dance DJs. Is it anyone I'd know? ... David Guetta? ... Calvin Harris?"

"Er, no, it's a bit different to the dance music you're thinking of," she said, looking slightly sheepish. "It's not exactly a clubbing event. It's called 'ecstatic dance' and it's kinda like a mind-body-soul thing — sort of like meditation — but dancing. Hey, no worries if it's too 'out there', it was just a thought," she concluded.

"Mind-body-soul dancing," I repeated, sounding interested. I thought back to the last couple of weeks since not going to church and how I missed having that feeling of *connection.* I thought back to my pledge to being a 'Yes Girl'.

"Sign me up," I said.

I pushed the doors to the community centre and immediately got a waft of sage. People were milling around in yoga pants, carrying water bottles and blankets. Some chatted in groups, while others sat alone reading or stretching limbs. A table had been set up in the foyer and a girl with big brown eyes and curly hair spotted me.

"Hi sweetie," she said, gesturing for me to come over. "Have you already signed up?" She asked with her pen poised at a list of names on a clipboard.

"Yes, it's Charlene, I mean, I might be under Tamsyn's name, she got my ticket for me, I think she's just on her way," I said, looking back to the door.

"Ah yes, here you are," she grinned. "I'm Sonia, let me know if you need anything. Go on through honey, help yourself to herbal tea".

I walked down the corridor which had various laminated A4 signs on the wall with things like: *'Please switch off your mobile phones'* and *'Namaste'* written on them. I could hear flute music coming from the left. It was the gymnasium, where it seemed the dancing would be happening. On the right was a kitchen and people were bustling and bringing in large dishes of vegetarian food. *Was I supposed to bring something?* I thought, and looked down at a sheet of paper I'd been handed when I walked in. Just then, Tamsyn came in behind me.

"Sorry I'm late darling," she breathed, last minute bloody drama with getting someone to cover the shop — all sorted now though".

"I only brought a bit of food for me," I whispered worriedly, holding a plastic triangle containing a cheese and pickle sandwich. "I think we were supposed to bring food to share...it says so here," I said waving the paper which was full of information about the weekend.

"Voila!" She beamed, producing a huge cobalt blue ceramic pot of homemade couscous which looked and smelt like it was straight from a market in Marrakesh. "I made this for both of us".

"You absolute star!" I said, relieved. "Shall we go in?"

The gymnasium was filling with people laying on yoga mats and sat in lotus position. One or two were already moving around in a kind of martial art way and others hugged and chatted quietly. The strip lights were off and curtains were partially drawn on the glass doors. The room glowed gently with Himalayan salt lamps dotted around the perimeter. I noticed the low table in the middle of the room; it was laden candles and incense, crystals and feathers, flowers, herbs and things I couldn't quite make out. The flute music I heard from the hallway came from a statuesque girl to the side. Tall with hair down to her waist that looked impossibly thick, she wore a simple Grecian-type dress which made her look like an understated Goddess. At the front, was a man with a goatee sitting quietly, smiling as people entered and nodded their acknowledgments. We found a space and laid our blankets down, already warm from the extra heaters which had been brought in.

"Feel free to sit for a while at the altar during your dance," the man said after a welcome chat. He had introduced himself as a Shaman.

Altar. That's what it is, I thought. I liked that idea; perhaps I would make a small one in my bedroom. I had been feeling the need for somewhere physical to go, to rest my mind and focus my spiritual thoughts; somewhere which wasn't a religious building, somewhere which wasn't my dad's grave.

The music started and he talked us through a meditation to relax, breathe deeply and start moving each part of our body, beginning with the toes and travelling up until we reached our heads. The music was serene and ethereal. I hadn't really heard anything like it before, except for maybe on wildlife documentaries. The sound of raindrops, pan pipes, soft percussion and chimes flowed around the large space which now felt very different to a school gym. Slowly we stood and began to move. Some people looked awkward while others made bold shapes. Although it was unusual and I felt slightly vulnerable, I was generally at ease; dancing had always been my comfort zone and where I felt most at home in my body.

Over time, the music changed subtly. It grew a little faster, the feeling was different, echoed by the crowd who also moved quicker. I could hear a sitar playing and my mind imagined India—somewhere I'd always wanted to visit. Now and then, a soft voice came over the microphone and reminded us to focus purely on our bodies and try to stay out of our heads.

"The voice of the ego may try to tell you that you are being silly, or that you look weird or unattractive, but just thank it for its words and try to ignore it. It will only restrict your free motion," he said in a friendly tone.

People closed their eyes as they danced, taking their minds away from the office, work, home life, and reconnecting back to themselves. After a while the music evolved again. This time there were Celtic sounds and a lightness filled the air. People spun, skipped and even laughed spontaneously. Later, a Spanish guitar came in, as well as a faster beat. A deep bass line struck my heart. Latin and R&B music was where my soul resided; it always had done. Immediately my hips circled and I felt sensual. I closed my eyes and let myself go even more, hearing sighs and quiet humming along to tunes as bodies moved past me. It was like being in a massive nightclub when your favourite song comes on and, for a moment, you're enraptured by the music, letting it take over you. Except this felt so much deeper and no one was caring how they looked or who was looking at them, and I could dance barefoot, instead of in four-inch heels, trying not to get stuck to sticky floors or stand on broken glass.

The guitar faded away and the beat became more intense; a tribal sound made with hand drums, accelerating by the minute. Dancers moved faster, feet hit the floor harder. The room was getting hot and the spaces between bodies seems smaller. The bongo drum reverberated inside me and sounded like a high-speed chase. People were stomping to the rhythm, thrashing around and starting to sweat. I could feel adrenalin course through my veins and my head tingled as if I had taken drugs. I threw my arms up and shook my core, urged by the need to move every single muscle and feel a release. In my own little sphere of euphoria, the surrounding area began to blur, I could hear shrieks, groans and even crying. Just as I my legs were losing energy, the drums stopped.

Silence.

Panting breath.

While energy still buzzed in the air, birdsong came over the sound system. Calming sounds of rushing water filled the hall. Gentle music quietly eased back in, as wild animals began to slow down and turn back to humans. Any unease which had been present before, completely disappeared. For a few precious moments we were one living, breathing, heaving mass; moving in flow in the aftermath of a storm. Slowly, slowly, dancers reduced their speed and made a few final movements and spins, like a sprinter unable to stop the momentum until after the finish line.

Instructed to move back down to the ground, I laid out on the hard floor, this time uncaring that there was no blanket or matt. The wooden surface felt so cool and solid to my effervescent skin. As the Shaman waited for everyone to become still, so that he could lead us through a closing meditation, I was in awe of what had just happened. Somehow, I had gone into a kind of trance where nothing else mattered except how I wanted to move. I felt like I had been in another world where there was nowhere I had to be, nothing to worry about, and no one else to think about. I had felt so incredibly free and it was as close to the feeling of being in the water as I'd ever experienced. It was primal. I was spent. All my muscles had been used. I drifted off and woke to the word: 'Lunch'.

During the afternoon session I felt even more relaxed and at home among the other dancers. As we were guided through different exercises to help us go deeper within ourselves and interact with the group too, I felt relief to be in such good company. Everyone had come to be there for many different reasons but the goal was the same. As I came to understand, by talking to various participants during and after the weekend, we all felt we had lost a feeling of *connection* at some point in our lives. Whether it was connection to ourselves, family, friends, jobs, creativity, spirituality, sexuality, nature, or the world as a whole; dancing in this way somehow helped to retrieve it.

In the following weeks and months after the workshop I made more and more friends within this little community of like-minded people. Each person was on their own journey. Some were working through grief, some through depression, some were searching for the purpose of their existence, some were trying to solve small problems of day-to-day life. Some were tackling control issues or confidence, some wanted to learn to trust, some had closed their hearts and yearned to feel love again. For some it was a regular spiritual practice, like prayer. Some just wanted to dance.

The beauty for me, was using dance to wade out of stagnant emotions. Normally, I would get into a bad mood and stay there for hours, unable to shift out of the sadness or depression, going around in circles over the same thoughts and the same self-abuse. I'd listen to sad or angry songs which — although had their place in feeling my feelings in the moment — heightened the negativity and took a grip on my heart, holding me captive in the misery. But this kind of dance forced me to feel the emotion, acknowledge it, embody it, and move through it. The evolving rhythms wouldn't allow me to wallow too long; my body knew better than my head and moved with the changing energy of the beats and melodies.

My soul came out the other end feeling heard, held and transported to a healthier place.

I thought about my dip into Christianity. The church and that gymnasium weren't so different. People were coming together in a building to worship. And if you wanted, you could dance at home in your bedroom or dance outside in the park, just like you could pray at home or pray on the beach too. The Shaman shared his beliefs, just like the Priest did. It was up to the individual to take on those beliefs or not. Essentially, they both offered positive and loving thoughts, ideas and encouragement to navigate your way through life. I came to realise that my beliefs spanned much wider than any doctrine, but there was no doubt that the mercy which I began to learn to give myself—and which was offered unconditionally to me by the church—saved me at that time. There is also no doubt that my leather-whip-loving friend had been a major catalyst for change in my life.

CHAPTER 11

"She's Very, Very Quiet"

So much happened to me over the next couple of years, and yet from the outside, it didn't look like much at all. I decided I needed to move out of town. More nature, less nightclubs. When the children I looked after grew old enough to make their own Nutella sandwiches, my lovely nanny job came to a natural end. Their mother Stella—who I'd become quite close to throughout her divorce and relocation to a large period property—was sad to see me go.

"There's a tiny cottage on the back," she said, as I helped unload books and computer games into her son's new bedroom.

"Oh really? That's so cool," I said, curiously. "What a bonus, any ideas what you'll do with it? Guesthouse maybe?" I probed.

"Well, it needs a *lot* of work," she said, eyebrows raised just at the thought of the potential costs involved in old buildings. I doubt I'll get around to it for years. Would you like to see it?" She added, knowing how renovations and decorating sparked my imagination.

"I LOVE it!" I sang, as I poked my head into the small, dusty spaces. "It's so cute and full of character".

"But it's a mess," Stella frowned, standing with her hands on her hips, trying not to touch anything in her designer office dress, or step on damp carpet in her beautiful suede heels. "And it's so gloomy. I'm not sure it's worth keeping to be honest. I may just get it knocked down".

"NOOOOOOOO! You can't!" I squealed. Stella pulled her head back in shock at my outburst.

"I mean, it's a tad run down—yes," I agreed, opening a cupboard in the kitchenette, which obviously housed a family of spiders. "But it's nothing a bit of white paint and a humidifier can't sort out. And maybe some deep cleaning...and perhaps this bit of carpet can go," I said, looking down at the black specks of mould climbing up the wall by the door. "It just needs a bit of love...and a few lamps…and a fair bit of bleach," she didn't look too convinced.

"Of course, it's up to you," I retreated, realising it was all very well me saying this, but she was a Managing Director with no time for scrubbing shelves, and no priority to update an outhouse when her whole home needed a refurb.

"If you want to use it as somewhere to paint, you'd be more than welcome," Stella offered on a whim. "A kind of art studio… if it's not too ugly," she added hastily.

"Are you joking?!" I asked, my eyes popping out of my head. That would be AMAZING! Thank you…are you sure? Thank you!" Stella laughed at my enthusiasm.

"All the time that it's still standing, you're welcome to it," she said. "And don't worry about getting paint on the walls, anything will be an improvement!"

I couldn't believe my luck. I'd tried to rent small studios before, so that I might actually be able to produce a decent volume of work to sell, but I could never afford it. Jersey was a costly place to live at the best of times, and everything had a price. But there was one thing on the island which was almost priceless: space.

"I'll leave you to have a mooch around," she said, heading back to the main house. "I'll be in the lounge, emptying *more* boxes. Would you like a cup of tea?" She called from the kitchen, which connected the two buildings.

As I moved around the little cold, stone dwelling and discovered the wonderful view of the garden from the much brighter room upstairs, an inspired thought entered my mind. I ran full speed down the tiny staircase and nearly knocked myself out on the low ceiling.

"STELLA!" I called out. "Stella?"

"Yes?" She replied, popping her head out from the door, spoon in hand. "Could I live in the cottage?" I said, slightly out of breath.

"*Live* in it?" She asked, baffled by my question.

"Yes, live in in it. I'd pay you rent, of course. And I'd clean it all up. Sorry…I'm being forward, it was just an idea. I'm looking to move out of my room in town, you see. But don't worry, you've got enough on your plate. I'll just use it as a studio…thank you…again," my waffling finally ceasing.

"You can if you *want*," She said with a concerned look on her face. "But it's really not very habitable. I'm worried you'll freeze, or get eaten by creepy crawlies. But if you think it's ok for you, then I guess we can get some sort of heating in there and arrange something".

I didn't particularly have many possessions since I'd left London, however, once they were all in the cottage, they suddenly seemed to double. Everything looked so large in the miniature abode. The living room was a small square with two large windows, an unused fireplace and one wall cut in half diagonally by the stairs. I soon realised that the best light was on the first floor, plus it had a sink and so, obviously, that would be my art studio. Downstairs, the only double bed that was going to fit was a futon, which I quickly sourced in the second-hand classifieds. Once the floor bed was made that left me just about enough room for a dollhouse-sized sofa under the stairs and wicker baskets bulging with art materials, piled up against the wall.

In the 'studio', which was basically a box room, I put up my large easel in one corner, dominating the room like an adult in a creche, and placed a desk in the other. The precious small built-in cupboard space had to be a shared occupancy. Clothes and shoes would have to give way to books and paintbrushes. This cottage, I decided, was going to be dedicated to my art and to my spiritual growth. I didn't need a TV or pretty things. I needed meditation and imagination. It was rudimentary but I loved it.

As my employment with Stella had ended, I made a bold move and quit all my other part-time jobs too; and with an empty schedule I threw myself back into artwork, just about scraping by with earnings from canvas and mural commissions. Sometimes I barely had any money at all but I didn't care, I was happy. There was a new feeling growing inside of me. I realised that although I had nothing, I had all I needed to start creating *anything*; as Nina Simone sang in her famous song: *I had life.* What more did I need?

My collections of beads, sequins, fabrics and paints started to take over every nook, making the boundaries between my living and creating, indistinguishable. There was no routine, no discipline, no 'switch-off time'. Painting slipped into the early hours of the morning; lunch was eaten at my desk while drawing; weekends meant nothing and were spent selling at markets or working on my website. Of course, on the flipside, I had complete freedom to relax any time I wanted too. In the same way that when you fall in love, it always seems to be an Indian Summer, it felt that way with the island once I moved to Stella's. With no one else to think about…or ask…or consult with…or make me think twice…or persuade me otherwise, I could follow my nose—and my heart, and my feet—wherever they took me.

Waking up in the cottage, where mornings could slip lazily into afternoons reading in bed, my attention would be taken by the sun outside. My bedroom was shaded by the main house, but the tantalising rays of light in the distance were enough to pull me from the covers. I stuck my head out of the door and felt that the air was already warm. The sea called. I quickly brushed my teeth and changed into my bikini with a sundress thrown on top. My ready-to-run bag already contained a towel, book, sunglasses, sun cream, notepad and pen. Topping up my water bottle and reaching for an apple, I was good to go within five minutes. No protesting boyfriend, no kids to contend with, no hair to wash, no dishwasher to load.

My little front door backed onto Stella's patio. Decorated with dreamy lilac wisteria which climbed over the walls and windows, the view from the door was nothing short of the *secret garden* you imagined as a child. Wild flowers, well-established shrubs and old trees around a lawn, led to a small white gate with a honeysuckle archway at the end. Behind the gate — to my further delight when Stella first showed me around — was a small lagoon-shaped swimming pool which appeared like an unexpected turquoise jewel. Almost untouched since it was built, the crazy paving, white-washed walls, vine-covered pergola and Pre-Raphaelite style statues dotted around the pool, gave a feeling of suddenly being in Italy; completely different to the English rose style garden preceding it. Tempted to shelter in the blissful

Mediterranean style oasis (as I often would while Stella was at work and the kids at school) I usually opted to venture further. The sea called louder than the chlorine water.

I walked out of the taller gate on the side of the garden and down the road, taking the next right which turned onto another lane. I passed a chapel, farmhouses, fields with horses nuzzling hay bags and Jersey's famous big-eyed cows munching on grass. The lane eventually tapered into a mud track, daffodils lining the sides of the entrance to a woodland. St Catherine's was a small wood by mainlander standards, but a much-appreciated change of scene by island locals who were so used to constant beachscape. Situated in a valley, it smelt of moss and wild garlic, and excited dogs pounded up and down the well-worn trail in search of things to sniff. A stream ran along the path and a mini waterfall formed from the hilly land either side. Stepping-stones took me across the stream, where the trees, once more, opened up and out to a lane, leading to St Catherine's Bay.

The first bay was stony, but if you found the coast path on the left, steps in the rocks took you up and over to a more secluded beach with more sand. Often, at the time of day I went there, when most people were at work or taking babies home for naps, there was just one other lady who loved to swim as much as I did; a retired nurse who believed in the power of self-healing. Sometimes we'd join each other in the sea and chat about the joy of the simple things in life, before wading off back to our respective sun spots. I chose a plot by the rocks, sheltered from wind by a stone wall with some shade from a tree canopy. There, I'd lay in the warmth, let my mind wander, thinking about all that had gone before and what might lie ahead. Living in a place where I could step out of bed, into a beautiful garden, walk through woodland and come out the other end to the sea, was beyond my wildest dreams. Each of the hundreds of times I would make the little journey, felt like a pilgrimage.

No fixed work. Basking in the sun alone. Painting day and night. I became introverted and even more thoughtful. My only routine was dance. I loved how freeing it was, and with each passing week I would go deeper inside myself. I was invited to many spiritual gatherings, ceremonies and holistic workshops; some of which I would attend, gaining knowledge on the lesser-spoken-about subjects. People would recommend or lend me books on subjects like chakras, the power of the mind, dream analysis, shamanic healing, meditation, prayer, higher beings, afterlife, trusting the Universe and how to start creating your reality. I devoured every page. Each line made me stop and question everything I had experienced so far, and contemplate how I could do things differently.

I began making a collage which eventually filled the back of my bedroom door. Using magazine cutouts, I applied a 'Creative Visualisation' technique, something I had read about which — being an artist — resonated with me. It portrayed a patchwork world I wanted to live in. The dreamy pictures included exotic beaches, galleries, exhibitions, women doing yoga, clothing I longed to wear, couples in love, cities I wanted to visit, artists creating, gardens in full bloom, sexy lingerie, bundles of money, beautiful interiors, cool bars and anything else that appealed to me. Sometimes I was surprised by what attracted my attention, but I never thought twice before tearing it out and adding it to the wall. My rule was: if it made me happy or excited to look at, then up it went onto the wall. It was a way to bypass years of out-of-date ideas about my life, to tap into my subconscious and find out what I *actually* wanted, not what I thought I *should* want. Later on, I noticed that so many of these images appeared in my life for real, in one way or another.

In the quietness of the cottage and the new stillness of my mind, buried traumas — big and small — began to resurface. I knew that if I wanted to move forwards, I needed to allow them to come. On recommendation, I went to see a therapist. I talked to her about things I hadn't thought about for years; things which I hadn't realised had moulded into fears and blocks in my life. She gave me tools to work through those things myself, knowing that I couldn't afford to keep seeing her; I was already on borrowed money. My bulimia resurfaced too. This time, I didn't let it scare me. Instead, I spoke to it kindly like I would a friend. *Why are you here again, dear one?* I would say. *What is it that you want to tell me? It's ok, I'm here for you.* This didn't stop it, but at least I was acknowledging it fully for once. Ignoring it hadn't helped at all; I needed new tactics if I was to make any progress. As I painted, my mind processed the new information I had acquired, forcing me to re-evaluate so much. As I churned through my past, I wondered how my bulimia had come about in the first place. *Why had I become someone who suffered from eating disorders? ... as opposed becoming an alcoholic, or drug addict or workaholic? What made food the friend – and the enemy?*

～

It was 1981 when my soul decided to enter this particular body. I'm not sure it knew what it was signing up for. It hasn't been the smoothest of rides. I was clearly an artist from day one, creating things from nothing and thinking deeply about everything. I experienced strong feelings and emotions about confusing things as early as I can remember. At night, I flew through different worlds, lived a million lives and had erotic dreams. But in waking life I was extremely shy. I literally turned crimson and flapped my arms at my sides in some strange motion—which I can only assume was to try and fly away—when anyone spoke to me. When they did, I barely uttered a word back. It's not that I couldn't talk, or that I didn't have anything to say. Actually, I had a great vocabulary and a lot of things that I wanted to express, but I was so scared of the reactions I would receive. I was sure that I thought about stuff that no one else did; and pondered peculiar things. As a toddler, I clung to my Mum for dear life and when I had to reluctantly start school, I'd spend my break times safe in the company of myself, just thinking or chatting in my mind to invisible beings.

"She's very, very quiet," the teachers would say on parent's evening. "She spends a lot of time on her own," they'd inform my mum in hushed tones. I never felt like I was alone though. My mind was always full of thoughts and ideas and questions. I needed to spend time by myself just to hear them all. The small privately-run school was situated in a converted Victorian house with hidden, narrow staircases connecting creaky rooms like a labyrinth. Governed mostly by stern old women, they would shout until red-faced, throwing chalkboard erasers and stomping around in their T-strap, worn-leather heels from the sixties. Often, I'd cry half the evening, unable to finish the gruelling homework, begging my dad not to go in and complain, in fear of the ramifications. Luckily though, the Headmistress was a kind and wise lady who kept the power-hungry battle-axes in check. That was, until she sadly passed away from Cancer. After that, us kids had no hope.

When my dad had enough of seeing me in tears, he went in to speak to my teacher. She was keeping me in detention every lunch break for a week; a punishment dished out for the heinous crime of not understanding the maths she taught from her prehistoric exercise books. Peering from behind the polished mahogany banister posts, which would have once been the main staircase of the old house, I stared at the door to the office which was closed. I heard Mrs P's voice warble higher and higher and then Dad's boom above hers. Then silence. It was unlike him. He wasn't one to ever shout or make a fuss. I don't know what he said to her, and I was petrified of what might happen once she got me alone, but after that 'chat' she never bothered me again.

The playground was lined with trees and hedges that pushed against an overstretched wire fence. Shoots sprouted and roots spread through the gaps to the outside, like zombies trying to escape a compound. Harshly chopped back on the inside to keep control of the spreading wilderness, I often felt like one of those trees: secretly wild, desperate to escape, nowhere to hide, back against the wall. On lunch breaks I'd wind my arms around the knobbly bark or climb and hunch up into a ball between the higher branches. I'd see faces in the trunks and was sure there were people in there with me. I never told anyone of course, I knew they'd think I was mad. I didn't know who those faces were but somehow, I knew that 'they' were on my side.

I didn't *always* want to be alone though, and I found it quite easy to make friends; I seemed to attract people without even trying. But I would only open up to those I felt a strong connection to. Not that I really knew what connection was back then, but it usually involved lots of colouring-in, roller-skating and making up dances to Madonna songs together. There was one friend who had been there from the beginning. I didn't know life without her, despite going to different schools. Our mothers had met when we were babies and lived next door to one other. Nina was my original ally. We loved each other so much that we fought like siblings. Hours flew by making water parks for our dolls and miniature gardens for woodlice. If we could get our parents to take us swimming, the day was complete. Goggles on, slinging our legs up and over the edge of the pool, we'd hang upside down like bats against the sides. Holding our noses and pointing out particularly funny specimens, we watched the strange reversed underwater world, where people looked like frogs swimming along the ceiling. Then, dropping from our perches, we'd slip down to the pool floor and skim along the tiles on our bellies, pretending to be mermaids. As the years passed, I would save her from fights with her older brothers and she would regularly pick me up off the floor when I passed out from smoking too much weed at parties. We had a quiet but solid bond. We would be friends forever, and I learnt early on, that sisters come in many forms.

My biological sister on the other hand, was the opposite to me. She was four years older and had, what our Dad liked to call, verbal diarrhoea. As fast as a thought entered that girl's mind, it was catapulting itself to the nearest person in earshot. She loved to talk, and I loved to listen, so it generally worked quite well. Standing in her jodhpurs, *Fruit of the Loom* jumper and velvet riding hat, she would call commands from the saddle of her broomstick pony. My cousins and I were sent on circuits, hopping over jumps made from cardboard boxes, milk crates and precariously placed bamboo canes, and ordered to perform dressage with side-steps and skips, horse noises included. As she grew, my sister entered real horse shows, had boyfriends, wore trendy clothes, got her hair permed and had big boobs. I longed to be as cool and confident as her. I also longed to have the gift she had.

Like me, she too felt spirits and energy, but her sight was much stronger than mine. Until she started school, she was so hyperactive she stayed awake most the night, always talking to 'imaginary friends' in her cot and driving my parents mad with sleep deprivation. Once she was an adult, she often chose to shut down her senses, too exhausted or disturbed by visits from those that had passed over. I felt frustrated that she would ignore such a gift, a gift which I worked so hard to cultivate in myself. When Dad died and he came to her and not me, I spent hours upon hours crying and trying to make tangible contact with him. Until I eventually understood that my gift was not *less* than hers, it was just different. I could also speak within other realms, but not with direct communication, mostly with feelings and sensations. The messages were sent differently but received just as clear.

My worst nightmare in the world was to be asked to stand on a stage or speak in front of people. I gave up one of my true loves, dancing, because I couldn't bear to be in any kind of performance where eyes would be on me. I also couldn't bear the thought of wearing the obligatory leotard. I was aware of feeling fat from a very young age and didn't want to be seen in any more Lycra than a pair of cycling shorts, which were a staple in every eighties child's wardrobe. Luckily, what I lacked in confidence was made up by my artistic skills. My desire to create things was constant; I felt it stronger than anything else in my little life and it remained that way ever since. I always had to be making something. It's a passion, an obsession, a compulsion, an itch that constantly needs scratching; an addiction that always needs fuelling. While I was creating, I could leave the outer world and live in my head.

The outer world was scary. I could sense other people's feelings, thoughts and emotions. I tuned in to other energies, including the spirit world, but I did not understand it. I had no idea this was unusual, that it didn't happen to everyone, that it was called being an *Empath*, and that it would affect me so much as my life went on. I just accepted that it was normal to feel extremely overwhelmed most of the time. Unless I was in a particularly relaxed or fun environment where everyone was happy, I spent much of my day feeling anxious and heavy. The weight of other people's fears and sadness, guilt or secrets, over-excitement and adrenaline, sent me on roller-coaster rides that I hadn't chosen to go on. It sounds sad to say, but the truth is, I didn't like being a child a lot of the time. It wasn't that I didn't have a good childhood — my parents were wonderful — it's just that I felt so much turmoil inside. I felt uncomfortable in my body; like I was just killing time while waiting to become fully-formed, waiting to grow in to my big teeth and my big fringe, waiting for my puppy fat to drop away, waiting for my breasts to swell, waiting for the years to reveal my true self, waiting until I was old enough to get on with what I was really here to do. I suppose I was a bit of a dreamer. I lived in my mind a lot of the time. But for some reason, which I cannot quite decipher, around the age of seven I swiftly became a realist. Perhaps it was my hypersensitivity to my parents' financial worries. Or perhaps it was my logical brain, which enjoyed figuring out how things worked on a practical level, that temporarily pushed magic and mystery out the window.

When puberty began to surface, it seemed that my body wasn't the only thing changing. As we entered the 90s my parents were hit hard by the recession. We moved into a smaller, rented house and I was moved to a state school. The children in my new neighbourhood and in my new classes were more streetwise and more rebellious than the ones I'd known at the private school. As the new girl, friendly teasing and flirtation from cocky kids pushed me to find my voice. I began to speak out and let myself be seen. And although it was still very challenging for me to be confident, I started to enjoy the new attention I was receiving, especially from boys. Immersing myself into the 'cool' group, I learnt to say the right things and quickly adopted a kind of shield which allowed me to be part of the action, while still just about keeping my emotions intact. It was out of my comfort zone to be more vocal and to edge a toe into the spotlight, but I knew deep down that I had things to say. I knew that if I didn't speak up, I would never be heard, never be seen, and never get anywhere if I continued to hide in my room or in my head. Soon, the fake confidence act became easier and false walls of self-assurance slowly built up around my timid centre, which would stay in place for years.

I also discovered the influence that the shape of my body had on the way I was treated and subsequently, how I felt about myself. I developed, what turned in to years of addictive eating disorders and yo-yo dieting and exercising regimes to lose weight and stay a size I felt was attractive and 'acceptable'. It gave me a big sense of control over something in my life when other things like jobs, money and relationships were becoming increasingly scary. Binge eating, starving myself, taking laxatives, arduous workouts and doing anything I could to be what the magazines and TV told me was the right size, became a big part of my life. It often dominated my thoughts and I felt like a slave to my flesh which seemed determined not to fit into a size 10 or be shaped like an hourglass, no matter what I did.

Plunging into water was always my comforting go-to, and I began swimming alone at the local pool 3, 4, sometimes 5 days a week after school. I had no desire to train or complete, only to stay slim and escape. The local pool was always busy; above the water, women gossiped loudly and men huffed and puffed with road-rage at the slow people swimming in the fast lane, but when I pulled my goggles on and dived underwater, it was all so beautifully fuzzy. Each time I entered the changing room, I would scrutinise my swimsuit-clad body in the long mirrors. *Was I thinner today?*

However, now I was an adult; dreaming again, dancing again. And I had a new question: *Was I HAPPIER today?* Generally, I *was* happier. But as money got even tighter and banks were hounding me daily, I reluctantly got back on the job search. Soon enough, I was waiting tables in cafes, pulling pints in pubs and taking on random roles like 'Bouncy Castle Supervisor'; only ever jobs which I could pick up easily, and which paid me weekly. As soon as I settled my bills, I would quit again. However, it didn't take much for me to become overwhelmed and beat myself up for choosing to be on the poverty line, when I was a privileged young woman with many options. The plunge into despair could be seriously fast and shockingly deep, giving me the feeling that there were bigger things at play here; things which needed to be dug up and looked at. I knew it was pointless patting them back down with a *sensible* career, monthly gym membership and nice car. My soul obviously had things it wanted to say, and I was only going to hear them when I finally stopped distracting myself…and listened.

Despite landing myself in Petty Debts Court, I knew I had to resist giving into a nine-to-five, and that what I really needed was to use this precious time to work on my self-care. After each time I freaked out and stuck my fingers down my throat, I thought of the words I'd read by ancient Chinese Philosopher Lao Tzu: *If you do not change direction, you may end up where you are heading.*

As Summer drew to a close, I realised I would have to replace my healing dips in the sea with something else. If I was going to stay positive and motivated throughout the cold and dark, I needed to immerse in nature another way. I'd read a biography by The Dalai Lama. In it, he described his daily routine. He woke at 3am to wash and meditate, then exercised at 4am, ate breakfast, read the papers, then prayed, then.....well, I can't remember the rest, but he had a pretty good start to the day. Granted, he was in bed by 8am, but nonetheless, I was inspired and decided that I could at least try to assimilate something similar which would work for me.

I started to get up at the ungodly hour of 4am to meditate. Often, I would fall asleep while sitting, but I kept at it until my body adjusted. Then at 5am, I would dress in warm and waterproof clothing, drive down the road and leave my car at one of the wooded carparks. I walked along the northern cliff paths for an hour, watching the burnt orange sun begin to rise, picking buds from the bright yellow gorse bushes which smelt of pineapple and coconut, before turning around and walking back. Every day it was different. Different skies, different birdsong, different feelings and different emotions. I grew to love it so much that waking up in the darkness wasn't agony anymore; I looked forward to the exhilaration of the cold air and how healthy and alive I felt. When I drove home, lights were only just starting to come on in houses. As I sat down to eat breakfast at around 7am, I felt like I knew a secret that no one else knew. This was my morning ritual. I was just starting my day and I already felt invincible.

Evenings offered an alternative kind of energy. Usually, I would have rested for a short period during the day, so I could stay awake late and continue my artwork or reading. If I was restless, I would take a torch and go for a late-night walk. The country lanes had very little lighting, and traffic fizzled out to almost nothing once it got past 10pm. I was drawn to being outside when no one else was around. It wasn't that I didn't want to meet people; rather, I yearned for more and more quiet and the subtle sounds of nature which can only be heard once the hum of modern living stops. Most people I knew would think it crazy to walk in the woods at night, alone—even in safe little Jersey. But I wasn't afraid. I was captivated by the beauty of darkness. All the harsh colours toned down to cool blue, indigo, grey and black.

As I took the path through St Catherine's Wood, which I knew so well in the daylight, everything felt extraordinary. The tree trunks smelt muskier, the wild jasmine perfume was stronger, the water trickled louder and small creatures rustling in the bushes seemed bigger. I looked up at the silhouetted trees against the moonlit sky, leaning over me like friendly giants. *What was there really to be frightened of?* I thought. Nature was reassuring me, speaking to me in her own language. I was seeing and feeling the world with new eyes. Everything was enchanting. I got to the point where meditation and prayer and life all rolled into one, and I was in a kind of constant communion. My new-found connection was like a comforting anchor; something I'd never experienced before. Until then, I had always just sort of been drifting and clinging onto the occasional rock.

Now and then, though, a storm would come, which even my anchor couldn't survive. I still hadn't dealt with my feelings about Dan. The sadness would temporarily subside. But once in a while, I'd hear one of our songs or see a photo of him online, or find out from a friend that he was making plans with his new girlfriend, and the pain would return — like a split at the corner of your mouth which pulls apart just as it is about to heal. And then, it would all go numb again. I would question all my decisions. I would scold myself for being so messed up. I would be full of fear out about my bleak finances. I worried that I was mad. During those dark nights of the soul I would batten down the hatches, get under the duvet, reach for my books and prepare for the worst.

Upon waking from one such episode I had a crystal-clear thought amidst the clouds and chaos. The meltdown had been spurred, this time, by a collection of items I had retrieved from Mum's garage. There were still a couple of boxes from when Lucy had driven me and my possessions out of London that night. Stuff I didn't have space for. Stuff I wasn't ready to deal with. On a short visit home, I had decided to take back with me, a hat box. The hat box contained every personalised thing Dan had ever made me. It was full. Both being art students with hopelessly romantic minds, we'd made each other a gift for nearly every birthday, Christmas and anniversary. Back at the cottage I made the big mistake of going through the box after a few glasses of wine. As I picked up a hand-written love letter which was tied up with a ribbon, dried lily petals fell out and a tsunami of memories and emotions hit me hard. The nostalgia and sorrow were unbearable, but the lid was off and there was no stopping it. I grasped onto each crafted gift and photo, and allowed myself to be taken over until they were done with me. Sat on the floor, surrounded by charged-up paraphernalia like a demon trapped in a pentagram, once again, I heard Lao Tzu's words: *If you do not change direction…..*

'ENOUGH!' I said out loud. 'THAT'S IT. I'VE HAD ENOUGH OF THIS'. *No more* I thought, *I need to change direction.*

I immediately text one of my new friends. I met Ellie through the dance workshop; we connected quickly, feeling something woven through both of us which was indescribable, yet extremely potent. A quiet, beautiful feline girl with psychic eyes and incense in her hair, I could see the long line of healers in the spirit world, standing behind her. When she danced she looked as if she belonged to a far-off tribe. When she laughed, her soul let off little sparks of electricity. Like me, she was intense and devoted. A fellow Scorpio with creativity running in her blood and heat in her loins. We had already become accustomed to carrying out full moon and new moon rituals, harnessing the power of the planets and ourselves, to try to better our lives. I knew I needed her to help me with this.

I looked at the wreckage all around me and considered what it would be like to simply be rid of it all. Instantly, I felt panic. *How could I throw away so much love? So much care? So much youth? So many good memories? Such a big part of my life?* I then looked at myself: sore eyes, clenched stomach, riddled with fear. I realised that these objects were no longer bringing me love, care, youth and good memories. They were only bringing me pain and paralysis. What would be the point in keeping them if this is how I was going to feel each time I opened the box? Was that going to help me? No.

I asked Ellie if she would do a fire ceremony with me. I needed to burn everything from Dan which was causing me heartache. It seemed like an extreme measure, but for me, it was a necessity. I had read a lot about the power of letting go; and a lot about the pain of *not* letting go. I knew that if I didn't release all that love back into the universe, I might struggle to find new love to replace it. Feeling slightly nervous—knowing that once those things fell into the fire I could never get them back—I knew deep down it was the right thing to do.

"What if you want to look back on these special memories, once you are old, and have moved on?" Ellie asked me gently.

"I don't want to wait until I'm old to move on," I said, staring at the flickering flames.

I had one last look at the pile and saw something poking out. It was a birthday card Dan had made me after we broke up the first time, and were still in touch. It was light-hearted and funny and sweet. When I held it, I felt a little tinge of joy instead of heartache, so I knew it was safe to keep. I tucked it away in my bag and turned back to Ellie. "Ok, let's do it". With Palo Santo smudging the air I threw a note into the fire first, asking for my treasures to be taken care of and for healing to be given to my soul. As I watched each piece burn, it was like burning lumps of my heart off. Lumps which were once healthy, but now were scar tissue and needed to be removed.

The next morning, I woke feeling lighter. I sniffed my hair, smelling the wood fire and smiled. I wanted to do something new on this fresh new day. I wanted to paint something different; something to show all my new feelings of lightness, darkness, visions, dreams, journeys, healing.

CHAPTER 12

You Are What You Are

Feeling less heavy than I had done in a long time, I found myself distracted from my artwork. Despite a head full of ideas for new paintings, I couldn't quite stay as focused on my craft as I had been before the fire ceremony. Something had definitely released, and space for something new opened up in its place. Solitude had become my norm while I worked on my inner self, but now I missed people; I missed having fun. I began to go to a few of the gatherings I was invited to instead of hiding away, alone in the cottage. Big farm parties, where details of dates and locations were on a 'if you know…you know' basis, went on into sunrise, blasting trance music in un-used poly tunnels, ravers dancing under the curved plastic, surrounding trees acting as soundproofing. Outside, Poi experts lit the wicks of their tethered weights, ready to swing them in hypnotic rhythm. Geometric light trails whizzed around their bodies like city night traffic caught on a high-speed shutter. Meanwhile, dried-out and salted magic mushrooms were handed out like crisps. Occasionally, I'd bring a boy home, breaking the unintentional celibacy. The next morning I'd move him on swiftly, before he started asking too many questions or his eyes adjusted to the obscure sketches on the walls.

Now and then I'd pick up a paintbrush and stare at the blank canvas, wondering where on earth to start, until a new message would ding through on Facebook about the latest themed party or arts event. Brushes were thrown down as I headed straight for the charity shops in search of Cleopatra wigs and sequin hot pants. During this time, I met a woman. She was well-spoken, well read and understatedly charismatic. We were introduced briefly at a meeting about an upcoming festival, where I was to help with stage set design. During the festival's closing party we crossed paths again while mutual friends chatted at the bar. Amidst strange costumes, rainbow lighting and 40s music, we talked about art and literature, before heading back to dance on opposite sides of the room, making occasional eye contact. We met up a handful of times after that, for business lunches in coffee shops and tucked-away restaurants, to swap ideas about big projects we wished to work on, and to see if we could collaborate and realise them somehow. But time and money always seemed to get in the way of bold creativity. I loved her voice; the elegant way she spoke and the way she talked about leaving behind a legacy with art.

"Time and money will always be a bother to artists. However, nothing can get in the way of passion," she said, as our ever-intensifying liaisons remained disguised as polite exchanges to onlookers.

On our last meeting we talked about 'magic pockets of time'. Moments which didn't exist in time as we knew it, with its controlled days and dates and years and hours and minutes. Pockets of opportunity which had no bounds, which you would never again get the chance to have. We agreed that you had to be daring, and often disobedient, and grab them in an instant or else they would disappear. We discussed how you might recognise such pockets because they felt special and sacred, despite any difficulty or controversy or apparent impossibility; and how they held such a feeling that was hard to put words to. These pockets contained a sharing of something precious and unique; perhaps something that just could not be. Something which would stay in your heart forever, in a place that was timeless and where no one got hurt, and where 'what-ifs' didn't matter. Allowing, just for that moment, to have a deep connection with another soul because you and the world were a better version because of it. Like delicate bubbles floating in the air which can't be held or they'll pop, for their fleeting time, they offered the potential to bring more wonder, mystery and joy into life.

We spontaneously spent that afternoon together in a sea view hotel room and never saw each other again. In an untitled email the next day, she wrote:

> *Not for her a watery end, but a new life beginning on a stranger shore.*
> *It will be a love story. For she will be my heroine for all time.*
>
> *- William Shakespeare, The Twelfth Night.*

November 2012

Staying with friends, in what felt like the middle of nowhere, I was taking refuge in a spare cupboard-sized room. An old house shared by a few mates near the stunning and secluded Plemont Bay in St. Ouen, was the perfect spot for emotional rehab. I had recently returned from a trip to Cape Town, where I had flown out on an impulse—and on a maxed-out credit card—to be with a man I had fallen in love with. He had been visiting friends in Jersey and I happened to meet him on his only night out at the beach club, falling instantly for his cocoa skin and corn rows. But as it turned out, I was not actually in love. Perhaps I had been a little hasty…. again. Heading into town to a coffee shop where I was a waitress once more, I shivered at the bus stop, missing the heat of South Africa.

St. Helier is the only town among the twelve parishes which made up the baby bailiwick island. Despite how tiny Jersey was, finance workers who lived near Plemont would still have to allow themselves an hour on public transport before reaching their hedge fund offices. The bus had to first embroider the coastline, winding its way around fields via numerous narrow green lanes to pick up the rural residents. I sat next to an older lady. She had a tanned bare face covered in lines and long hair tied in a plait; I struck up polite conversation with her. We exchanged the usual info: where we were going, what we were doing that day. I told her candidly about my failed African romance and possible plans to head out to New Zealand, where — at thirty years and ten months old — I had just enough time left to apply for a one-year working holiday visa. I figured that I needed more adventure, more nature and more and inspiration if I was to pull myself out of a post-failed relationship pit again.

Half expecting her to roll her eyes at my carefree attitude and obvious rebellion against routine and discipline, she looked at me kindly and replied in earnest with, "We are what we are Dear".

My heart had ruled my head once again. Deciding we were in love and that we needed to be with one another, we had agreed that I would come to Cape Town. He too held dreams to work elsewhere in the southern hemisphere, and so it seemed to make sense that I would come to him and that we would go somewhere from there together. I had left the cottage and given away everything I owned. Ridding myself of all my possessions had become a bit of a habit, a compulsion, a way to keep starting again; re-inventing myself, having no responsibilities or chains. I discovered that freeing myself of excess *stuff*, freed my mind too. Beautiful clothes, jewellery, shoes and favourite old CDs were donated to charity. Duvets, blankets and cushions were given to friends. Old paintings and art books were handed over to fellow creatives.

Stopping over at Mum's before heading to Heathrow Airport, I cleared out the last of my things in her garage. As she watched on with worried eyes and questions about my safety, I threw away sketchbooks and portfolios of artwork from years of school and college, deciding that they held no use other than to dust off and show my children one day— *if* I even birthed any children at all. I kept just one container which held a selection of photos and sentimental items from family gatherings and travels. But aside from that, I *had* to feel like nothing had a grip on me anymore, physically or mentally. I didn't want any old memories to haunt me or hold me down. I needed to feel like I'd just landed on Earth and was starting from scratch.

Thinking back, I suppose it wasn't all that different to my bulimia. Donating, selling and opting out of everything that I owned, rented or belonged to, was the ultimate purge to cleanse myself of the past, and of the debris that cluttered my head and heart. It was my way to be free. I was going to travel, live out of my backpack and do casual work.

When I excitedly reached my destination, I got hassled at immigration for only having a one-way ticket, which my new beau had assured me would be fine. The South African officer glared at me like I was about to get a gun out and shoot down the entire airport. Suddenly, things didn't seem so peachy. They took my passport and escorted me through to Arrivals to find my boyfriend so he could lend me the money to buy a return. I probably should have taken heed of the obvious omen right there: DON'T DO IT. Within a week, I realised that I had made a big mistake. He wasn't what I thought he was. I probably wasn't what he thought I was either.

Falling back on my spiritual practices to get through days of uncomfortable silence and arguments until my flight home, I wondered what had happened. I picked up my sketchbook which was balancing on top of my half-packed backpack. Flicking through the pages I saw a theme: unfinished drawings. Lots of ideas and not many completed pictures. I had been blinded by that old friend who I knew so well: impatience. I wanted a new life and I wanted it NOW.

I always dived so fast and so deep into everything I did, be it love or work or friends or art, or anything for that matter. I believed in no regrets; no regrets for NOT doing something. I could handle making a fool of myself and I could shake off embarrassment, because I preferred to always try something new or trust someone I felt strongly about, rather than *not* try or trust at all. But diving fast and deep had its pros and cons. It led me straight to the bottom of things. It revealed all the underlayers right at the start. When you can see everything, you soon realise when something's not right, and if I felt something wasn't right, then I'd act on that immediately too. That would often mean changing my mind drastically on big decisions, swallowing my pride, eating humble pie, letting go of a whole load of plans, losing money and going back to square one. I was prepared to do those things if it meant I would have no regrets and I could live each day to my fullest.

On my return to Jersey, my friends were amazing. They lovingly refrained from expressing their previous doubts about my jetting off to another continent to be with a man I just met, who I assured them was 'T. O' again. They welcomed me back that November, fed me warm winter soup and let me stay in their homes while I reassessed my life.

That kind, wise-looking woman on the bus who listened to my sad love story, told me that I must be the person I am; that I must do what I must do, and repeated the phrase, "You are what you are," many times during our journey. As we arrived in town I thanked her for such lovely company and we went separate ways. I walked off with her words ringing in my ears … *You are what you are.*

Slightly sheepishly, I asked Stella if I could move back into the cottage. "Of course," she reassured me. "In fact, I could do with someone to look after the dog when I'm away, if you don't mind?" And so, with a gorgeous white Cockapoo in tow who missed her owner, we both nestled back into the cottage, both with tails between our legs. Kiki became a good friend of mine, walking with me to the woods, licking my tears when I cried. Now that I was back, settling into my old routine of solitude, books and music, I knew it was time to embark on the collection of paintings which I'd never gotten around to; I also needed money if I had any hope of going to New Zealand. A deadline was in order. I booked to have an exhibition at a large hotel. I would use the walls of the ground-floor spaces and pay a commission on any sales. For the second time, my luck was in; the Victorian seaside building was in the midst of refurbishment. The eighty-two bedrooms and beach-facing conservatory were priority, and the lounges were the last to have a face-lift. The lovely lady owner was happy for me to hammer nails into the dated cream wallpaper, seeing as it would be torn down soon enough. With Stella letting me paint in the cottage and the hotel allowing me to hang my work to sell, it seemed like fate was on my side. Maybe Fairy was around again.

I immersed back into meditation; this time making notes of the visions and feelings they invoked. I recorded my dreams and even set timers throughout the night to wake and remember each one. I was amazed at how much was going on while I slept; a whole other world of past, present and possibly future. Sometimes, entire paintings would come to me in a flash and I'd have to speedily sketch the image down before it faded away. In the morning, the child-like drawing would be enough to jog my memory and I'd set straight to work to re-create it on canvas. Other times, I'd see words in a language I didn't know, and would have to translate them from the scrawl in my journal. They were usually Latin-based, with old dialects and messages for my waking life. The results of my paintings were surprisingly good; I'd never been so clear on what I wanted to achieve with my artwork. The collection was growing nicely and my mind was expanding. I kept thinking about the lady on the bus. Her words popped into my head at random times. *We are what we are.* Why was it so penetrating? What *was* I?

As I worked on a piece inspired by female Sangomas (the traditional healers I'd read about while in South Africa), I thought about the way every place and every culture had its own wise women, herbal remedies, alternative therapies, magic, myths and legends. When I first visited the island and Gemma drove me around, showing me points of interest like a geeky tour guide, I remember we stopped at a dolmen. An unusual arrangement of large stones which dated back to the Neolithic period, it was like Stonehenge — only on a dwarf scale. She told me the island had lots of these sites and apparently witches still used them. *Witches?* I thought. "What...like Pagans?" I asked.

"I Don't know," she shrugged. "I suppose so". We took some obligatory piss-taking spooky photos of each other and moved on.

The dolmens intrigued me. *Were there really witches in Jersey's history? Did they still exist?* Some sources suggested that witch trials took place in Jersey from 1562 – 1736. The Channel Islands, it seemed, held the title of being the witch-hunting capital of Europe, with 67 cases in Jersey and 111 in Guernsey (far more per head, for the population, than anywhere in Europe). The accused were usually held in Mont Orgueil (Gorey Castle), before being burned or hanged. The more I read, the more I wanted to know about what made a woman a so-called witch. How did they decide?

The sad truth was, that so many things were considered reason enough to label a woman as a witch, and therefore, evil. The list of possible signs was endless. From what I was reading, it seemed that if you were a healer, a clairvoyant, an artist, an ally of other women, an enemy of other women, single, without children, financially independent, openly sensual or sexual, out-spoken, overly passionate, too wild or even too introverted— you were an outcast and a suspected witch. You were different because people didn't understand you. You were a threat to a tightly controlled religion or community and therefore you would go to trial. I was shocked at this discovery and dumbfounded as I read about more and more about the treatment of anyone who didn't fit into the one mould. I thought about myself and how I might have come across; I would have had to keep very quiet about my visions, my dreams and my senses. I certainly would not have been able to be single *and* have a sex life. It was clear that, back in the day, I would have been a witch.

I decided to use some of my daily walks to visit the dolmens. Circling these New Stone Age sites, I could feel the air thick with ritual. I looked at the large misshapen pillars, posts and slabs surrounded by grass-covered mounds — which once served as chambers, alters, and sacred graves — and imagined the secret words spoken and blessed offerings made. The sites were often positioned according to ley lines and planetary alignment, and the low-lying stones placed in two wonky lines in an aisle fashion, acted as passageways. I could almost see hooded figures walking slowly down them.

On one afternoon outing, where the sun was gleaming through the trees, I sat in the middle of a stone circle, thinking about my unknown heritage. I felt an affinity with the island, I could feel a connection to the many gifted and sacrificed women. They were my sisters.

Just as the last few rays of sun eked out their time before sinking into the ground, a shard of light hit my face. I realised that not only would I have been considered a witch back in the day, but I WAS a witch — *today*.

CHAPTER 13

Hotel Cleaning Happiness

A mutual friend sent him along to my Art exhibition, determined that we were a great fit. I wasn't looking for *yet another* boyfriend since my bad romance in Cape Town, but she was adamant that we must meet. A quiet boy from Slovakia with a fire in his belly, we did in fact fit, and found a strong connection somewhere between art, photography and marijuana. I didn't particularly have a *type,* but Adam was definitely different to the majority of my exes. I either fell for the creative and outgoing ones: the ones with all the chat, the ones who could dance or play music or write or paint; or I went for the ones who were straight forward and did what they said on the tin: looked tasty, although not always that satisfying in the end. But Adam was introvert and intriguing with pale eyes that pierced through you. He was into Pink Floyd, conspiracy theories and Buddhism. He preferred me without make-up, naked, rather dressed up in sexy lingerie, wearing flat shoes that I could traverse and explore in, instead of impractical heels.

By mid-December 2012 my exhibition had been a mini success and I found my way to New Zealand—with Adam. Our plan was to first stay with friends who lived in the South Island while Adam bought and fixed up a van. Then travel for a while. Then find work. Then travel again. The vehicle he found wasn't a campervan with space to sit or stand or make a cup of tea. It was literally a small van with seats upfront, and the full area in the back was turned into a high-level bed; belongings would be stashed below in the custom-built space. When you sat cross-legged on the mattress your head had to bend down under the roof, so reclining was the comfiest position. Saying that, it was cosy. Blankets, fluffy throws, a pile of pillows and walls covered in fabric made it into a sweet little love den.

In my usual style, after paying for the flights, I was already on borrowed money and trying not to worry about how long it would last. Holly and Joe, the couple we stayed with, were old mates of Adam's. They moved to New Zealand to set up a yoga and massage retreat and chose the hot spring region of Hamner Springs for its beautiful mountainous backdrops and healing waters. Unexpectedly, Holly asked if I wanted to help her do some treatments.

"You're definitely a natural," she said, while I rubbed her shoulders one evening after a long day. "I can tell you have the gift". I'd kind of always known I was good with my hands — in more ways than one. I suppose it came with the strong intuition. She gave me tutorials in relaxing and hot stone massage, and told me she'd pay me to help her through her busy period. I was amazed at how quickly I'd acquired another skill, for free, and in something which I enjoyed … *and* I was making money! After reading so much about creating your own reality with positive thinking and positive actions, it confirmed to me even more that the Universe always provided if I allowed it.

Long hugs dragged out to the last minute as we said goodbye to Holly and Joe at their beautiful home. It had been an amazing couple of months with yoga in the garden, heart to hearts with like-minded people, and group meditations to see in the New Year. We drove off and my heart soared. We were free. We could go anywhere. The Southern hemisphere Summer was in full swing and I hung my head out of the window while Adam drove down wide roads with no traffic. The country was rugged and raw, towns were funky and relaxed, the warm air smelt like alpines and the horizon looked like Middle Earth. I grew up in a suburb where 'going for a walk' meant a gentle stroll across the common. Adam grew up in Slovakia where he'd hike for miles to get to his mate's house. He introduced me to a whole new world of wild living which would change me forever.

'Freedom Camping' areas—where you could pull up anywhere and stay the night—were sadly in decline due to reckless tourists leaving litter on natural sites, but we did our best to find them anyway. I loved rising out of bed just metres from the water's edge. No hum of electricity, no instant appliances, no noise. Instead, a wake-up dip in the cold lake water, exotic birdsong echoing off the mountains and a slow-boiling kettle on the camping stove for fresh coffee and biscuits. I felt so alive. This new existence was a bizarre reality for me; I couldn't quite believe that I was there. This was something I would never have thought to do, or been able to do, without an organised group. Cities and beaches were my comfort zones. I was a very practical person, but I knew nothing about survival in the wilderness … or countryside for that matter. I watched in awe as Adam navigated obscure tramping trails, pitched tents at the bottom of glaciers, waded through rivers and lit fires. He filled a black sack with water from a brook and placed it in the sun to warm up for a solar shower. By the evening the water had heated through. He hauled the liquid load up, hung it onto a tree by its handle and draped the hose, with its small shower head, over a branch. "There you go madam!" he smiled, proudly. "One hot shower". Undressing in the middle of the woods, I braced myself against the cold which was creeping in fast. Reaching up for the valve, I let the water flow.

"It's hot!" I screamed.

"I told you!" he laughed. I didn't really think it was going to be that warm. I thought maybe it was just a gimmick. He handed me an eco-friendly soap bar and I bathed my whole body after days of quick washes in sinks and freezing cold hair washes under outdoor taps. I turned 360 degrees, looking up to the sky as I lapped up every drop. I was surrounded by trees, my bare body was on show to nature, my bare feet were on leaves, the sun was setting and there was no one there except us.

"This is so, so amazing," I said to Adam, as he held out a fleece blanket, ready to wrap me in, once I'd dried off. That night, we ate sausages speared on sticks, drank whisky from mugs and listened to *The Doors* through our portable speaker. Inside the van, we made love with restricted head room and unrestricted noise while rain beat against the metal around us.

~~~

We were halfway through our year-long visa when Adam and I moved into a small studio for the winter. It was fast turning cold and peeing outside under the stars in the middle of the night wasn't 'adventurous' anymore, it was just bloody Baltic. I got a job as a cleaner for luxury holiday apartments in Queenstown, and I attended a craft market on the weekends where I sold my paintings to tourists. The cleaning job was hard graft. I'd never done anything so physically demanding before, except for maybe my partying effort during the first semester at Uni. The apartments were high-end and had to be cleaned meticulously which meant working in pairs, scrubbing, polishing, bed-making, sweeping, mopping, vacuuming and lugging the industry-sized equipment up and down the stairs as there were no lifts. Finding used condoms that had wedged themselves in sofas and between bed sheets, became a new skill added to my CV.

Each apartment had a balcony overlooking a beautiful vista, and we were instructed to open the sliding doors to let fresh air in while we worked. At minus five degrees, with wind sweeping in from the snowy peaks, thermals were essential. By the end of the Winter season I had chapped lips and nose, my tan had faded to white and I looked like Coco the Clown.

You see some interesting things when you clean hotel rooms; sometimes I was scared to open that door. But regardless of the exhaustion, the monotony and the dirt, I made a vow to myself to be nothing but positive. I wanted to activate the *Law of Attraction* again and magnetise good things. I'd done more research into the theory which was also known as 'Cause and Effect' or 'Newton's Third Law'. Today, people were seeing things less as Karma in action, and more as *science* in action. It was being proven by scientists that our thoughts and intentions had a direct physical outcome, and that our life was a result of them. I still wanted so much more out of this trip. I wanted Adam and I to get on better; things had started going sour already and I couldn't bear the thought of ANOTHER relationship going down the drain.

Something had changed soon after we moved into the tiny studio flat. I welcomed the creature comforts which were a novelty for a while, and we definitely both enjoyed the proper bed with space to jump around, but Adam became agitated when I talked of moving on. I was surprised to discover that he didn't handle travelling so well. He was amazing at making a camp and living in the wild, but he struggled with the unpredictability of being on the road, stressing about where we were going next, where we were going to spend the night, when we would be able to find work.

"But that's the whole point!" I would say to him. "That's why we're doing this...to live for the moment, to go where we please, to be free. We've got a van, that's our bed. Everything else is easy! Just trust babe, it'll all work out great," I smiled broadly, excited by the prospect of no plans; curious as to where unknown roads and wrong turns might lead us — and *who* they might lead us to. Infinite opportunities awaited.

"I've got a good job here as a decorator, my boss says he can sponsor me so I can stay longer, I don't like not knowing what we're doing. And I hate getting lost," he would reply, and my heart would sink. We had opposite dreams. To him, the flat was perfect; a predictable base where he could go to the same job each day, plan his cycling and hiking trips from, and then safely return to. To me, it was a cage in the middle of paradise. I wanted to experience all the things that New Zealand had to offer. I wanted to go back to Australia when our visas ran out. I knew the truth was that we needed a miracle for all that to happen because I had very little money. I knew that Adam was just being logical. However, I also knew deep in my heart that it *was* all possible if I just let go and trusted the flow. If I just kept saying YES to life. If I continued to be open-minded. But how could I show him what I saw in my visions? How could I expect someone else to have the same risky beliefs, and take a leap with no guarantees?

Despite the depressing prospect of cleaning every day, I committed to positivity and practiced gratitude that I had a job at all. I reminded myself that the physical work was keeping me fit and, in fact, I was getting stronger all the time and developing strange muscles in my back and arms that I didn't even know existed. I made sure that I got up a little earlier to do just five or ten minutes of yoga every morning so that my limbs wouldn't give up on me. I had a reoccurring knee problem and pain in my shoulders which I couldn't afford to prevent me from working.

This is NOT what we signed up for! I could almost hear my body saying to me.

It's ok, we'll take care of you, yoga replied.

I put my heart into every room and cleaned as if I was cleaning my own home, paying attention to details and going the extra mile. I made an effort to always chat to my workmates; I joked with them to lift their spirits when they were fed up or when the weather was gloomy. I asked them things about their lives back home and got them to talk about their hopes and dreams for the future. I trained new employees who were fellow backpackers from all over the world, often speaking minimal English. Some were totally disinterested and some were just utterly clueless. Remembering my goal, I trained them with patience and enthusiasm. I insisted that no matter how busy we were, no matter how hungover anyone was, each time we started on a new room I made everyone stop, open the large glass doors onto the balcony, step outside and take in the stunning view which was right over the massive Lake Wakatipu. I would remind them that although we were all reluctantly doing this job for the same reason: to make money, we had to remember why we were there: to see the magic of New Zealand. Lastly, I made it my ritual as we finished cleaning each apartment, just before closing the door, to stop, look at the space, smile and imagine how happy the new residents would be when they walked in and first saw the beautiful, clean rooms. I imagined that it was me coming to stay in them. Then I would lock the door and say "Thank you". My colleagues rolled their eyes and thought I was crazy, but I didn't care what it looked like. I knew that what I was doing was an important spiritual practice.

∾∾∾

I started to see '1111' flash in front of my eyes everywhere. Every digital clock in the holiday apartments seemed to call me to look at them just as they switched to eleven minutes past eleven. I'd look at my phone and the time would be 11:11. My laptop clock, town clock, cooker clocks, microwave clocks…anything with a clock, started to do the same. Number plates, phone numbers, addresses, all seemed to have four ones in them. At first, I joked about it as a weird coincidence, but it became incessant. *What the hell was going on?*

As soon as I hit the Google button, a million results came up about it. Apparently, it was some kind of heads-up from the Universe or angels or whatever you believed in. A sign of awakening, a symbol of alignment with a higher truth, a message from the stars to inform you that you were going through some kind of metamorphosis; or you were about to; or perhaps that you *needed* to. There were many explanations for seeing these numbers which millions of other people were seeing too, but the same theme rung throughout: inner transformation.

The tension between Adam and I grew by the day. I felt heartbroken that it wasn't working out. By then, I loved him dearly. I thought we could make a life together; some sort of life anyway. One where I would paint and he would train for triathlons; I would read and maybe he would stop smoking so much weed. It might not have been a fairy tale but I was ok with that. I didn't expect things to be perfect.

Couples always had their challenges, I knew that. But at that point in time, at thirty-one years old — even though I knew I wasn't exactly over the hill — my friends were all tying the knot and popping out first-babies by the dozen. I began to wonder when I was going to find 'T.O'.

Adam had an abundance of wonderful gifts which he hardly recognised himself. He was creative, inventive and romantic, but that often went hand-in-hand with moodiness and pent up frustration which he internalised. He was also trying to give up pot; something which was proving to be a lot harder than he had anticipated. He was a deep thinker, an athlete and a loyal friend. He was a free-spirit and passionate about getting out in to the wild, testing his ability to survive. He was spiritual and curious; willing to explore anything from transcendental meditation to tantric sex. He thrived off living simply and getting off the beaten track. He longed to climb every mountain and cycle every terrain. He cared for me, I guess I knew that deep down, but his heart had been broken badly in the past and he fought his own fears to open it up again to let me in.

Not long before I met him, he had hit a low. Suffering a bad sports injury meant he couldn't enter triathlons for some time, and he felt uninspired with his photography; a combination which left him without direction or purpose. In an act of anger and depression he cut off his long, naturally grown dreadlocks. I understood why he decided to lose them; after all, I'd done the same when my dad died, but I wasn't so sure it had helped him to move forward. Chopping his beloved hair, meeting me, and planning to move to New Zealand was supposed to be a new chapter for him, but he kept his severed locks in a bin liner like a cadaver in a body-bag. As we packed, in the weeks leading up to our departure from the island, he assured me he would do something with them. The bag didn't move from behind the sofa until the last day, when they were put in a box with the rest of his stored possessions.

To me, those dreadlocks represented an old life; one he wasn't ready to let go of. I wanted him to forgive the heartache from his ex-girlfriend so that we could take things to the next level. As he packed the dead hair away, deciding to 'bury them in the ground later,' I should have known I was fighting a losing battle. I longed for Adam to want me in the way I wanted him, but his wounded heart took him on constant journeys which I was not a part of. As time went on, we'd be together physically, on walks and hikes and fishing trips, but often his mind was elsewhere and his heart even further. The only time we always connected emotionally—the only time he really dropped the barriers—was during sex. After, he held me tight against his beating chest and I'd feel momentarily comforted. But in painfully stark contrast, outside of the bed, he'd become even more distant.

Then, out of the deep, dark blue, news came that his father had passed away suddenly. His family were back in Slovakia, and Adam made the tough decision to stay in New Zealand. I temporarily abandoned any ideas to leave him. I wanted to make it all better for him; for us. I'd lost my dad when I was young, I knew the pain and confusion and I wanted to be his rock. But as I tried to get closer, he withdrew further and I felt isolated beyond belief. I'd heard people talk of feeling more alone *with* someone than without them, and I knew what they meant. My conscience told me I *shouldn't* leave him when he needed me the most. My heart told me I would fade away again if I stayed.

CHAPTER 14

Magic

We got word that The Dalai Lama was visiting New Zealand. Back in the day, it would have been a *Stereophonics* concert that got me all excited; now it was Dalai Lama on tour which sent me into a spin. This special monk, the spiritual leader of Tibet, 'His Holiness,' believed, by his people, to be the 14th reincarnation of the bodhisattva of compassion, was giving a talk in Dunedin, a city just a couple of hours drive away. A few of us were curious to see this Buddhist in person, who was renowned for being a peaceful and humorous humanitarian, so we made the trip to see him.

I'd made a couple of really good friends at campsites; girls from Hamburg and Amsterdam who, like me, had followed the call of their wild hearts and stepped out of civilisation in search of a more primitive experience. Kaja—who later became a manager in conservation—had given up her urban existence as a designer by day and guitarist in a band by night, to devote herself to yoga and nature. We agreed on the relief of living more simply, leaving the pressures of a speedy, media-driven world behind; but also empathised with each other on missing big comfy beds, long hot baths, late-night jazz haunts, and reassuringly expensive Vodka Martinis. Sitting around a fire, eating molten marshmallows with huge countryside laid out right before us, I don't think either of us could really decide if one life was better than the other.

When we reached the hostel in Dunedin, we were handed the key for room number eleven, and my seat in the auditorium was, of course, eleven; this 11:11 craziness was getting out of control. The Dalai Lama's talk was altruistic and uplifting, albeit, emotional. The journey to see him was the final trip Adam and I made together.

I was feeling overwhelmed with confusion of what to do about my perpetually turbulent love-life, and I was experiencing deep emotions that—despite having gone through more tragic things than boyfriend problems—were taking me to unknown places of sadness inside myself. This was obviously more than just a break-up. I was having another kind of awakening. But as with all awakenings, I was sinking deep in to the most hidden places within myself first; the parts that were calling to be seen. The dark before the dawn.

During our time camping and trekking in peaceful and wild surroundings, we had no smart phones, no Instagram, no Facebook; just the present moment, like it was before. Without connection to Wi-Fi I felt an earthly connection to my own deep roots, ancestors and ancient wisdom. It felt like all the positive thinking I had been doing was making a huge difference to my overall ability to be more open, psychically. It seemed to be activating a kind of doorway for more levels of life to come in. With plenty of time to myself while Adam was out riding new tracks or fixing his bikes, I would wonder alone in to the woods, down by the lake or to a waterfall; wherever I could find water. We had been living in mountainous areas for months and I missed the sea. I pined for the salty air, the uncluttered horizons and the deep, unseen mystery of the ocean. The sea could always clear my head and soothe my heart. But I made the most of my surroundings and spent much time meditating, journaling, thinking, swimming, running, walking and just being in awe of the stunning landscape all around me.

On a cloudy Saturday when Adam was out, I felt like the weight of the world was on my shoulders. I had tried so hard to follow my heart but began to wonder: *Why was it breaking again?* With all my intuition, I was still getting it wrong. I didn't know what was happening, but I knew something was coming to a head. I ran through the woods and cried. I cried and cried the more I ran. I realised I hadn't cried for some time, which was unlike me; I was the kind of girl who cried at weddings, soppy films and TV adverts; but there had been a drought lately. Possibly, I was scared of what tears might show me. Now it was pouring out of me in torrents. When I couldn't cry anymore I sat and took out my journal.

Pen poised at the paper, I didn't know where to start. I had so many thoughts whirling through my mind that I was getting even more frustrated for not being able express myself. If I wrote every single word that was going through my head, I'd be writing a Bible-sized book. I took a long, deep breath and, in the way I'd read about in one of my self-help books, I surrendered all attempt to control the situation. There was a pause in my thoughts. Then, without thinking I began to write. To my surprise, I was writing a poem. I hadn't written poetry since I was a child, but now it was flowing out of my hand like a babbling brook. It came out in a song of words. The words were unusual; different to how I normally expressed myself. They spoke of intense and untold secrets. They spoke of other realms and mysterious lands. When it stopped, I was stunned; my pain had subsided and my mind felt clear. Rather than cramming page after page with endless paragraphs of muddled thoughts—only to still feel confused at the end—I had filled just one page of poetry which had somehow satisfied my heart and emptied my head. Ordinarily, I fell back on filling and emptying my stomach to get the same relief. Not only that, something within me had just awoken. It felt as though a portal for a far more expanded perspective of life had appeared. Like at school, when I first learnt that the Earth was just *one* of many planets floating in a big black lagoon of stars and constellations and comets. It blew my mind.

This new-found magic in my life served me very well. I was writing poetry every day and connecting to nature in a profound way. My bulimia felt redundant. The void I had felt before was beginning to be occupied with a unique sense of power. My heart was still breaking but my spiritual self was mending during the daily communion with divine energy. I did private little ceremonies, prayers and rituals, using whatever I could find to make offerings: candles, flowers, fruits, wine, poems tied up with ribbon or string. I made detailed declarations of my desires and gave gratitude for my gifts. I had no magic guide book telling me what to do or say; I didn't follow any witchy recipes. I just did what seemed right and what made me feel alive and excited again.

I deeply respected the traditions of the Craft that I'd read about, but I believed that using magic or performing spells were not activities only for organised Covens, which seemed so out of reach for others, and they didn't *have* to follow the same rules. I did agree though, that it was something to be respected deeply and practised with kindness and integrity. As someone who has always done things her own way — listening to her gut (and rarely anyone else) for guidance — magic would, most certainly, be a personal and eclectic practice for me.

From what I understood, spells were essentially connecting deeply to your soul, to other souls, and working in tune with nature. They were a way to pool energy, and even scientists were understanding that we could do some of that with our brains alone. I knew that if I was in the right frame of mind: positive and undistracted, I could pool my energy very well. Most of the time our energy is scattered between so many things and thoughts. By pooling or funnelling my energy, I knew I could set strong intentions and stand more chance of seeing them materialise. By working with the moon, the seasons, my spirit guides and all the cycles of life, I was honouring myself as sacred piece of the Universe; a piece who has just as much right and as much power on this planet as every mountain, every ocean and every tree.

During one of my meditations, I used a practice of simply allowing anything to come in to my mind, anything that might offer insight as to what I should do next. It was a technique I liked to use; no structure, no visualisations, no set idea on what state I *should* be achieving. Just free-flowing thoughts and observation of anything that seemed to be particularly interesting. The name 'Nancy' came to me strongly, before vanishing again. I didn't know anyone by this name, and afterwards I wondered if it was a message for someone else. I mentioned it to Adam and to my friends, to see if it meant something to them, but no one found a link. I put the thought aside, aware of not hanging onto anything too tightly, but felt it was something I should at least remember.

Waiting at the bus stop at an out of town shopping centre, I was the only one there on a cold Sunday afternoon, until a figure popped out of the blue. A tall guy, maybe late twenties, with white dreadlocks, pale skin and red albino eyes, came and stood beside me. I said hello and immediately noticed he was wearing, what looked like, layers of summer clothes. He had the appearance of someone who had piled on half the contents of his holiday wardrobe at the airport, in an attempt to get away with carrying hand luggage only. A long-sleeved shirt with a surf vest on top, full leg thermals with board shorts over them, and flip-flops over socks. With his unusual looks and wardrobe malfunction, he was definitely a suspicious sight, but I kept my mind open as it wasn't so strange to see some unique ensembles in the backpacker community; especially those that had been on the road a while.

"What time is it?" He asked me in a laid back and slightly monotone American accent. I went to pull out my mobile to check, but before I did he said, "I have a clock," and produced a digital alarm clock from a white plastic bag.

"Oh," I replied, wondering: a) why he would want a large digital clock if he was indeed, travelling light, and b) why then, he was asking me for the time.

"It's broken. I came to buy batteries for it," he paused for a moment. "But they don't fit". Then silence. I was about to question why he didn't just ask the sales person for the right batteries, it looked like a pretty standard machine, but thought twice, once I'd concluded that he was possibly very stoned. Feeling cold and bored at the prospect of the bus ride home, seeing this rather amusing blanched stranger made me smile. The bus arrived, and being the only two people on it, it seemed to me absurd not to sit next to him; anyway, I needed some entertainment. He began telling me about something that had happened to him last week—a bizarre and abstract tale. I listened politely and responded by raising my eyebrows now and then. Shortly after finishing his account of events he looked up to the corner as if he was remembering something and then he added, "Or was that a dream? I'm not sure". I couldn't contain myself and laughed out loud at his surreal story, which broke the ice and we chatted more freely.

I asked him where he was from and why he was in New Zealand. He said he lived in Maui, worked as a stonemason and that he surfed most months, travelling to the slopes to snowboard the rest of the year. He went on to say how much he loved his island, that the people were so wonderful and kind and that he wouldn't want to live anywhere else in the world. I nodded in agreement and told him about my travels so far. After that, it was like he was on some sort of mission, he just kept telling me about how great Maui was and that I should really go.

"Yeh, I'd love to go one day," I said, "I've always been fascinated by Hawaiian culture. And it just looks incredibly beautiful".

"You MUST go, you really should go," he'd reply adamantly, as if this was a message, he had specifically for me.

Finally, we reached our destination, Queenstown, and as we pulled up to the bus stop I waited for the usual exchange of names, numbers and 'we should hang out sometime,' which was pretty standard when you meet fellow backpackers. But as I turned to grab my shopping bags I looked back up and he'd gone. I stepped off the bus and squinted both ways. I could just about make out his white dreadlocks far off in the distance and stood there in amazement at the speed at which he must have moved. They say Angels sometimes walk the Earth. If this was, in any way, preordained for my benefit, then whoever sent him obviously knew me well. An albino Hawaiian space-cadet who wears socks and flip-flops, is definitely my kind of Angel. *Why do these 'Messengers' always ride on buses?* I thought to myself.

Eventually I bit the bullet and told Adam I was leaving. I wanted to help him through his issues but our relationship was too unbalanced; it wasn't fair on me to suffer while I waited for him to open up fully to me. And I suppose, it wasn't fair on him to feel pressurised to do so before he was ready. Although we were amicable, and although Adam told me to stay in the studio flat as long as I needed, I decided I would move out asap. In my experience, co-habiting after a break-up just prolonged the agony and prevented life from progressing.

Once again, I didn't know what on earth I was going to do. I had no money for a deposit on a new room, only enough from my wages to pay a small monthly rent. I wasn't proud of always being so skint, but it was the way I always seemed to end up. So, I just did what I always did: I meditated and channelled all the energy I could muster, in hope of some sort of positive outcome. I decided that whatever happened, I would stay for a month, then leave. I couldn't bear staying in the same town. I needed yet another clean slate.

The Manager of the complex where I cleaned was a lady called Jackie. She lived on-site in one of the luxury apartments which she owned. The other staff misunderstood her and found her intimidating so they didn't really speak to her. But from the first time I met her, I saw with my knowing eyes, a woman who—underneath a stern and quiet exterior—was kind, funny and hard-working; people were rarely what they seemed. Her demands for high standards (handing us toothbrushes to clean mould from shower corners) were often mistaken for punishment by her employees. The truth was, she just took pride in the buildings and in the business. I made an effort to get to know her and I discovered she had a great sense of humour and a naughty side which appealed to me. We'd sometimes hang-out at her place or go for a drink in town, and she seemed to really appreciate the company.

When I broke up with Adam, I held off before telling Jackie that I'd be leaving the job, as I wanted to figure out my plans first. I made various appointments to view rooms in house-shares but the outlook was pretty dismal. Either the homes were in an awful state, the housemates were not the kind of people I wanted to be sharing with, or the price was just way above what I could afford. The following week I came in to work and went to the office where Jackie was sitting at her computer. Taking a deep breath, I told her what had happened, that I was having a tough time and that I would be looking to leave in a month or so, but that I'd carry on working until then. I also told her that if she knew of anyone who had a spare room to rent then I'd be interested.

"That's a real shame," Jackie replied with a sincere look in her eye. "You know, if you wanted to work in the office here, we could sponsor you to stay in the country". I felt like she wanted me to stay as a friend, as much as an employee.

"That's really lovely… and I will think about that," I meant what I said. Considering I had wanted so much to see more of New Zealand, this was a perfect and easy solution which had popped out of nowhere, but my heart told me that I must leave.

"I have a spare room you can stay in," Jackie added. "Regardless of whether you stay on or not. It's an en-suite with kitchenette at the back of my apartment".

"Seriously?" I asked.

"Yeah of course. You'll be nice and close to work too! …until you leave, I mean". Thrilled, and almost in disbelief, I took her up on her offer and told her I'd pay her the going rate. But she dismissed my words with a shake of her head and just told me to give her what I could afford. It was a wish come true. Relieved that I had somewhere to go with no financial pressure, I put aside any fears of my non-existent future plans and concentrated on this gift currently being placed right in my hands. It felt like fellow women were always looking after me. Sisters were always at the right place, at the right time.

Within a couple of days, I had moved my things in to Jackie's and settled in. I had a beautiful new room with a big bed and my own bathroom — with a bathtub — Praise the Lord! I couldn't remember the last time I'd had a bath. Jackie said I could use her spacious apartment and balcony as I wished when she was out or away, which was actually quite often. And not only that; the complex had its own gym and outdoor hot spa on the terrace. She casually mentioned I could use them if I wanted (she never bothered using it herself).

As soon as I had the chance, I took myself up to the terrace, whipped my towel off in the freezing night air, lifted the lid off the hot tub and submerged myself in to steaming hot water with its dreamy blue lights shining beneath the surface. Sinking into the moulded seat, I closed my eyes with bliss as I leant my head back and allowed the heat to soothe my muscles which were tired from physical strain. Opening my eyes again, I was taken aback; the night sky was awash with a million stars. It was so clear and crisp that I could make out the snowy peaks of The Remarkables Mountain Range in the distance; the Milky Way swirled in indigo hues around a slither of crescent moon. I was awestruck. Suddenly, there I was, a broke backpacker, sitting in a private hot spa, overlooking the mountains, staying in a luxury apartment. It was incredible. I invited my girlfriends over one evening to share some food, wine, music and a spa session, and we all agreed that whether it was *The Law of Attraction* or magic or bravery or just pure luck, something unseen was sure as hell at work.

CHAPTER 15

———◆———

Couch Surfing

A ustralia was on my mind. I'd lived there for a year and a half when I was nineteen and always wanted to return. I had worked as a Nanny for a mother with twin baby boys. Zahra was thirty-six and I was still in my teens when we met, yet we connected instantly and became good friends. She and I would chat about everything: life and love, boyfriends and husbands, art and travel. She loved to hear about all my flings and holiday romances. Being from a devoted Jewish family, her love-life prior to meeting her husband was not quite so colourful, so she took much joy from listening to me recall my own capers. Eyes narrowing with both hands around her coffee cup, "Tell me *all* the details," she'd say in her Aussie accent, as I folded the laundry and mentioned a Brazilian who asked me to marry him, one night in in a swimming pool in Bali.

I had a fair bit of knowledge of childcare. From the age of twelve I helped look after my young auntie's kids, and then later on, my sister's. In-between that, I spent many weekends babysitting in my local area. I was confident that I could handle most things they threw at me — or threw-up on me. Zahra's own babies were her first real experience of children, and she often looked to me for guidance. Sometimes it felt like I was the thirty-something and she was the teen.

I came to help her through a nanny agency; she was going through a challenging time as one of the boys had broken his little leg. At one and a half years old, one twin, who had just started walking, would be bounding off like a puppy in all directions, while the other, with the broken leg, needed to be carried everywhere in his ridged and heavy plaster-cast which covered his belly, his entire left leg and half of his right leg. Poor little thing, he looked like a mummified starfish. I adored the twins and I became like part of the family over the months that I worked with them.

When I made the decision to leave Queenstown and go to Sydney, I didn't yet have enough money for the flight but I was determined to make it happen somehow. Employing my extreme optimism, the first thing I did was to email Zahra and tell her we'd finally be reunited. It had been a decade since we'd seen each other but we had always kept in touch with letters and photos. Even though the twins were so young when I left, she always spoke about me so that they would remember; now they were teenagers themselves. I had a reply from her the next day, telling me that they were going on a long-awaited family trip to Europe around the same time that I was looking to visit.

"NOOOO WAY! You *can't* come when we're not here," she said when she found out. But I assured her that I would plan it so that I would see her at least a couple of days before they left or just after their return. She then wrote back with an incredible offer. They needed a house and dog sitter while they were away and still hadn't managed to find anyone suitable. She asked if I would come and stay, covering the cost of my flight over as payment. I was gobsmacked. Once again, the Universe had found me a way to follow my heart. And not only that, I would be helping Zahra out too.

However, things changed rapidly. Zahra's husband suffered an injury which forbade him from travelling, and so they had to cancel their plans. They were devastated, they lost a lot of money and I was totally gutted for them. My flight to Sydney had already been booked and was non-refundable, so I could still use it, but they would no longer need a dog-sitter. The circumstances were obviously not happy ones, but the fact still remained that I had a flight to Australia by unexpected means. And thankfully, Zahra and her family did manage to make their dream trip to Europe a couple of years later.

~~~

With altered accommodation plans I set about organising my move over to Sydney. I decided to check the *Couchsurfing* website (yet another brilliant brainchild of some free-spirited Californian entrepreneurs). *Couchsurfing* allowed you, as a traveller, to contact anyone who signed up, offering their spare room or sofa to crash on while you trotted around the globe. It's was a beautifully refreshing and free exchange, which all members did for the pure fun, kindness and karmic sake of it. That way you got to hang out with a local and get a more authentic experience of the place you were visiting too, rather than spending all your time with a bunch of Brits in the Irish pub. People often asked me about *Couchsurfing*, and how you knew you weren't going to be staying with a total psycho; or get robbed. And well, I guess, you didn't really know for certain. But as with most online pursuits, everyone had a profile and gathered feedback, and if a host were to do anything untoward, they would soon be ousted and banned. But really you had to use your head; any travelling you did alone had its risks. You did what felt right, you tried to keep risks to a minimum (e.g. arranging to meet your host in public first) and used your intuition. If it felt weird, then it probably was.

While still in Jackie's apartment in Queenstown I contacted a chap called Tom who lived on the stunning north shore of the city in a place called Dee Why, right near the beach. *The beach!* I thought excitedly, I couldn't wait to be in my happy place again. We exchanged a couple of emails and I tried to get a feel for his personality. He seemed like a nice enough chap; when I told him I'd be flying over on the eleventh of June—because eleven was my lucky number—he replied excitedly, explaining that his life had been ruled by '11:11' for the last twenty years. Had I not known what he was talking about, I may have assumed he was a complete nut-job, made my excuses and left the conversation. However, after my personal 11:11 experiences, I took it as a good sign.

Tom offered to pick me up from the airport, and when I came out at Arrivals, I scanned the crowd and then did a double-take. He was standing there, beaming with a massive warm smile and piece of copy paper in hand, with 'CHAR 11:11!!' written in bubble writing with stars all around it like a three-year old's birthday card. This was either going to end up really great, or with my face on a milk carton.

Tom was brilliant. He was everything you'd hope from an Aussie, with his leather brown tan, broad shoulders and an even broader accent. He completed his stereotype perfectly by greeting me with a loud, "G'DAY!" He let me use his flat as I pleased for the week that I stayed and inspired me with his tales of living in Maui. *This is strange,* I thought, *someone talking to me about Maui again already.* He had worked as a surf-gliding instructor in Hawaii in the eighties, but he suffered a near-death accident which left him with serious — but luckily only temporary — injuries, and unconscious in hospital. When he woke up, the first thing he did was look at the clock and it was '11:11'. From then on, his life changed and since then he had been seeing '1111' everywhere. Tom went on telling me about Maui and urged that I should really go there someday, exactly as the albino boy on the bus had done. This was the second time in two months that someone was banging on about Maui to me. I wondered what it meant. *Was my dream man there? Was my dream job there? Would I find the meaning of life there?!* As I got ready to leave Tom's, with sand between my happy toes once more, he picked up my backpack for me, expecting it to be heavy. "Is that it?!" He laughed. "You don't leave much of a footprint, do you?"

Continuing on my Couchsurfing Quest I went to meet an old friend in the centre of Sydney. Fifi was from London; a stunning and talented performer, we became friends when I exhibited my artwork at Burlesque shows around the city. As it happened, Fifi had come to Australia on a working holiday and so we arranged to meet up. Sydney was hosting an Annual Burlesque Festival and she was in the line-up. I decided that it would be a brilliant thank you to Tom for his amazing hospitality, and a fun night out (as he'd been though a rough patch with a painful divorce) if I got us tickets. He'd never been to anything like it. The room was filled with more nipple tassels and seamed stockings than you could shake a tail-feather at. To say Tom loved it, was the understatement of the century.

Fifi and I decided to do a few of the tourist spots together and visit the Blue Mountains, which were only a couple of hours away. We met at the central train station and I noticed that we looked quite odd as travelling buddies. There I was: stripped of make-up, bronzed skin from hiking in winter sun, wearing my worn-at-the-knees leggings, bobbled thermal top, knitted mitts, beanie, backpack and boots. And there was Fifi—all six foot of her. She had sleek victory rolls in her hair, china white skin, berry-stained lips, wearing a skin-tight black wiggle skirt. She looked something akin to a beautiful modern day Morticia Addams, wheeling her carry-on case behind her while holding a parasol above her head to shield her porcelain skin from the UV rays. But somehow, in our opposite ways we worked, and our company was so easy, fun and relaxed. When she asked if I wanted to stay in a hostel up in the mountains, I suggested *Couchsurfing* as an alternative. It was a new concept to Fi and she was dubious but willing to try. I managed to contact a host who sounded interesting; a young eco-warrior who ran a small farm near Katoomba, the nearest village. He said we were more than welcome to come and stay and that he'd meet us in town at the Winter Magic Festival, which was on at the time. *Perfect*, I thought, we'll be among lots of people so if we're not sure about him, we can make a safe exit.

We arrived at Katoomba which was brimming with hippies, live music and bearded men dressed as wizards. Market stalls sold colourful knitted scarves and crystals, while festival-goers streamed through the streets with tie-dye clothing and glittered faces. Revellers danced to acoustic bands and clutched steaming cider to keep warm. The atmosphere was crisp and fresh, and I found myself feeling relieved to be breathing in the air of the snow-capped mountains, which surprised me after longing to get away from them in New Zealand. We met Rob, the eco farmer, in a busy pub and soon got chatting. He was kind and intelligent and we felt fine about the prospect of staying with him. Once the festivities came to an end we followed him to his truck. Dumping our bags in to the Ute, we headed off to his pad. The night was drawing in and the roads were getting longer and longer. "Is it quite far?" I asked, as Fifi glared with big eyes in my direction. I could tell she was feeling unnerved by the darkness and distance.

"I live quite far out of the town," Rob answered. "You did read that on my profile, didn't you? I did say that I was quite far from town," he repeated. In all honesty, as I thought back to sitting in the internet café in Sydney, scrolling through the *Couchsurfing* website—trying to max out my connection time which cost $4 per hour—I had been a bit rushed and didn't read *everything.* I guess I got a good initial vibe from Rob's personal profile and forgot to study the details about the accommodation. "We'll be there soon," he reassured us.

Fi was getting more and more agitated. Every now and then I'd feel her poke me in the back with her finger as we passed by some derelict old house. I turned around and smiled, mouthing, *Don't worry.* Truth be told, I was starting to freak out a bit myself. Finally, we arrived and piled out of the truck, onto muddy ground. The small farm was pretty basic and Rob showed us inside his self-made home. The bedroom, lounge and kitchen were all open plan, and I knew that Fi and I were thinking the same thing as we eyed the double bed, veiled with a mosquito net: *Where would we be sleeping*?

"You guys are OK with compost loos, right?" Rob asked as he opened a door to show us the toilet.

"Yeah, fine," I replied. I was used to basic facilities with my recent adventures. Visiting 'the little girl's room' while camping, usually meant a walk in to the woods with loo roll and a plastic bag. Fi poked her head into the rudimentary bathroom and came back out looking like a rabbit in headlights.

"You're going to have to show me what to do with that thing," she whispered worriedly to me, as Rob went to put the kettle on.

We soon established that Fifi and I were happy to camp down in our sleeping bags, despite our host offering to sleep on the floor and give us the bed. After an hour or so chatting about life on the farm, sustainability, conscious living and, of course— Burlesque dancing—we all hit the sack. Fi wore to bed, a long black silk robe and eye-mask, zipping herself up in the sleeping bag all the way, until her head was covered. "You look like a bat!" I joked. It was totally impractical but I loved her for it. She was so glamorous, even out in the sticks. I admired her for stepping out of her comfort zone and taking the chance to experience something new, which, after all, is the true essence of travel.

Due to the multiple layers of clothes I wore to bed, I slept like a log. Meanwhile, Fi tossed and turned throughout the night. I woke up early, and seeing that my little bat friend was fast asleep in her cocoon, I padded quietly over to the glass doors to check out the view, which had been in blackness when we had arrived the night before. At daybreak, the previously ominous-looking land now looked enchanting. The sun was yet to rise and the air was cold and damp with dew drops covering the long grass in the distant field. To the left were chickens in their coop and to the right were sleeping pigs. I gazed out to the horizon and absorbed the peace and freshness of the countryside. A small kangaroo hopped out in to the field, fifty metres away from where I was standing. I froze. Then another appeared. Then another. I watched as they bounced around and boxed with each other, my feet glued to the ground in fear of scaring them off. When it seemed that they were going to stick around, I turned to look at Fi; I had to show her. Shaking her softly, she groaned as she emerged from the sleeping bag and lifted her eye-mask. "I'm knackered," she rasped.

"Look at this," I pointed to the door. Reluctantly, she wriggled free from her cocoon and wrapped her arms around herself tightly against the cold air.

"What"? She grumbled. But then she saw the 'roos; one with its baby. We both stood there, captivated by the wonderful wilderness that played out right on our doorstep, and I could tell from that moment, she knew it had been worthwhile getting off the beaten track.

CHAPTER 16

Peter Pan Saves the Day

The next day, Rob gave us a whistle-stop tour of the region in his truck, and this time, we both felt at ease. We were on a tight schedule due to Fifi's performing commitments back in the city but as it turned out, the mist had come in and there was barely anything to see anyway.

"Well, I'm sure it's a really beautiful view," Fifi said dryly while standing at Echo point, staring at grey and white cloud where the famous rock formation should be.

"I'm so gutted you can't see it, Fi." I said sadly. "The Three Sisters really are a stunning landmark".

"Guess I'll just have to come back, won't I?" She said with a cheeky smile.

A few hours later we said our goodbyes at the train station. "Thank you," she said as she bent down to give me a squeeze, her tassel shrug tickling my face. Little did I know that I had just planted a seed which would grow and turn her into an avid nature-lover. Dancing by night, travelling by day, she continued to explore Australia, and the world.

Sitting on the steps to eat a sandwich, I watched the sun burn the big white tiles of the Opera House, and — as if to complete some sort of cycle — headed straight for my favourite Astrological shop, where I had my fortune told the first time I came to Australia with Lara. We stumbled across the mysterious little outlet when we arrived in Sydney back in 2001, after spending a psychedelic month in Thailand with temples, utopian beaches and a shed load of local whiskey. I had a sudden memory, transporting me back to South East Asia, filling my senses with sandalwood incense and reggae music.

"How far is it?" I remember asking the girls, as we meandered down the dusty track back to our beach hut, after what seemed like ninety-eight hours of non-stop dancing at the Luna Bar in Krabi.

"About another twenty-five minutes," answered Krista, one of the two well-travelled Danish girls we met on the boat from Koh Phi Phi. The four of us got on well and decided to share accommodation so we could get a bigger chalet.

"TWENTY-FIVE minutes?" I protested, dragging my heavy feet along the ground. The soles on my *Havaianas* were wearing thin from all the walking through hot sand and dancing on rum-drenched floors. I could feel every little stone on the road through the tired rubber; the middle plug between the toes kept popping out of its hole, causing my foot to propel forward. It was as if my flip-flops were ganging up on me, tripping me up, probably so that they could have a god damn rest. I pushed my sweaty hair back. Even dressed in a mini sarong and halter-neck top the size of a hanky, my body was overheating in the monsoon season humidity.

"Twenty-five minutes?" I asked again, slightly confused. "But I'm sure that it only took us *five* minutes to get to here from Ao Nang".

"Noooo Stupid!" Krista laughed in her American-tinged Nordic voice. "That's where we were *last* week. We're staying in Railay Beach now. It was cheaper, remember?"

Thailand brews its own whiskey which is poured lavishly into beach buckets for consumption with Red Bull via a straw. We got through... well... buckets of the stuff. We later realised it contained amphetamines. I don't remember sleeping much that month. No wonder I was confused as to where I was from one day to the next.

It was a transitional time for us in Sydney. We'd upped and left our young lives in the UK at eighteen years old to fly the nest, venture across the globe and into the unknown alone. We'd dived head-first into Thailand, cutting our travelling teeth in prison-cell style hostels on the back streets of Bangkok; and being chased by rabid dogs across fields in Koh Pha-Ngan. Having our palms and tarot cards read in a small neighbourhood called 'The Rocks' which was situated in the shadows of Sydney Harbour Bridge, felt like the most logical next step on our trip which had already proved to be somewhat shady and surreal. We were only just beginning to really discover ourselves and explore our boundaries — or lack of them. Some divine guidance felt like a good idea at that time.

Today, the historical corner of the city, crammed with old sailor's pubs, craft shops and barista cafes selling soup bowls of flat whites, The Rocks attracted tourists, social media students and brooding artists. I spotted the familiar gold serif signage of the astrology shop beyond the crowds. It looked exactly the same, which made me pause and flashback to my teenage self for a moment: *did I look the same as twelve years ago?* Not that different actually. I had a bit more ink on my body now and a bit less bleach in my hair, but aside from that, not much had changed on the outside. *Inside* was another story.

I darted in to the shop to grab a new book. I didn't have much money left, but I put books in the same category as good friends: invaluable. They inspired and supported me and I needed that on my daunting journey ahead. I found a fairly chunky paperback about a Balinese Shaman which caught my attention. With all the devotional practice I had been doing in New Zealand I was keen to learn more about the power of ritual. Book in hand, I left The Rocks and jumped on a bus to a backpacker's hostel in Bondi Beach. I wanted to re-visit an area—and a time—where I had lived, worked, and first discovered the deeper layers of my sexuality.

Bondi always reminded me of a t-shirt I wore to death: sun-bleached colours, well-loved, and a little bit tattered around the edges; an old favourite that you always return to. Nostalgia kicked in as I spotted *Gertrude and Alice Bookshop*, where—when it was once more of a dusty nook than the spacious store it had become—I used to go for cappuccinos on my days off and sit in the old worn velvet armchairs, leafing through thumbed, second-hand pages. I followed my memories which led me down a quiet side road to *Siren Song*; relieved to find that the little shop full of silver jewellery, beaded dresses and mermaidy knick-knacks was still there. Heading for the sea, I walked along the coast path which took me past *Bondi Icebergs Club* where the large outdoor swimming baths filled and emptied with the pounding Pacific each day. Named for the 'icy' temperatures—which rarely ever fell to single digits—members (aka 'Ice cubes') plunged into the pools throughout the Australian winter and 'braved' the chilly waters, come rain or storm. *Had they even felt British waters?!* As I wandered, I thought about how many times I'd trodden that coast track, past the smaller Tamarama Beach where the more experienced surfers gathered; and further on to Bronte Beach where yummy mummies hung out to drink green tea between yoga classes and playgroups. After two days of reminiscing, I was ready to move on.

The problem was I had no money left. I had come over to Australia from New Zealand with faith alone that it was where I needed to be. So far, things had turned out well and the Universe seemed to be providing nicely for me; but I was down to my last few dollars which would only buy me two more nights in a hostel, and after that I had no idea where I'd be sleeping. Most people would consider this to be an absolutely ridiculous situation to get yourself in to. But I had been listening to my heart, acting on it and following it religiously. I was leaving my fate in the hands of others because, quite frankly, I didn't have the strength to determine it myself. I was going with the flow; seeing where life took me; trusting that the current I fell into would be going the right way for me. I just needed to let go. I needed someone else to run the show for a while.

I had no possessions except what I carried in my backpack. I'd been meditating every day and following the messages I received without hesitation. You're in a different mind-set, and you act in a very different way to 'the norm' when you live like that. Logic takes a sidestep and intuition takes over. You dismiss all thoughts or opinions that what you are doing, might be absurd. After reading numerous spiritual books, and months of continuous mindful practice, I came to the strong belief that we — everyone and everything — are in fact all 'one' on this little planet we call home; and that our little planet is part of the much bigger 'one', which we call the Universe. Like atoms floating around within large solid structures, I felt like I was an individual person, yet just a teeny part that made up the whole. Within that whole there might be stronger parts and weaker parts, smaller parts and bigger parts, nice parts and not-so-nice parts, parts that shone bright and parts that ducked in the shadows, healthy parts and diseased parts. But we were still all in this structure together — all coming from the same place. I believed in the cycle of life; in Karma; that all the joy, friendship, hard work, help and love that I gave out — would come rolling back around. I knew I must be vigilant and guard my safety as best I could, but I also truly believed I was looked after, and trusted that everything I needed would be provided somehow. All I had to do was not worry. Easier said than done.

The money I had would buy me two nights with a roof over my head…or…it could buy me one more night and a bus ride to Melbourne. I was digging deep in to my gut feelings; my next decision needed to be a trust-based one and not fear-based, if I was to get through this desolate patch. My heart was saying *Melbourne*. The first time I came to Australia, despite living in Sydney for nearly a year, I didn't manage to make it to Melbourne in the neighbouring state, as I was working all the time and saving my money for further travels. I had always wanted to visit the city which was renowned for being more arty, more cultured and played-down cool. At that moment I just felt the need to go there, even though I had no clue what on earth I'd do in terms of a bed, food or plans once I arrived. To stay in Sydney just felt wrong and that was enough to make my mind up.

With little else to do anyway, I concentrated on pushing any worries aside and followed my feet to *Peter Pan's*, a travel shop with a slightly worn out Disney-esque fascia, and looked at the bus listings. Getting to Melbourne would use nearly every dollar I had, *but where would I sleep when I got there*? I thought. The eleven-hour journey meant I'd be arriving close to midnight. I didn't like to rely on *Couchsurfing* in these situations; if something went wrong I'd be stranded in the darkness. But then, just below that listing I spotted another bus: Sydney – Melbourne Night-bus. *NIGHT-BUS!* I re-read enthusiastically. I could get to Melbourne *and* have somewhere to sleep. Two birds, one stone! I had never in my life been so excited by such banal information. The word 'night-bus' used to fill me with horrific flashbacks of gruesome journeys at 4am, trying desperately to get home from the centre of London after way too many Bacardi and cokes. A whole other species of human crawls out from the woodwork at that time. But not now; now the night-bus was like a friendly apparition appearing from the horizon. Who knew what the hell I'd do the next night, but I had just bought myself one more day to figure out my future.

I felt good; the fear in my stomach had taken another step away. Queuing at the desk to speak to an advisor and book my ticket, a slightly harassed-looking girl popped her head up at me from behind her customer and apologetically told me she'd be with me as soon as possible. It was busy in the shop and she seemed to be doing about five jobs simultaneously. "No worries," I said, "No rush". She smiled gratefully and pointed to a bench with a couple of computers and desk chairs.

"Please feel free to use the internet while you're waiting…check Facebook or whatever you like," she added in her cockney accent; probably another English girl who tried to escape the rat-race of London. Same rat-race, opposite side of the planet.

At that point in time, owning a device with its mystical mobile data was just a twinkle in my eye, and being able to go online was still a luxury. I sent a couple of emails back home, checked Facebook messages and read my horoscopes. I spun around in my chair, expecting to be beckoned over to the counter, but the poor girl was looking even more frantic. "I'm so sorry!" She called over to me with a stretch of her neck, "won't be long now". I smiled and waved my hand in friendly dismissal to her comment.

"Really, don't worry, it's fine," I said. Turning back to the screen, I did the only thing one can do in these situations, I scrolled further down my Facebook feed. As I caught up on the lives of all my friends: baby snaps, holiday sunsets, extreme close-up selfies, quotes from Buddha, pictures of vegan food — all the usual stuff, something jumped out at me. Below a yoga picture that Holly had posted, I noticed a person named Nancy who had commented on it, and it made me stop in my tracks.

∼∼∼

The name 'Nancy' bared no significance back in New Zealand when I first heard it in my meditation. But seeing it now sparked something in my subconscious. I clicked on Nancy's profile and saw that she lived in Melbourne, which seemed way too serendipitous to ignore. Then my intuition said very clearly: 'Ask her if you can stay with her'.

OH NO! I thought, *there's no way in hell that I'm going to write to a complete stranger... sounding like a proper stalker weirdo... asking if I can come and stay in her home... that's just insane!* But that's exactly what I did. Cringing as my fingers typed the words, I reluctantly wrote out a message something along the lines of:

"Hello Nancy, my name is Charlene. I hope you don't mind me contacting you like this but I'm a good friend of Holly's. I have been travelling in New Zealand where I stayed with her for a while. This might sound utterly crazy, but I did a meditation a while ago and the name 'Nancy' came to me. I just saw your comment under Holly's photo and I got a feeling it was YOU that the meditation was about. Perhaps we are supposed to meet? I am currently in Sydney and I'm just about to travel down to Melbourne. I don't have any plans and not much money (I lied there – I couldn't bring myself to say I actually had *no* money at all) *but I'm following my heart and it's telling me to go there. This is a really big ask and PLEASE, of course, just say no if it's out of the question, but is there any chance you have a spare room I could stay*

in for a couple of days, or would you know of anyone who does? I cannot pay you but I can offer a wealth of services to exchange! I can do cleaning, cooking, babysitting, painting, massage… anything you might need help with. I know this is really unusual, but I guess if you don't ask you don't get, right?! …. Char xx"

My finger hovered over the *send* button, I screwed up my face, wincing at the thought of her reading my creepy message; then I hit SEND. There. it was done. The voice of my late father came in to my head. We loved the TV show *Only Fools and Horses*; and Del Boy (the main character) always used to say to his brother Rodney, in his East End London accent: "He who dares Rodders…He who dares," as in the original 'He who dares, wins" SAS motto. My Dad loved to repeat this phrase and I could hear it now, urging me to dare to be brave and ask for help in an uncomfortable way.

A few minutes passed and I thought about the unlikelihood of hearing back from Nancy. But my luck was in. Soon after, I had a message in my inbox; it was her. I glanced over my shoulder and luckily the frantic travel agent was still snowed under, giving me more precious internet time. Nancy said she was excited about me calling to link up with her; she was intrigued by my meditation and welcomed a conversation to see where it might go. She offered me a bed in her home and told me she'd call me to discuss further.

In a very brief telephone conversation Nancy told me she had plenty of room in her large home, as all her grown-up children had recently flown the nest, and to get the train from Melbourne Central to her town, Hampton. I would be arriving at the unsociable hour of seven-thirty am; however, she said she would be delighted to meet me early at a café just outside the station. I could barely thank her enough before I had to hang up.

The girl at the travel desk was finally free and I didn't want to miss my slot. I booked the overnight bus, walked back to my Bondi hostel to eat one-dollar cup noodles and pondered over the latest additions to my non-existent itinerary. I was so grateful for Nancy's hospitality but at the same time I was petrified about having absolutely no money to arrive with. I did my best to keep positive and went to bed chanting affirmations.

The next evening, I packed up my bag and headed for Sydney's main station. I checked in for my journey at the bus depot with loads of time to spare, and so thought I'd have a wonder around the streets nearby. I was still chanting my positive mantras in the back of my head continuously, because—as much as I didn't want to admit it—I had no idea how I was even going to eat that night. I had exactly one dollar left. One lonely dollar. How I was going to eat the next morning, tomorrow lunchtime, tomorrow evening and beyond, was also a mystery; but at that point, I could only think as far ahead as the present moment or I'd crack. Eckart Tolle, a spiritual teacher, based his entire teachings on the power of NOW. He explained how the power of the present moment is all that ever really matters. He said that anything which happened even just one second before *right now* — and anything you think might happen just one second after *right now* — is of no concern. Whatever is going on, whether you are in the midst of chaos or the midst of despair, the second you take a breath in to your lungs and realise you are still alive, is the moment you can change everything by the thoughts and decisions you make there and then. That's how I was living at that point in time. I was in survival mode.

As I walked, my belly was already beginning to grumble. It took all of my will to stay focused and not berate myself for getting in to this situation by choice. I could easily scold myself for allowing my life to come to such extremes. People were starving in the third world. They would walk for miles to get water, rice and building materials; and here I was letting myself go hungry and risking being homeless because I had *chosen* to leave my privileged life, my job, my home, and jet off around the world on the budget of a five-year-old's piggybank. But I couldn't permit any self-loathing or I'd sabotage all my efforts to follow my heart's true voice and continue to activate the *Law of Attraction*. When you decide to take a leap of faith and trust the Universe completely, there's no room for a half-hearted approach; you have go ALL-IN.

I kept my chin up and walked on, remembering all my learnings of how to keep the faith. Paulo Coelho (Author of *The Alchemist*) talks a lot about looking for 'signs,' and in the *Celestine Prophecy* series, Author James Redfield's stories revolve around signs and synchronicity. I called upon these practices while I walked, and as I passed a newsagent I did a double-take at the shop window:

Lucky Lotto! read the sign of a lottery advert. I turned to continue walking but then remembered that with signs and intuitions it's best not to second-guess your first reaction or gut feeling. I went in to the shop. Pulling out my one and only dollar from my purse, I asked the cashier for a scratch-card. My heart was beating fast, despite my calm exterior. I thought about how the cashier had no idea this dollar was all I owned. I thought about how that dollar could have bought me a cheap snack — which would have at least sustained me a bit longer — but brushed that unhelpful thought aside. I left the shop, ticket in hand and coolly kept walking. I waited until

I could sit down somewhere private. I had no expectations either way as I slowly scratched the panels off.

I WON TEN DOLLARS! I *actually* won ten dollars! I had just multiplied my total finances by ten. Ten dollars, at that moment, felt like ten million. Ten dollars meant that I could buy myself food and coffee that night. Ten dollars meant that I had trusted my gut, and the universe had my back. Having allowed time before my bus left, I was able to go back to the newsagent and collect my *massive* winnings. I can't express how happy I felt at having just ten dollars; happiness really was a state of mind.

Boarding the bus, I settled in for the long journey ahead; I was in seat number eleven—of course. Smiling and resting back, I turned my head to gaze out of the window at the night sky. It was a full moon and the enormous sphere seemed overly big and bright; I felt hypnotised by it. I had always been moon-sensitive, feeling the push and pull of her cycle to my very core, but on this night, it felt even more potent; as if it were a spotlight on a stage which followed my every move. It felt comforting and intimidating all at once. I wasn't sure if it was glaring at me fiercely—desperately trying to warn me of what I was letting myself in for by handing over my welfare to the universe—or, if it was watching over me with the loving eyes of a Fairy Godmother, assuring me with, "There, there … everything will be fine my child". I chose to believe the latter.

With my heart still pounding whenever my mind moved out of the present moment, I decided to use the beautiful, luminous globe watching over me as a focal point for my mantras. During the entire journey I stared at the sky each time I felt fear rise in me, and recited my magic words. We stopped at a service station around dinner time and I ate my pasta and drank my Americano in reverie of the ten dollars that had fallen from the sky. When I finally arrived in Melbourne Central at six am, I immediately looked for the station platform to catch my train to Hampton, as Nancy had directed. It was only when I sat down in the carriage that it suddenly occurred to me: with my attention completely consumed by just getting to Melbourne (and rejecting all thoughts that I would actually be homeless if, for some reason, I missed the connecting train), I hadn't even looked on the map to see where Nancy actually lived! I didn't have a clue where Hampton was. I just knew I had to get there.

Having hardly slept on the bus, I soon dozed off on the train as we left the city, feeling much more relaxed now that I was on the last leg of my journey. I awoke from a slumber of abstract dreams shortly before my stop and couldn't believe what I was seeing out of the window. The ocean. Nancy lived in a village near the beach; for some reason, I assumed she'd be inland. It couldn't be more perfect. I hopped off the train and followed Nancy's clear directions to the coffee shop we'd arranged to meet in. She was waiting outside with a big smile and welcomed me with a warm hug which I melted in to, as if Mother Nature herself had manifested before my eyes and taken me in to her bosom. I hadn't realised how much energy I was using just to hold it all together, until her arms allowed me to let go.

CHAPTER 17

Visionaries

A s we went in to the café, Nancy ushered me towards a table of ladies who were all beaming at me. 'These are the girls!' she said with her friendly Canadian voice, and I was greeted with a chorus of 'Hellos' from the middle-aged women. Nancy was part of a group of 'Visionaries.' They were entrepreneurs, holistic therapists, coaches, innovators, trainers, parents, teachers and anyone who wanted to create a more conscious future. The women around the table were all part of this non-religious group, but more importantly, were simply good friends who gathered regularly to exchange ideas, share visions, channel energy and offer support to one another. It was unsurprising then, that Nancy had welcomed my message from Sydney. But the way in which I had been guided to her out of nowhere, still took my breath away. Once again, like in the hot tub in Queenstown, I sat in awe at the way I had trusted completely, and been taken care of.

As soon as we reached Nancy's house I knew I needed to be completely honest about my situation. I told her, diffidently, that I had no money but that she shouldn't feel obliged to help me anymore than she was comfortable; I would, as always, work something out. In the meantime, however, I assured her that I could offer a variety of ways to help in exchange for putting a roof over my head.

Three weeks later and I was still there. Nancy was a healer and physiotherapist; her husband an osteopath. They shared a studio in the village and kindly offered me use of the space to do massage. She asked her friends if they'd like a treatment— trusting that if Holly had tutored me then I must be good—and I had a line of readymade clients. The way things were working out, was bewildering. Being positive and trusting life was a daily practice which took a lot of effort, but it was proving over and over again, to be fruitful.

I helped Nancy with deep cleaning the house, which she was finding a bit harder since having hip trouble. Her and her husband lived in a beautiful big weatherboard home in the southern Melbourne suburb. A veranda extended along the front of the building and large windows made the spacious living room a bright hub in the middle. But the glass was getting misty from the sea air and the porch had gathered cobwebs over winter; the light that shone through into the lounge was producing rays of floating dust. She also owned, what seemed like, a million crystals. Everywhere you turned there were precious stones of all shapes, sizes and origins, winking like little sage people from around the world. Some were pea-sized and piled in bowls; others were as big as pineapples, sitting proudly and heavily on shelves and mantle pieces. I took on the task of cleaning the all the windows and washing every crystal. Nancy helped me outside, wiping the lower panes while I hopped up on a ladder to reach the tops. We laughed together while she told me, in her un-faded accent, tales of her past as an adventurous teen growing up in Canada. She told me about meeting her Aussie husband, a free-thinking, surfing osteopath who came to work at the clinic where she had just entered her career in physio. And about being a young New Age mum to three children. She was fierce. I loved her attitude and schoolgirl humour.

I listened to her with deep respect and deep longing for such a satisfying life. I may have had more freedom than her as a single girl in her thirties travelling the globe, but I envied her role as a mother who'd nursed her babies into the world. I yearned to feel the fulfilment that perhaps only a parent could feel. *But why was I bothering to even think about such things?* I thought. Men were dropping like flies out of my life and I wasn't exactly attracting father material for any potential children. Any child of mine would have to arrive through bloody Immaculate Conception at this rate. Nevertheless, I wished for a feeling of completeness that lasted longer than a meditation or a honeymoon period; I wanted to feel whole—all of the time. I wondered whether motherhood brought that. Or whether children would, in fact, leave behind an even bigger void once they checked out of my womb, and later on, out of the nest.

After washing the expansive collection of crystals, I polished them dry. I imagined receiving high-vibe energy from every single piece as I held them in my palms, benefiting from the individual power that each one gave. Once I'd finished, the sun shone in and flooded the room with fresh light. I looked at Nancy who was smiling from ear to ear. I felt like I'd just helped to bring even more Summer into her already huge, warm heart.

The 'girls' decided to take me on a trip along The Great Ocean Road. They said I couldn't come all the way to this part of Australia and not experience at least part of the famous coastal drive. In Nancy's car I watched a never-ending stream of spectacular views out of the rear passenger window. Stopping at little villages to drink coffee, eat cake and check out the boutiques, I breathed deeply, taking in the stunning cliff-edge vistas with their huge, sweeping beaches and crashing waves below.

Innuendos bounced back and forth—as they always do when you get a bunch of vibrant, lively women together—and howls of laughter filled the car as we flew down the open road. Helen was a potent healer and Seer; a gentle soul but hugely powerful. Highly sensitive to changes in energy, she wore rose quartz around her neck to help protect her from negativity. "I bought a new wand the other day," she said randomly, while sitting up front next to Nancy. "It's a shamanic one...with crystals and feathers, bound together with leather. I knew it was meant for me, it vibrated when I picked it up," she said earnestly.

There was a pause. Then raucous laughter.

"IT VIBRATED?!! shouted Nancy... "NO WONDER YOU LIKE IT!!"

"Where do you keep it?!" Rita chipped in. "Do you sit on it... to keep it warm?!" she screamed, answering her own question.

"A vibrating magic wand... I didn't know you could get those in the alternative healing shop!" Nancy added with a massive grin. Everyone was howling.

"Trust you lot to make this in to something rude!" Helen laughed, and our eyes all streamed with tears at the way she'd told us about her special purchase with such innocence.

At lunchtime we found a Hipster café with gourmet burgers and views of the ocean. Claire, who was also one of the girls and lived nearby, came to join us. I had warmed to her immediately during our breakfast when I first arrived in Hampton. Not one to mince her words, she was upfront and direct with a filthy sense of humour. Tall and lean with cropped grey hair and big eyes, she was an advocate of yoga and sex. She'd travelled to every corner of the globe, exploring new places and new things at every opportunity. These Visionaries, who each lived distinctive lives, were a force of nature and I hoped to be some kind of student among them. It felt so good to relax and laugh and talk with women who had gone through more of life than I had. It was such a relief to be in the company of these *teachers.* I was intrigued by Claire and her free-wheeling way, wondering if perhaps that's how I would end up. She was so rebellious that she seemed reluctant to even be quizzed about her lifestyle — as if the mere verbalisation of it would take away its magic.

One of Nancy's friends, Sandy, reminded me a little of my mum as she had the same soft, kind and quiet way about her. She came to me for a massage and we talked about her late husband, whom she had adored. I sensed in Sandy's body, a real need for pleasure and movement again; it seemed that the loss of her soulmate had caused her feminine joyfulness to stagnate. I suggested that she danced, whether in a class or just at home to music that she loved. "Get your hips moving again!" I said. "Your Sacral chakra needs opening!" and I placed my hands on her lower back to send some much-needed zest to her saddened pelvis. "This chakra is all about creativity... do you paint or draw at all?" I asked her. Sandy loved to paint and had a real talent for it; she had paintings all over her home, but struggled to pick up a brush since her husband passed away the previous year. I told her that if she liked, I could help her get back into it.

She took me to her stunning holiday home on the Melbourne Peninsular where we stayed for a weekend. The one-level house sat up in the hills with an almost 180-degree panoramic window over green fields and sea. We walked the wild beaches, talked about family and love, we ate delicious food, drank good wine, meditated together, listened to music and finally, we painted.

Sandy was a nurse-turned-psychotherapist. She'd always loved to help people and therapy was a natural progression for her. It was something she'd never really set out to do—having loved working with a variety of patients in hospital—but life had evidently edged her toward the internal root of illness, rather than the physical symptoms; probably due to her intuitive gifts. Her way was gentle and measured. I spoke to her about my past but never felt she was 'working on me,' she simply listened as a friend. It was a healing couple of days for both of us, and by the end of it we both had large canvases filled with colour and hearts full of new inspiration.

This is it! I thought, *I've finally found the wise counsel that I've been looking for.* I'd always wondered why I didn't have elders who I could turn to. My Mum would have done anything for me but I was stubbornly independent and rarely asked her for advice. I didn't really think she'd understand what I was going though because I was so different to her. My grandmothers both died when I was young, and none of the other women in my family seemed to act the way I did. No one else had broken away from our home country, or used their spiritual gifts openly, or been vocal about their darkness and disorders, or chosen not to have children. I didn't blame them; they probably didn't have as much freedom or privilege as I had; or maybe they just didn't *want* the things I wanted.

I suppose I was a pioneer of sorts in our family. But nonetheless, I felt alone and misunderstood. I seemed to be on a journey which was poles apart to everyone else's. I didn't seem to think like everyone else. I didn't seem to find healing or fulfilment in the same ways other people did. I was always hoping that someone would come along and be my mentor. But it never happened. It was me who always ended up giving all the advice. When I fell into the lap of this group of wise women, I assumed I had found them so they could help me get through life.

On our journey back from Sandy's holiday home, I poured my questions out to her in a cascade as she drove. "What do you think I should do?" I asked her. "I loved Adam but he's not right for me … Do you think I'll ever find someone who doesn't make me crazy? … I adore kids, but I don't think I want them … do you think I have issues or is that normal? … I need to feel grounded and secure, but I need to feel completely wild too … is that even possible?"

She looked at me sympathetically.

"I can't answer your questions, darling," she sighed. "You and your life are so unique. I don't think you have issues. I just think you are living the way you want to live … and I admire that a lot. My life has been very different to yours—a very good life—but different." I felt deflated. My fantasies of being taken under a wing, fizzled away. Every time I looked for role models, it became more and more apparent that I would have to be my own inspiration and look for guidance from the spirit world.

The only other place I ever found relatable advice was in books. I could always rely on books. I decided from that point on, I would have to learn to harvest knowledge and wisdom myself. I would have to be my own Oracle. Only *I* knew me, inside and out. Only *I* knew what was best for me and my well-being. I would take golden nuggets of intelligence from sources wherever I could find them, and gain an eclectic comprehension of what it was to be human. But ultimately, I would keep coming back to me. I would keep listening to my gut; that was all that mattered.

CHAPTER 18

My Way

I left Australia in July 2013. I reluctantly borrowed money off my mum to get the cheapest and longest flight home. She didn't have much spare cash herself, but she didn't hesitate to help. I'd never asked my parents for money when I travelled in my teens, or when I went to Uni in my twenties, and part of me felt like a failure, especially now I was in my thirties. *Wasn't I supposed to have it all figured out by now?* But recent events told me to hold my head high, we all needed a hand sometimes; the women in Melbourne had taught me that. They may not have been able to answer my questions or make all the confusion go away, but they gave me food, shelter, laughter and love when I needed it most.

I felt I had come to, what seemed like, a natural end to my time on the other side of the globe—and the other side of my brain. I had gone through some big transitions and yearned to be with my friends and family, in order to stop, take stock and get some sort of grounding of it all. Mum was relieved to see me. It had been a worry for her, knowing I was out there alone, not knowing what on earth I was doing. She respected that fact that I was a grown woman but would never stop being my mother.

Spending time with Nancy and her gang was unparalleled to anything else I'd done, spiritually. In-between road-trips, massage and cleaning crystals, I began joining them on their meetings and meditations. Connecting remotely to other *Visionaries* all over the globe via conference calls, they showed me how to push my psychic awareness even further and how to trust my visions even more. This wasn't something they did in private; this was a way of life for them. It was so refreshing to be around people who spoke openly and matter-of-factly about their other senses, as if it was just another way to see, hear or smell. I could almost feel my mind physically expanding; whole new rooms opening up inside the house that was my brain.

Soon enough, I moved back to Jersey — the island that continued to call me back, no matter how far I roamed — and back to the cottage. I was always astounded when Stella welcomed me again and again. To me, so much had happened and so much had changed and I couldn't imagine simply slotting back in. But I guess, back on the island not that much time had passed and not that much had changed. As far as the island was concerned, I was still the same Charlene, and there was still a little gap waiting there for me. And so that's what I did. I filled the gap back up. I slotted back into my spot and caught up with the people I loved, and I painted for my supper.

But it wasn't enough.

And I wasn't the same.

I came back home with a new sense of power and magic running through my veins. But there was a problem: I didn't know how to approach dating anymore. I'd tried everything, and each time I picked the wrong ones. Over the course of a year I worked my way through a hot BDSM enthusiast who looked mean on his motorbike, but couldn't get off in the bedroom unless he was in complete submission; a six-foot-something rugby player who stimulated my body but not my mind; and a good-looking, mature divorcee with four kids who turned out to only want a bit of fun—with whatever pretty young thing he could get his hands on, it seemed. I was feeling pretty pissed off with being let down again and again. I was fed up with my thoughts being dominated by the pursuit of a perfect partner.

Scanning over my sorry finances, I dropped my head on the desk. Looking back up, I stared at the search engine on my old laptop which was over-heating and making whirring noises. Sometimes I worried that it might explode. Sometimes I worried *I* might explode.

Bored of my mind churning over ex-boyfriends, I looked to the internet for distraction. Giving my fingers something to do so I couldn't bite them anymore, I typed in the familiar words: '*Female escort work, London'*. Working as an escort—a call girl—was something I had often thought about, and actually looked into a few times. I always felt that the act of entertaining men (or women, for that matter) wouldn't be so far removed from what I found myself doing naturally a lot of the time anyway. Leaving nightclubs with boys I didn't know had been a fairly common occurrence in my twenties. It wasn't so different; the risks were the same. At least I was a bit more streetwise now I was older.

I was comfortable with strangers, I was good at making interesting and intelligent conversation, I was great at making people feel at ease, I was fun to be with, I was attractive, and I had a high sex-drive. Most of all, I was great in the sack. Not by my own admission … I'd been told … a number of times. I put it down to my passionate, artistic side. *So why not make money from it?* The more I thought about it, the more viable it seemed now, than ever before. My mind was the most open it had ever been. Far from spirituality steering me away from 'dark' deeds; on the contrary, the changes I had gone through in the last few years made me realise that I could make up my own rules to live by, and that embracing your 'shadow side' played a massive role in becoming whole. My sexuality was a big part of who I was. My lust was a force capable of moving mountains. My curiosity to discover more about my body and subconscious drove me to all my edges, seeking out just how far I could go in any one direction before falling off.

I meditated for some time on the idea, challenging the concept of what *was* and *wasn't* 'acceptable,' and began to question the foundations of what people said you *could* and *couldn't* do. A lot of the time people simply repeated the opinions of others, not even stopping to really think about whether they truly agreed or whether there was any evidence or knowledge to back their ideas. Beliefs, attitudes and viewpoints were so often passed down through the family or within peer groups and societies.

I abandoned the rigid templates and guidelines, which the majority of people seemed to be living by, and allowed myself to imagine doing things in whatever way I pleased. When I actually disregarded my own stereotypes and conditioned opinions, my morals became something that were malleable. I held the standard for myself that as long as I wasn't hurting anyone, and as long as I looked after myself, I could do whatever I wanted. I was the driver of my life, no one else. Sex work was legal in the UK. If you wanted, you could make your escort job a profession, declaring your income and paying your taxes just like everyone else. I wondered: *was using your body in such a way really so bad, when people were selling their souls to bosses, gruelling work schedules and corporations every day?*

Then the fear would creep back in and I would also worry: *was there anything shallower than selling sex?* As a feminist, this potentially went against everything I stood for. But if the world was now supposedly so pro-female liberation, then surely *true* equality meant that a woman could decide for herself exactly what she did (or didn't do) with her body, without judgement. I thought about how the world would view a woman who hired a male escort for good sex and companionship. *Was it frowned upon in the same way?*

I thought back to what I had learned about 'witches'. Most of my female ancestry had probably lived in suppression; suppression by society, by religion, by war, by men. Part of me wanted to do it for them—make the most of the freedom which they never possessed, and which had been gifted to me, simply by the generation and privilege I was born into. I wanted to show them that I would honour their sacrifices by using my freedom to help myself, and subsequently, others. I would use men to *my* advantage. Their weakness would be my gain. I wanted payback on their behalf, using the powerful female body — the thing that had been so abused throughout history — but this time taking charge; doing things on my terms. If I was really honest, I wanted payback for the men who'd used *me* and caused *me* pain too. Most of all, I just wanted to do it, so why the hell shouldn't I? I knew that girls were often victims of the sex industry ... but that wasn't always the case. I decided that I would do it, and I would be a not be a victim, I would be victorious.

Initially, I contacted a female escort agent called Anne who I'd found online, and who boasted strong vetting of clients and offered high security. We spoke on the phone and I felt comfortable that she sounded friendly and professional. On meeting, I was surprised to be faced with a man in a bomber jacket.

"Are you Helena?" He said as he walked up to me, looking side to side first. I'd chosen the pseudonym based on Helen of Troy. It seemed fitting.

"Yes," I said, hesitantly, slightly confused.

"Yeah, hi, sorry, Anne couldn't come. I work with her," he said. It became quite clear that Anne was the administrator and was employed merely to make girls feel more relaxed and draw them in. He was basically a glorified pimp taking half the money; and the 'security' was him driving around, dropping various girls to and from jobs and waiting for text messages to say they were ok.

"So, what if I wasn't ok, and you were off somewhere else?" I asked him.

"I'd be nearby. Look, are you interested, 'cos I have to get back to work," he sounded frustrated. After weeding out some more information and discovering that the website which the 'agents' used to find clients, could just as well be accessed by me, I told him I'd call Anne to make arrangements and left. I would not be calling Anne, that was for sure.

I headed from the tube station, straight to a large chain store and straight to the lingerie department. The cheap garments weren't to my taste but they'd have to do until I made some money. Anyway, they'd do the job. In my experience men rarely noticed the *quality* of your underwear; mostly only other women appreciated real silk, luxe lace and a well-fitting bra. The smaller the better was the case with most guys. Next, the shoe department. Black plastic stilettos for the bedroom, which I'd never be able to wear in public—let alone walk in them without going arse over tit — would also suffice for now. More subtle shoes would be worn for meetings. Next, the pharmacy. An array of condoms in various sizes, flavours and textures. The cashier didn't bat an eyelid as I rammed my Santa sack of Johnnies into my bag; this was London, not the island. After my flight, hotel and shopping, I was virtually out of cash.

Researching other escorts, I set myself up online with a selection of smart-clothed and semi-naked faceless photos. My profile outlined my services and 'strengths.' I wasn't worried about the work — I knew I could do that just fine; my only concern was safety. *How would I avoid being murdered in a hotel room?*

My plan was simple: speak to clients for some time on the phone first. Perhaps it wasn't the most fail-safe plan, but it was my only plan. My intuition would have to do its best to weed the wheat from the chaff — or the 'normal' from the psycho. Meeting strangers didn't scare me; in fact, I enjoyed it. I had a knack for connecting with people really quickly. I could always find common ground and could always relate in some way, no matter how contrasting our lives were. Maybe that was down to travelling at a young age, or all the jobs I'd done, or maybe it was just my strong senses.

When it came to the pants-off-part they already felt good about themselves and I already felt I knew them in some strange small way. They always came back for more. Some guys wanted to have dinner at nice restaurants first, some wanted to drink champagne in chic bars, some asked me to come straight to their hotel suites, and some only wanted to visit to my room for an hour. Each service was priced accordingly; only intelligent and polite callers got a look in. It was far from being a glamorous or easy job all the time though. Anyone who thought it was, was disillusioned. Any glamour involved was short-lived or superficial. Essentially, I was paid to do what my clients wanted me to do. I just made sure it was still on my terms.

"Maybe you'd like to freshen up first?" I'd suggest, counting and hiding the money I'd just been given while they were out of sight. Gazing at the them while they awkwardly undressed, I liked to make the men feel ever-so-slightly intimidated by my watching eyes, feeling the power in my hands, instead of theirs for a change. In the room, I played Alicia Keys and Kelis, using their music to get me in the right mind-set and fill the background with a soulful, sexy vibe. The music was for *me*, not them. The right words, melodies and bass lines could take me from lonely artist to potent temptress within seconds. Failing that, I'd grab the remote control and put Kiss FM on the hotel TV; couldn't go wrong with old-school 90's R'n'B.

Whether I was taking a submissive role or acting shy, it was always me who was in control, even if they didn't realise. One wrong move and they soon knew about it. Despite the 90s music which reminded me of my basement club days, I wasn't a teenager anymore. I wouldn't be pushed around.

Each day I focused my mind on willing only good clients to me, engaging the *Law of Attraction* for a slightly less chaste cause. I focused on men who were respectful, straight-up about what they wanted, generous with tips, nice to talk to, clean and — ideally — not butt-ugly. Usually, it worked and things went pretty smoothly. Occasionally, it didn't, and those days I definitely earned my money. But occasionally I would genuinely connect with someone; the single and attractive ones who didn't want the guilt of a one-night-stand. The lively ones who just couldn't get enough. The curious ones who wanted to be with a girl they could explore their sexuality with.

Some had wives they loved, but who didn't want sex anymore. With some, I had great conversations, and with others I laughed my head off. Often, in that room, as two strangers doing something so intimate, we understood each other. We saw one another as two sexual beings who were both craving excitement, seeking something to help fulfil our passion for life. There was an unspoken trust. I was impartial and non-judgmental to their secret fantasies, worries or sensitive situations, and they understood why I chose such a line of work. Sometimes, when the right song came on, the feeling was good, and the connection was there…it was just as hot and as explosive as it was with lovers I'd chosen.

As I waited for appointments, I continued my mindfulness practise and spent the precious time thinking, reading and writing in my journal. Lounging on the bed, wearing joggers over my lingerie, when I received a booking I'd take my glasses off, put my books away and slip my heels on. Switching from meditation to mistress wasn't as bizarre as it sounded; both were like transcendental states: stepping beyond the ordinary. Once in a while, a man would ask to bring his wife or girlfriend. A joint fantasy which led them to seek the help of a 'professional'. I enjoyed those meetings; the dynamic was completely different to being with a man alone. The women were always tentative at first, but before long it was the men who drifted into the background while strong female energy took over. It was in those sensual and electrifying moments, when I was experiencing new intensities and trying out new positions and techniques, that I had to pinch myself and remember: *I was being paid for this.*

Browsing in the Kensington branch of Ann Summers, a striking sales assistant with fish-plaited hair came over. "Have you found what you are looking for?" she asked in a friendly London voice. I thought about this question for a moment and heard it, in my head, as something way more profound than I'm guessing she had intended. *Had I found what I was looking for? No…not quite…not yet anyway,* I thought.

"Erm, yes, I think so," I said looking at the nipple clamps and leather harness I held in my hand. Some of my clients had very particular kinks, and I realised that I needed more 'equipment' if I was going to keep them satisfied: coloured stockings for foot fetishes, neck ties for naughty secretaries, latex gloves for a touch of dominatrix.

"We do have a lovely, real-touch dildo to go with that harness if you'd like to see it," she asked, and I noticed she had a beautiful tattoo of a diamond in the centre of her chest. Before I could stop her, she was marching off to the other side of the store and grabbing numerous boxes. "Or… this one is even better!" She said, eyes opening wide and holding a neon pink object. "Come over here," she summoned, taking me over to a promotional stand. "This one is made from velvet-soft flexible silicone, has advanced vibe technology with SIXTEEN intensity levels, and it has a waterproof USB charging socket…no batteries! ... Touch the tip," she said excitedly, "good, huh?" My finger vibrated all the way down my arm.

"Cool," I nodded.

"And watch this," she went on, holding the dildo in an expert manner which indicated the amount of times she had performed this manoeuvre. Turning it upside-down, she began lowering it into the 3D stand. I peered in, confused. There was a bowl of water on a shelf which she was poking the tip of the toy into. "Look at the ripples?" she beamed. See how concentrated they are, and how many patterns the different settings make".

"Wow," I said, suitably impressed and mostly surprised by the unexpected water show within the shop. The sales assistant looked very pleased with herself. Mission accomplished. "I guess I'll take it," I said involuntarily, feeling helpless to her well-rehearsed pitch, despite the hefty price tag.

Back in the room I inspected my new purchases. Things had come a long way since my first clunky, plastic rampant rabbit with noisy moving pearls. Now you could operate sex toys with phone apps and buy vibrators that looked like sleek desk accessories. It was reassuring to know that ever-evolving technology and engineering was helping women to find more pleasure. Not all was lost in the modern world.

A regular client introduced me to 'private functions,' where invites were for couples only. I served as the perfect no-strings partner who wouldn't be insecure, jealous or reserved. He liked to watch me go off and enjoy myself among the crowd and I got high off the freedom and chance to explore. Naked waiters covered head-to-two in gold body paint handed out champagne and canapes at parties; dark stairways led down to 'dungeons' in sex clubs. For a time, I felt like I had ultimate independence. I was using every ounce of my power, and my confidence shot to the roof as I received masses of compliments. My clients were diverse but there was a continuous theme: they all preferred a girl with natural shape, and so I felt at ease in my soft body. They said that women like me always seemed to be genuinely enjoying themselves, as opposed to the ones who were too concerned with calories to eat gourmet food, or too hung up on belly roles or thickness of thighs to really let go and have fun.

Moving between Jersey and London, I had a delicious secret. I was living between worlds, pursuing excitement, going into unknown adventures. I wanted to give my body everything it craved to experience. Nothing was off limits. I could do anything, be anyone. I felt like anything was possible. I needing nothing but my body (and maybe a few X-rated accessories) to survive. I was chasing thrills, following my pussy like a man followed his dick. I was outside of the mundane, outside of normal routines. I was also making the most of it — because I knew it wouldn't be this good for long.

It would have been easy to get carried away with it all, but I knew this was a reality with a time-limit. Soon enough this adventure would become mundane too … and routine … and laborious … and my luck would run out … and I'd get pissed off with it — just like every other job which wasn't my true calling. Plus, I didn't like the deception. Not that I was particularly lying to anyone, but I wasn't exactly sharing the truth either. I would tell my friends and family that I was working in London, or that I was about town with new friends and acquaintances; I just withheld the *finer* details. But it didn't bear thinking about, if something bad were to happen to me. The danger. The consequences. The impact on those around me. I would get out as soon as my heart told me to.

The money I made went into funding my life as an artist. I wasn't greedy, I didn't want to make piles of cash. I only earnt as much as was necessary to cover my rent, bills, pay off some debts and buy art materials. My priority was still to have a creative life and — although it might have seemed in conflict with what I was doing — my priority was also my wellbeing and spiritual development. I may have been selling my body but my mind was sacrosanct. When I wasn't with clients I continued my personal growth studies with mediation and reading. Earning decent money in short spates allowed me to focus on my real passion the rest of the time. Two or three days of work each fortnight allowed me to spend hours-on-end in my studio. Not a day would pass when I wouldn't feel grateful for the chance to pour myself into my art.

On a crisp Spring day, when Londoners were wearing short-sleeved shirts and scarves, and pockets of sunshine broke through the cold chill, a client in his twenties arranged an appointment. Apparently, it was his first experience with a call-girl. I told him I'd come downstairs; not something I'd normally do but I had a feeling he might end up lost in the hallways if I left him to his own devices. The minute I saw him standing in the hotel bar I was weirdly struck by his presence. Not that he looked that unusual or any different to the usual punters— apart from being good-looking and obviously in great shape—he was an average guy. But I suddenly got a small lump in my throat and my tummy did a nervous flip. *Come on Char,* I told myself, *get it together babe.* He headed for the reception. *Oh bloody hell!* I panicked, *don't ask the fucking receptionist which room 'Helena' is in!* I went in quick to make a diversion.

"Need directions?" I said to him quietly with a smile.

"Just meeting the boys for a stag do," he said, one side of his mouth curling upwards towards a cheeky smile back.

"I'm Will," he added, in a less cocky tone as I began to turn on my feet.

"I know," I replied, and walked to the lounge area.

CHAPTER 19

Rose Tint

We sat on the tan leather sofas and Will was doing his best to look relaxed. He smelt good; a strong aftershave marketed at guys like him—fresh, sexy and a bit of a bad boy. I wore a simple black vest with skinny jeans and converse trainers, deducing from our chat on the phone that he wasn't the kind of guy to turn up in a suit. It was always important to 'match' your client in public. The girl-next-door look was spot-on; I felt pleased with myself for getting it right. And under the vest, which I could tell he was already trying to see, a peephole bra, matched with a lace thong.

"You're gorgeous," he said.

"Well, I'm not being funny, but surely you could get any girl?" I asked. He looked over his shoulder.

"It's the army; it makes things so complicated," he replied, bringing his dark brown eyes back to me. I felt uneasy, in a good way, and nervously tucked my hair behind my ear. It wasn't normally like this. Usually I felt completely in control.

"It must be such a strange life." I said, as we eased into conversation. "Everyone else is just walking around, doing their thing, shopping, eating out, watching movies; just thinking about themselves and their little lives. And there's you, in Iraq, surrounded by… fear," I said, for want of a less serious word, given the nature of our meeting.

"I'm used to it I guess. Anyway, what about you?" he laughed, "Your job isn't so *normal* either!

"I'm used to it I guess!" I quipped back. "Shall we go?" I nodded upwards.

We dealt with the money and I peeled off my outer layers in seconds while he was in the bathroom. Sitting back on the bed in my black lace, he moved towards me and my belly did a little flip. *This is new*, I thought, *I feel like I'm on a bloody date.*

"God, I'd love to have a girlfriend like you," he said, and suddenly he wasn't so shy anymore. He kissed me, in exactly the kind of way I loved to be kissed. Part of me wanted to say, *I could be your girlfriend!* But I shut the ridiculous thought down. We had sex and the chemistry was intoxicating. It seemed too good to be true.

～～

"I do it because it gives me total freedom," I explained, lying on my side with my hand on his stomach.

"I totally get it," he said, "I don't think it's bad. I think you're amazing … just going after life, getting what you want, making things work for you. I wish I could be more like that. Shit! … the time," he said, jolting up.

"Don't worry about that. It's fine. The meter is off now," I whispered. "If you don't like the army, why don't you just leave? Who's stopping you?" I asked, genuinely not knowing whether soldiers signed some sort of contract which tied them into months, years or decades of service. "You're young, you could do anything. It's your life. You only get one chance at it—well, at least I think so anyway— unless you believe in reincarnation… which I kind of do…but I don't think you are aware of the life you've just lived…so it's irrelevant then really, isn't it?" I stopped, aware that I may have divulged too much, and looked at him for his thoughts on the matter.

"I can't," was all he said.

"Why not?"

"It's complicated," he said stiffly, "I can't just leave," and his passionate energy closed down. I paused, not understanding and not wanting to come across naïve.

"Will you come and see me again?" I asked vulnerably. I didn't like how out-of-character I sounded. "…When you're next on leave?"

"Of course. Try and keep me away!" he said, piping up, giving off charged vibes again. I almost forgot he was a client and nearly climbed back on top of him.

"I have to go," he said solemnly.

I didn't stop thinking about Will from the moment he left. I fell into complete infatuation, once again. The next time he visited, was just as heated. Sex with him was feverish and intense and we talked deeply afterwards. His eyes were sad about something but he wouldn't open up fully.

"I've just not been myself the last year," he said. "I keep looking for things to make me feel better. I bought a new car and normally that would make me happy …but I'm not fussed about it at all. And that's when I decided to see a …. see you," he stuttered, not wanting to use the word *call-girl*. "And I just can't believe how awesome you are," he looked down. "I never expected that".

I felt strange when he went to hand over the cash. I shook my hand to say no, but he insisted. "Don't pay me next time, ok?" I said, sheepishly.

"Why would you do that?" he said.

"Because I like you, you idiot!" I laughed.

"Really?" he sounded surprised. "Babe, I can't give you what you deserve," he said, looking away.

"I know, but that's ok. Things have a way of working themselves out," I replied.

"And I don't expect you to give up this job. It's your freedom. Just save the best bits for me," he added, with a grin.

Never in a million years did I imagine I'd meet someone I actually saw as a potential boyfriend, while working as an escort. *But why the hell not?* I thought. I'd tried meeting partners in every other way. Maybe the most unlikely situation would be the right one. When he walked out the door I felt hollow. I wanted more time with him but he always had to go. I looked at the next day in my diary and sighed: *Friday - Nick - Twickenham - 7pm.* I didn't feel like seeing anyone else now. Without a second thought, I decided that I would quit. Right there and then. No more. I didn't have to finish anything; it was never all about the money. I'd gotten so much out of the experience but now it was time for something new. And just like that, I cancelled my next appointment and never looked back.

I thought about all the things I'd done before and reminded myself that the Universe always supported me whenever I made big decisions and bold moves. I'd go back to Jersey and commit myself to my creative endeavours, full-time. Now that my finances were a bit more settled I could afford to focus on new projects. Whether I could focus my wandering mind away from being in bed with Will—and towards lucrative design work—was another thing. But I'd give it a good go.

At the airport, I drifted through duty-free, images flashing through my mind of my recent stay in London. I headed for the perfume aisles and towards the men's section. Picking up random bottles and sniffing them, I stopped in my tracks. I found the one he'd been wearing that first day we met and my head rushed at the stirring scent. Taking a piece of sample card, I doused the entire strip with the spray, folded it tightly and tucked it into my wallet. While waiting for my flight I sent an email to Will, telling him that I wasn't going to be working as an escort anymore because it didn't feel right since I'd met him.

I don't expect you to stop doing this work if it means you can live how you want to live, Will said in his message back. *Don't give it up for me. I can't give you what you want*, he wrote.

Blind to what was so clear to others, my loved-up heart saw only what it wanted to see; it read his words only as kindness, and overlooked the obvious: he didn't want me to give up anything for him because he sure as hell wasn't going to give up anything for me. He couldn't give me what I wanted because it was all, in fact, lies.

Pining away in my little cottage, I created a world for myself where I would wait patiently for my hero. The thought of him got me up in the morning; visions of us reuniting got me to sleep at night. I sent him texts with no replies and put it down to his job or lack of phone signal. An overriding rapture blocked out any doubts and carried me through days and weeks until I heard from him again, when we'd arranged a time and location to next meet on the mainland.

I invited him to the island and fantasised about showing him all my favourite beaches, but he always said he wouldn't have enough time. I ignored the *Magician* which kept popping up in my tarot readings—which, in its more formidable form, represented shapeshifters and ill intentions—and chose to see its favourable traits: talent, strong capability and resource to succeed. When the death card made an appearance, I re-shuffled the deck.

All the while, I threw myself into my artwork, feeling happier and more at peace than I had done in a long time. Committing myself entirely to my ideal of what Will and I could one day be, I was completely uninterested in any other men. It served me very well; having been distracted by sex for so long, now I could just sit back and get on with other things.

My painting took yet another route. I was so romantically inspired in my work that I started to paint dreamy scenes with beaches, sunsets, tropical flowers and mythical-looking women — pouring all of my emotions into the ice-cream coloured skies and turquoise seas. I began printing the images onto fabric, turning them into framed textiles and cushions; and creating a small online shop to sell them in. I worked on my platform, teaching myself to build a website and promote it on Facebook. I felt so driven to make money from my new quirky enterprise, and it felt so good to follow my intuition into another new chapter. I loved how one minute my heart could be leading me in to sex work, and the next it was urging me to paint mermaids.

Others would think I were mad if I told them everything I had done in the last few months, but although my actions suggested haphazardness, I felt more in alignment than ever. My soul was talking and I was listening. Online orders through my *Etsy* shop were from all over the world but they were small and sporadic. Learning how to reach a wider audience, I started using Instagram for most of my advertising. I went crazy with hashtags: #sunset #sunrise #beachlife #mermaids #surf #dreamy #interiordesign #kidsbedrooms ... I spent days taking styled photos of my stock around Stella's beautiful home and garden, and hours editing them on Photshop.

As I sat in my pyjamas late at night, working in total darkness except for the glow of my laptop screen, an email pinged through. The subject line read: 'Artwork'. I assumed it was marketing company who had found my website and added it to the thousands on the bulk mail list, ready to try and sell me web packages or domains. The sender introduced herself as Brooke, owner and swimwear designer for *Peace of Paradise Creations*. She said she'd seen my posts online and loved my illustrations. I sat up straighter; this wasn't the usual templated sales pitch.

She continued, explaining that up until recently she had been sourcing her swimwear material from stock fabrics, but that now her business was growing and she had recently won a fashion award, she wanted to produce her own prints with unique designs. She loved my style and asked if I would be interested in creating images for repeat patterns. Also, she was massively into body positivity, and so her garments were made from sizes zero to twenty-two. My heart was pounding and my mouth was open; not just because this was extremely exciting news, but because this swimwear designer was based in no other place than....Maui. I couldn't believe it. Of all the countries, cities and islands in the world. I was also blown away that she was passionate and pro-active about body acceptance in women's fashion. It was literally everything on my dream job wish-list. Brooke had been searching for artists work on her project and my #hawaiiansunsets and #hibiscusflowers attached to my paintings had led her to me. I sat for a few moments in reverie of what had just happened, before replying enthusiastically to her email.

In the morning I went straight back to re-read the first email. It was beyond coincidence; beyond synchronicity. I felt as though I had somehow summoned this event to me; although I hadn't even known what I was summoning at the time; I just knew that by following what made me happy, and by ignoring negativity, I had magnetised something brilliant. I suddenly felt like anything was possible. I also felt that anything was *more* possible when you had a heart full of love. My feelings for Will and determination to see him had me in a state of permanent euphoria which I wouldn't let anyone break. My little world was rose-tinted and I liked it that way.

Stretching paper onto board, I squeezed out every last drop of Summer as I sat day after day in the courtyard, creating tropical designs while listening to audio books and YouTube talks on my portable speaker. I had become interested in the brain—with regards to habits, patterned behaviours, beliefs and depression. I was fascinated by its ability to actually carve *new* neural pathways when we really worked on changing what we continually thought about. Hour by hour, minute by minute, second by second, we could determine our future life with better and more constructive thoughts. I knew that some people saw me as overly optimistic, but I knew that if I was able to see the best in things, then it always paid off somehow.

The artwork fees for my designs were fairly humble but I was ecstatic, seeing my work go from sketch to finished product. Brooke sent me previews of her swimwear photoshoots, where surfy Hawaiian models posed at the water's edge with my illustrations adorning their beautiful, diverse bodies. I was so proud of myself; there was my art, bobbing around on boobs and bottoms, in Maui!

Excited, I messaged Will. I told him all about my miracle email from Hawaii and told him that this was a new start for me...for us; I was going to make an 'honest' living, doing something I loved. He didn't reply. I waited and waited, but still nothing. I decided, in my pink-sky mind, that he was obviously still away and that if there was any future for us, then I would need to be closer to him when he returned for his brief visits home. It was no good me being on the island when he only had a short time to see me *and* his family. I needed to be back in the UK.

But what on earth was this Maui thing all about? I wondered, as my rainbow brush strokes touched the clean white paper. After years of practice, I knew precisely how to make the paint spread in one big wash and pool at the edges, to get that distinctive and dreamy watercolour style. I mean, I could just *go* to Maui. But that wasn't it. It seemed like Maui kept coming to *me;* and that it was telling me something.

Yes, it was just a place on the map, but it felt more like a message. Since my magical awakening in New Zealand, each time I went through a positive transition, Maui popped up like a signpost or a beacon … or a buoy, marking the way as safe. It had told me (via the albino space cadet at the bus stop) that it was safe to leave Adam when my heart was breaking; and it had told me (via Couchsurfing at Tom's place) that it was safe to leave Sydney when I had nothing in my pockets. But now, I didn't know if it was telling me that it was safe to follow Will, or whether it was showing me that my career would flourish more in Jersey. Like the unwelcome tarot cards, I put the negative thoughts to the bottom of the pile and booked my ticket to England. I decided that my design work could be done in any location where I had a surface to paint on and WIFI to connect to. So I did what I did best: cleared out, packed up and left no trace behind. Mum took me back in her flat, as she always did, and I stressed the fact that it would only be temporary — just until I found somewhere to rent, closer to Will's barracks.

Sitting in the pub toilet cubicle at my friend's party, the message from him came through. It was all over. I woke from the dream. The rose tint turned blue. And I realised what my 'Maui code' had really been trying to tell me.

CHAPTER 20

Carpentry

October 2015

"*I don't understand... I just moved back to the UK to be near you,*" I wrote, clutching on to the last threads of our conversation which wasn't even face to face. He sent one final message, telling me he was in a mess and that he was sorry. Sorry—such a small word for such a big lie. He tried to explain that when he first came to see me, he'd wanted to be someone else and never expected to feel so strongly. But that didn't justify the way he'd let our meetings continue; or let me think he was at risk in Iraq; or have me believe that we were more than simply escort and client. It didn't justify the total disrespect for my trust and my heart. I was pissed off with myself too.

After all I'd been through and all I'd learnt, I was still letting men walk all over me and rule my life.

"Why Will? Why did you need to do that?... tell all those lies? Why didn't you just break up with your girlfriend? Why couldn't you just be yourself with me?" .... And there they were: the same string of words that Dan had said to me five years earlier, when I confessed I'd cheated on him. The same hurt and confusion as to why someone you loved would do such a thing. I was now on the other end.

I felt stupid for ever thinking it was a match made in heaven. I was so mad that he had deceived me all that time. But really, it was *all* a lie. We had both been behaving in a way which was undercover. I didn't like pretending to family and friends to be elsewhere or doing different work. When all was said and done and I really thought about it, it was no wonder then, that by living a covert life, I had ended up in a false relationship. There went the *Law of Attraction* again. I wasn't being punished, it was simple Cause and Effect.

But even through the heartbreak, I looked back on the period of time I was 'with' him, and how I had experienced such euphoric feelings. It was during that heightened state that I attracted a dream design commission. I believed more than ever, that happiness was a state of mind, not circumstance. Life was what you made it, not what it made *you*. Will was merely a piece in the puzzle which showed me the bigger picture of how to find more inner joy. People may say that looking at life through rose-tinted glasses is a foolish thing to do, but for me it was a gamechanger. It made me focus only on the good things so that I wasn't distracted by other people's stuff. It made me more open, so that what was meant for me could come pouring in. It made me repellent to negative energy, so that anything toxic would naturally fall away.

And fall away it did.

The right person would come someday. Someone who would appreciate my love; someone who would respect my trusting and open nature. For whatever reason though, I was back in No-Man's Land. The last decade of my life had been a myriad of jobs, countries, homes, lovers and soul-searching quests — which had brought me both bliss and pain. I wasn't about to give up now. I'd come too far.

～～～

Back at Mum's flat I had a long bath in her small tub and drank endless tea — because tea always makes it all better. She asked me what went wrong with my latest boyfriend. I simply told her it 'didn't work out,' because I couldn't bear to tell her the disappointing truth. I cried but I recovered surprisingly quickly. My tears were bored of being shed over men. Then she cut a chunk off my long hair, (she is a hairdresser, not an evil witch) because that's what you do when you need a life overhaul — you get a new hairstyle. I told her that even though I was thirty-four years old, and even though I was back on her sofa-bed for the hundredth time, I was not going to let this get me down or stop me from pursuing my dreams; although slightly unsure as to what those dreams actually were anymore. I went bed early, because when you've tried bath and the tea and the new hair-do and you're still sad, sleep solves everything.

Luckily, Mum and I get on extremely well and although it isn't the most ideal situation for a thirty-something woman, I made the most of sharing quality time with her and remembered every day to focus on the positives, and be really grateful that I had a family at all who loved me, even if they didn't always understand me. I would make her dinner and she would make me more cups of tea while I painted. My design work for Brooke turned out to be short and sweet; she had all she required for her new swimwear collection and so I would need to find a job again. I trawled the local online recruitment agencies and looked at temporary office roles but they only filled me with dread. I needed something uplifting; a fun or creative environment; somewhere I could be myself and not pretend that I had a five-year plan involving promotions, pensions and property ownership because—let's face it—it was highly likely that I would bugger off again pretty soon.

I put the laptop down and thought about when I was a teenager. I was always working evenings and weekends around my school hours to pay for my next outfit, trip away, or to fuel my ever-diminishing vodka and orange fund. Back then I'd simply meander through town, squinting at shop windows for vacancies and walk straight in as soon as one caught my eye. By the end of the day I would have half a dozen application forms and by the end of the week I'd have a job. I dumped the search engine and instead, headed for to the large shopping centre. Nothing wrong with going back to basics.

Sweet Enchantment was a new small boutique chocolate shop and they were hiring. Luckily, Claire the Manageress was a wanderluster like me and as soon as she read on my CV that I'd worked in Sydney, we were comparing countries we'd visited and discussing the thrills and perils of being a single female globe-trotter. Sitting on stools in the tiny staff room, which also acted as the store room, I glanced around while she filled in paperwork during our impromptu chat. Boxes with labels like *Strawberry Champagne Truffles* and *Chilli and Lime Dark Chocolate Bars* were piled up high. Transparent bags filled with mis-shaped pieces had written on them: *TESTER - Peanut Butter Pots.*

"You have to try all the flavours," she said, noticing that I was homing in on the *100% pure cacao buttons.* "So that you can advise customers".

This is perfect, I thought, feeling chuffed that my manifesting powers were obviously still in action. I mean, it wasn't exactly making the most of my art degree which had put me in debt until old age, but it was about as close to fun as I was going to get from an in-between-things job. Claire knew what a backpacker's brain was like, so she understood that I wasn't going to work in Woking forever. Plus, I had the duty of eating my way through testers while delivering happy customers their chocolate fix. It could be a lot worse.

She finalised the brief interview which had mostly consisted of us talking about travel, and I continued to look around at the over-filled space. Next to the kettle, on an unstable stack of files, I spotted an Angel card deck. It must have been hers but I didn't want to pry; she was, after all, now my Manager, and I wasn't sure of the boundaries of this new friend/colleague. But the presence of the cards comforted me, and I knew I was where I needed to be.

"The only thing iiiis," she said slowly, "is that I can only currently offer you one day a week. I really hope you still want the job," she said with worried eyes. "I mean, I'm sure we'll need you more in the future," her words speeding up, "and I think one of the girls is going to leave soon". She looked at me eagerly for a response. I suppose she was just as relieved to have found me, as I was her.

"I'm sure it will all work out," I said and smiled. She beamed back at me and dived in for an unexpected hug.

By the end of my first shift I knew everything about Claire's love-life—and she about mine. We sympathised over each other's inability to spot a bad boy, and our huge capacity to dig out their endearing features. Mostly though, I worked with Teigan, the twenty-year-old Assistant Manager. With her vampy style, dry humour and head usually buried in a fantasy novel, I loved her sweet and smart company. Having already managed a store in London and living in a flat with her boyfriend, I could easily forget that she was still just a kid really. She would often come to me about personal matters; I almost felt like a fraud giving her advice when my life was so reckless. But I suppose, despite lacking material success, I was fairly knowledgeable in the how-NOT-to-do-things department. She asked me about building confidence, having more faith and taking risks. I tried—with my relatively limited thirty-something years on earth experience—to pass on some sort of wisdom that my twenty-year-old-self might have benefited from.

Teigan and I stayed at the shop after-hours one evening, preparing for a stock count the next day. As we replenished chocolate coin jars and filled shelves with Valentines hampers wrapped in pink, black and red ribbons, inevitably we got onto the subject of sex. She was another fellow Scorpio; I always seemed to home in on them. No matter how polite conversation began, when two Scorpios were in one room, conversation nearly always turned to nocturnal matters.

"I'd like to be a bit more...y'know...*active* in the bedroom," Teigan confided. "... Or not even in the *bedroom*... maybe the living room... that's my point...it's all got a bit...safe...and predictable...if you know what I mean?" She looked back at me from the mini stepladder as she placed another heart-shaped box on the pile. "But I don't want to offend him. I mean I love him and I'm not complaining or anything ..." she trailed off.

"...But you need some FUCKING EXCITEMENT!" I burst in.

"YES!!" She screamed.

"Look. We are women. We have strong needs...desires. If we ignore them, then we...well...shrivel up—not just physically, mentally too". Teigan screwed her face up. "We are so lucky to be alive at this time," I continued. "Listen babe, women long before us had NO say in what they wanted, and if they *did* say…or worse still, if they actually *acted out* what they wanted, they were labelled as witches and were cast out of society — or killed".

"That's a bit bloody extreme!" She laughed.

"I know, I know, I'm just saying that we have to speak up. We have to voice our feelings. We have to exercise this precious right to speak and be heard, to do what we want, to be who we want to be. We've all been hiding for far too long".

"Blimey". Teigan stopped what she was doing for a moment. I took a breath and thought about my Great Grandma. I was telling Teigan all this, as if I had it all worked out but I didn't…nowhere near. I was voicing words that I needed to hear myself.

I was pretty happy at the chocolate shop. It wasn't what I wanted to do for the rest of my life, and I was on minimum wage, and I was still trying to process all that was going on (or not going on) in my personal life, but it was simple and light-hearted and I could switch off from it as soon as I walked out. Just as Claire and I had hoped, I was soon working five days a week and my bank balance let out a little sigh of relief. I had no savings but at least I could get by and pay my bills. On my days off I painted, sitting on a sheet on my Mum's lounge floor with my canvas propped against the radiator. Occasionally I would sell a piece, bumping up my income. No matter how bad things got, no one could take away my creative talent and my determination to use it.

Whenever possible, I would dust off the old bike that I'd left in mum's garage since before I could drive. It was one of the only possessions I hadn't turfed out over the years; I couldn't bring myself to give up something which offered instant freedom and escape for when the walls closed in on me. It was a touch too small, my knees nearly hitting my elbows, but it was good enough. On my days off I cycled along the canal which ran through the town. I needed to get outside, to get nature's healing. I also needed to be alone. I had much thinking to do. In order for me to change direction again in my life I needed stillness within, this was how it always worked. I wasn't one for talking through my problems with everyone. I needed to let it all sink in…find its place in my heart; only then could I begin to move forward.

I loved watching how the water and the surrounding foliage on the canal were always changing with the seasons. Small water birds and swans glided along as I rode the bumpy track to West Byfleet, a neighbouring village. I hadn't been there for years. Close to Weybridge, where the rich and famous liked to collect property, and not far from Waterloo, West Byfleet was a humble but busy little place with a multicultural handful of shops and restaurants. As teenagers, Lara and I would meet the local Italians there in bars nearby, which were owned by their fathers, uncles, brothers and cousins. They drank wine and Limoncello while the other boys drank pints, and we thought they were so cool and sophisticated.

Coming off the canal path onto a small lane, I pulled out onto the station road where the train whizzed through to London every half hour. I noticed a new cafe, *Taylor's Coffee House*, nestled in alongside hairdressers, estate agents and butchers in Edwardian buildings. I had a fiver left in my wallet and a copy of *Harper's Bazaar* Magazine in my backpack which I'd been devouring page by page, since I had spent the remains of my wages on it. It was my only treat. The female edited, intelligent articles and gorgeous photography satisfied my hunger for more knowledge about creative women taking lead in society, and filled my tank with artistic inspiration. Deciding that coffee would be a good investment for my last few pounds, I checked out the little café. Decked out in minimalist retro furniture, with black and white prints on the walls, it had an eclectic mix of sleek Art Deco and funky 60s lounge style. I ordered an americano and found a laid-back chair by the window. Reading my magazine, I felt a sense of excitement. I had nothing to my name, I'd recently made another big love-fail, and my career left a lot to be desired. But something stirred in the air and somehow, I felt exhilarated again. It was as if I could sense the presence of exciting times coming my way. Perhaps it was a premonition. All I knew, was that despite being low on life goals, passion was still running through my veins.

At times like this I always felt my connection as part of the Universe again. Life was 'talking' to me in some other language, like when a song speaks straight to your heart. I closed my eyes for a moment and asked, in my mind, for a sign; a sign of what I needed to do next. I did this a lot, but especially when I felt so aligned. When distractions subsided and fears drifted away, I could hear divine wisdom so clearly. After a few moments I sipped my strong Columbian coffee and continued to flick through the pages of my magazine. I came to the centrefold; it was a feature titled, *Under the Sea.* The contents nearly popped off the page in front of me, I was mesmerised. Of course, it wasn't unusual for me to be drawn to anything revolving around the sea but this was different. The feature was about unfathomably expensive jewellery, with emerald rings, pearl bracelets, aquamarine earrings and sapphire brooches in shapes of sea urchins and jellyfish; all way out of my league of spending. However, the accessories were set on an underwater backdrop which drew me in like a magpie. Behind photos of the precious gems were vintage watercolour illustrations of seabeds, and quotes from the original Hans Christian Anderson version of *The Little Mermaid.* I stared at the feature continuously while thoughts whirled through my brain and I tried to catch them. The sounds in the café turned into subterranean music. The jewels on the page turned into a twinkling ocean and I could almost smell the saltwater. In a clear vision I could see pages and pages of writing... a story that was so magical and yet so real. I could feel mystery and romance, adventure and laughter, sadness and suffering. I saw so many life experiences — good and bad, successes and failures — that had been collected along the way. I felt a sense of hope and faith, of overcoming obstacles.

It was *my* story.

And I felt a yearning to share it. I didn't yet know that it would be an entire book, or even what the ending would be, but I knew I must begin to write it anyway.

I began to visit the little coffee house frequently and made notes and sketches on these new visions. It felt like my little hideaway. Somewhere I could write. Somewhere I could dream. Somewhere I could remember. Somewhere I could to begin to carve out meaningful anecdotes from the big gnarly tree that was my life so far.

Before I knew it, I had a reason to briefly hop over to Jersey again. The island never stopped beckoning me back and like all my previous infatuations, I always dropped everything to run to her. I had been asked by a woman who bought my artwork in the past, if I could paint a large mural for her little girl's bedroom. It was a brilliant opportunity to make good money and a great way to see my Jersey friends; I was already planning my next escape to work somewhere else in the world, so it would be good to catch up with them before another period of long-distance friendship.

I stayed down by Gorey Harbour with my holistic therapist friend, Sonia, the one who I'd first met at the ecstatic dance workshop. She'd recently given birth, and so in-between working on the mural and catching up with everyone, I offered her a bit of respite from sleep deprivation and held the baby while she showered and made meals.

While spooning tahini, chickpeas and various other health foods into a blender, Sonia mentioned that she had a friend called Tony coming around the next day to put some shelves up for her. The baby had been poorly and she asked if I could let Tony in and show him around if she happened to be busy with breastfeeding and nappy-changing. In the morning, the doorbell rang, and hearing the baby cry in the next room with the sound of her mother's voice gently trying to soothe her, I hopped downstairs to get it.

"Hi, you must be Tony," I said smiling, once I'd opened the door to a man in jeans and lumberjack shirt. I clocked his eyes straight away and had the strangest feeling. The very first thing I thought when I looked at him, was that it seemed like I was somehow looking in the mirror. It was bizarre, but something in his face instantly seemed recognisable to me — as myself. I couldn't quite comprehend the sensation. *Was he reminding me of someone? Had he been on TV? Did I know him?* I assumed I must know him and had forgotten who he was, which was a common occurrence when you'd lived on a small island. Immediately, I became conscious of my appearance. I was wearing a particularly sexy combo: grey jogging bottoms (the type that have seen better days and the bum has gone baggy), a cardigan which had some smeared banana on it from when I last held the baby, and oversized knitted slipper socks which were fraying at the edges. To top it off, my unwashed hair was piled on top of my head. I suddenly felt very awkward standing in front of him. He had a warm face and was magnetising in a quiet way that I couldn't quite work out.

CHAR! I screamed internally to myself, *Give it a rest, will you?!* The LAST thing I needed to be doing right now was looking at men. I needed time out from all that.

"Have we met before?" I asked, as I let him into the hallway, expecting him to give me good reason as to why I felt the way I did. *Ah yes…I did some work on Stella's house*, I thought he might say; or, *Yes, we met in the pub down the road once*.

But no.

"No. Pretty sure we've never met," he answered quite definitely, to which I felt unusually offended by. He seemed so certain that he didn't know me — and seemed so unaffected by my presence. But I felt sure that we did know each other… was I *that* forgettable? I quickly gathered that I was alone in the recognition. I did my best to compose myself and tried not to stare into his eyes while I searched for his clues to why I felt this way. He had a lovely aura but it was too early to read his *story*.

"I'm Charlene…I'm just staying with Sonia for the week. She's a bit tied up with the baby, I'm afraid," I explained.

"Ah, ok," he scratched his chin and looked around.

"I think she wants the shelves in there," I pointed to an alcove in the living room. "Would you like a cup of tea?"

"Great, thank you," he said, moving his tools over to the wall.

I went in to the kitchen and took a deep breath as I flicked on the kettle switch. *He must be a carpenter…I like carpenters*, I thought. Sonia hadn't said anything about Tony; only that he was 'a really nice guy' and would be putting up some shelves for her as a favour. *STOP IT!* I scolded myself again for allowing my mind to wander. I popped my head round the door, "Normal tea?" I asked.

"Yes please, that'd be lovely, thanks," he said loudly, bent over, searching for something in a canvas bag.

"Milk…sugar?"

"Milk and two, thanks," he answered, retrieving a tape measure.

"Feel free to put some music on," I shouted from the kitchen, "there's a massive stack of CDs in the corner".

"Excellent! Will do," he called back, and within a minute I could hear a very familiar sound.

No. Way, I said to myself. *It can't be…it CAN'T be.* The first few chords of a song came on the stereo and it was none other than my favourite song of ALL time: Jamiroquai, *Space Cowboy*. I froze, shocked by the unbelievable chance that he would pick my favourite song. *It's just a coincidence*, I convinced myself. Shrugging it off and scouring the cupboards for 'normal' teabags, I soon realised that Sonia possessed more herbal tea than an Indian ashram. However, Tetley or PG Tips or anything remotely similar, seemed to be out of the question. Oh God! I thought, I can't give this man herbal tea.

"Won't be a second," I said and dashed upstairs. Sonia was desperately trying to calm her crying baby. "Hi Honey," I said, "Sorry to bother you, but Tony is here—it's fine, I've shown him in—but I want to make him a cup of tea, and well...you don't seem to have any".

"I think there's still a small jar in the cupboard with regular tea in it," she offered, while rocking the baby back and forth. "Thanks Char, I'll be down soon".

"Okay great, no worries," and with that I bolted back downstairs. *Right, small jar with normal tea, got it.* The teabags looked ancient but they would have to do. Just as I was filling the cups, Tony came in to the kitchen. "Do you know what height these shelves need to be?" he said, pointing to the alcove with a pencil.

"Erm...no," I answered, feeling a bit embarrassed. "Let me just check". I ran upstairs again, two steps at a time, nearly tripping over my slipper socks.

"Sonia says, whatever you think," I relayed, breaking into a sweat, knowing how that information wasn't really going to help.

"Okaaaay," Tony scratched the stubble on his chin again. 'No problem. I'll just go for standard," he said and smiled. His eyes twinkled and I had to look away.

Tony began measuring and I carried on making the tea. *Right, milk and two sugars*, I reminded myself. The least I could do was make this man a great cup of tea for his kind efforts. If there's one thing us Brits do well, it's a cup of tea. I went to the fridge and was horrified to discover that there was only a dribble of milk left in the carton. That, and various dairy alternatives: coconut milk, almond milk, rice milk, soya milk. My heart sank. *Ok,* I thought, *I can handle this, I'll just explain that there was no milk left – that I DO actually make a decent cup of tea under normal circumstances.* Okay now we just need sugar. *Oh Holy Mother of…!!*……It seemed that sugar was also off the menu in Sonia's vegan kitchen. I rummaged around the cupboards and managed to find a packet of fruit syrup which resembled something that might be mildly palatable—about six years ago—judging by the best before date. There was no choice. This was an emergency.

I reluctantly passed the mug to Tony, apologising profusely for such a crap brew. I didn't know why I was so hung up on impressing this man with my tea-making skills; I WASN'T LOOKING TO IMPRESS MEN! I kept reminding myself of this fact. And anyway, it was highly likely that he was married because he was obviously a fair bit older than me....and I was living in England now....and I was probably going away again....and anyway....I WASN'T LOOKING FOR A MAN. *What was wrong with me?*

I heard him locking his toolbox and wondered why he was clearing up so soon. He came and stood in the kitchen with me, drinking the last of his manky tea; pretending very politely to enjoy it. "I'll need to come back tomorrow," he said. I tried not to look excited and went for a surprised expression. "The shelves are the wrong size for the space," he added, "I'll have to get some wood and make them up".

I slapped my forehead into my hand. "Oh god! I'm so sorry!" I cried, "Didn't Sonia...?" I stopped mid-sentence. Bless her, she was so tired.

"It's fine," he said, placing the empty cup in the sink. I don't mind doing it.

The next day Tony arrived with an armful of timber and I put the kettle on again, having been to the shops to buy tea-making provisions fit for the Queen.

"Did you *make* those?" I asked, pointing to the shelves.

"Yup. In my garage," he said proudly. "I can pretty much make anything in there…providing it's a shelf!" He joked.

"You're so kind," I said. There was a brief silence and suddenly I felt a bit awkward. I could feel a tense energy between us so I quickly started chatting. As we spoke about my artwork, why I was in Jersey and how we both knew Sonia, I discovered that Tony was not a carpenter. He was retired from the police and Special Branch, and now worked as the island's Coroner's Officer. "So, you look at dead people?" I asked, intrigued, hugging my tea and glancing at his ringless wedding finger, out of habit.

"Well… yes…that's often part of it," he laughed. I thought about telling him that I sometimes *spoke* to dead people but thought better of it. I told him I was planning on travelling more, although not definite on where yet. The small talk turned into a more personal conversation and the words flowed easily between us. He told me how he had gone to see Sonia for back massage therapy after a particularly stressful time in his life, and she had opened his eyes to the emotional pain we carry in our bodies. He was going through a separation and recently lost his father too. His energy was both strong and gentle. I couldn't help noticing how much depth and warmth there were to his eyes, and how he had a witty sense of humour, similar to mine; and how he held his body in a good posture; how he spoke so intelligently; how we seemed so similar and yet had such different lives, and how there was obviously a chemistry between us. *But why was I sizing this man up when another relationship was the last thing I wanted? ...and he was only just separating from his wife?* More importantly, why was this person being put in my path *now*, when I'd been waiting for someone like him for years? It all seemed like terrible timing.

"I'd like to see your artwork," he said as he put the hoover back under the stairs, leaving the area where he'd been working, spotless.

"I'll add you on Facebook," I said casually, trying not to let on how happy I was that he had shown an interest. "It's all on there".

"Have you got any nice plans for the weekend?" I asked as he headed for the door. "Well, things are pretty quiet on the home front at the moment," I nodded, showing that I understood. "It'll probably be me, my daughter and my two dogs Romeo and Maui...and a curry with the rugby on TV!" He laughed.

Sorry...Romeo and who? I asked quickly, ignoring the rest of what he was saying.

"Maui. Romeo and Maui are my two little Yorkshire Terriers," he smiled broadly. "They are such little monkeys...love 'em to bits...I'm such a softy when it comes to them".

I laughed forcefully, desperately trying to sound natural. But my adrenalin was pumping. *Maui? What the...? Seriously?*

"Well, good luck with your travels, and I'll see you again sometime...or not ...I guess...depending how far you go!" Tony smiled and put his hands in his pockets and looked to the floor briefly before picking up his tools. I closed the door and breathed deeply.

Baffled by the Universe with its mysterious ways and annoying timing, once he left, I sat and stared at the boats in the harbour from the living room windows. *A dog called Maui. I'd never known a dog called Maui. I guess it might not be so rare. Maybe it wasn't a sign. Maybe it was just coincidence.* I dismissed my thoughts about Tony as anything other than just a new acquaintance. I wasn't going to jump to the wrong conclusions and get carried away again. *I'll just block it out*, I decided. *It's for the best.*

CHAPTER 21

Malibu Dreams

Mum rented one of the ground floor corner flats. It was pure luck that she got it, rather than one upstairs or sandwiched between two others. I was so relieved when we moved her into the housing association block, that it came with a small garden. A light amidst the darkness. Gardening had always been a love of hers and I couldn't stand the thought of her not having somewhere to be outside or potter after dad died. When sadness struck and the small rooms became claustrophobic, she could, at least, get some fresh air and be among flowers. She had natural green fingers, as did her mother, and her grandmother, Fairy. Without using books, she found her own way around plants using trial and error and a lot of intuition to understand what they needed. They seemed to like her. Roses bloomed and small shoots shot up; vines wound around bamboo and cactus doubled in size. Even small creatures were attracted to her and I often laughed at how she was like Snow White in the woods, birds singing on her fence and squirrels even becoming tame, running up onto the decking to eat nuts that she left out for them.

I too, inherited the green fingers, although I didn't use them much. Somehow, I usually knew what to weed and how to cut back, despite being clueless to what any of the plants were. I'd also learnt, after years of war with my stomach, to listen to my body and feed it the vegetation it needed to be healthy and *happy* — as opposed to a particular size. Green leaf salad seemed to balance out my fluctuating weight. Herbs like coriander and parsley seemed to make my gut feel good.

On my day off from the chocolate shop I sat outside and put my face in the sun. The neighbour upstairs started shouting at the TV which was on loud with the windows open, and I frowned momentarily before relaxing back into the warm rays. I looked around the garden, impressed with Mum's recent efforts. She'd planted different coloured pansies which were glowing in the daylight, and cleared the leaves off the stepping stones which led to the gate just a few metres away from the backdoor.

Seeing all the terracotta and blue glaze pots always reminded me of Nanny. She lived in a static caravan on a well-kept retirement park by the River Thames in Chertsey, and having spent most of her adult life on the move, her permanent garden was her pride and joy. I could almost hear her whistling continuously in that melodic way that only old people seem to be able to do; and almost smell the unique scent of sweet tomatoes in the tiny greenhouse, river moss in the air and a faint whiff of a cigarette, which she smoked as she picked and pruned. Occasionally, I *did* actually smell tobacco, even when I was indoors, where no one smoked, and no windows were open; a sign that she or someone else I loved from the spirit world was still nearby.

Snails were a constant battle; they were Nanny's enemy, but I secretly loved how they invaded like a friendly army, using watering cans as shelters and feasting on her wild strawberries. I remembered how, even though she had a garden full of plants, she still crammed succulents inside the caravan wherever she could. Only now, years after her death, did I realise that she was obviously a botanical witch. After Nanny died, Grandad lived on into his nineties but I only ever saw him at family gatherings. I went back to the caravan just once but everything felt different. Everything was so small and the magic had gone.

I thought about her mother, Fairy, and wondered what it would have been like to know her in the physical. She lost her husband at war and it broke her heart. The trauma went to her bones, eventually killing her young too. He was in the Navy. I might have known that she would be in love with a man of the sea; her soulmate, I suspect. At Grandad's funeral, my Uncle pulled me to one side and said he had something for me. Out of a piece of tissue, he produced an unusual ceramic medallion.

"I found this when I cleared out Mum and Dad's caravan," he said. It was rough, unsymmetrical, with a small hole at the top and obviously hand-crafted. "Look at what's on it," he pointed. I looked down at the clay disc and gasped. Carved into the front was a woman in the sea, pouring water from a vase. Although you couldn't see below her hips it looked like she had the top of a mermaid tail. "I'm not sure what it is; only that it belonged to Mum's mum and it just popped out of nowhere," he smiled. "I have a feeling it's supposed to be with you".

When I researched the origin of the coin, it turned out to be something which mothers put over their newborn baby's belly buttons once the umbilical cord was cut, to keep them neat and tidy. They threaded a ribbon or string through the hole in the clay and tied it around the baby to keep it in place. It's likely that all of Fairy's and Nanny's children would have worn it, and that Fairy's husband must have made it while he was away at sea. The history behind it made it all the more special. I couldn't think of anything more magical than a mermaid relic, made by a seaman, which held the energy of newborn babies.

"Thank you so much," I hugged him. He had no idea how much it meant to me. To me, this was another major sign. A sign that I was on the right track. A message through the ether from Fairy, telling me to share my story.

That night, before bed, I meditated and had some sort of out-of-body experience. Fairy came to visit me. Anyone would say I fell asleep and it was *just a dream*, but it was much, much more than that and I knew it. She didn't have an appearance as such, more of a presence. I could sense her, smell her, hear her; even dissolve *into* her. I could feel every single one of the atoms in my body, vibrating and moving around, making it suddenly so easy to comprehend that I—like everything on the planet— was made up purely of energy; that Fairy was too, and she still existed, only, in a different dimension which most humans couldn't see...or had forgotten how to see.

The air turned warm and I heard quiet trees rustling and water trickling, despite being indoors. I could smell lavender and bergamot, and my closed eyelids saw brightness. Sensing her energy close in around me, as if being in her embrace, she shared wisdom with me in a language without words. She told me not to be afraid of my desires, even if they seemed illogical or impulsive. She told me that others may not understand my actions, but I mustn't allow them to push me off my path. She said that controlling men wasn't the way to get respect from them; neither was seeking out payback from them. She advised me not to put up barriers to love, just because I had been hurt by it in the past. Most of all, she encouraged me to show my true self; that hiding parts of me would only ever lead to disappointment and unfulfillment.

As my eyes popped open and I came out of my meditation, I lost all sense of time and space. For a good minute I was floating in beautiful nothingness; my body, weightless. In that moment I had the strongest knowing that and I would never actually die — not in the way we learn it; that the atoms of my body and the soul inside, would simply move on… into another form, becoming one with the Universal energy. I sat and stared at nothing, trying to absorb the experience. I breathed slowly, using the inhale and exhale to process the new knowledge. I'd learnt in a workshop once, that breath — our life force — is the key to deal with anything. Bit by bit my consciousness came back to earth and I felt the heaviness again. I would never forget what had just happened. I was changed forever. I laid down and allowed myself to drift into sleep, trying hard to get back to the place where Fairy was.

I woke with a shock. I thought I could hear a knocking on the door... continuous knocking, banging, getting louder and louder. But it stopped as soon as my eyes opened, as if waking up had answered it. Then I heard words.

"You know what you have to do," said a deep, calm and certain voice buried somewhere below my abdomen. I froze. A rush of memories and feelings flooded my whole being. The block I'd implemented, burst open.

Fuck! I thought. *Yes...I do.*

My heart had whispered to me, from the day I left Sonia's, that I needed to tell Tony how I felt. But my rational voice berated me for immediately thinking about another man, when the tears from the last one were barely even dry. *Have a fucking break Char!* My inner Miss Rational scorned. *How about just chilling out for a while?* She said sarcastically. Miss Rational liked to remind me of why pursuing this man would be a bad decision: He was nothing like I imagined my life partner to be. He was approaching a divorce, he had a teenage daughter, he was almost twenty years older than me, he lived across the Channel, he used to be a police officer, he probably frowned upon people like me who lived their lives in a nomadic and unplanned way, he might cringe at my spiritual beliefs, he could be shocked by my sexuality, he might be disgusted by my highly controversial job in London.

However, my heart was having none of her negativity and the whispers gradually turned into shouts. My heart told me that I must be more open-minded if I was to find true love; that it may come in a different package to what I might be expecting; that if I wanted things to be different, then I needed to start doing things differently. Against all reasoning, I had to speak to him. I had to tell him how I was spellbound when I met him; I had to tell him how I'd felt like I'd known him all my life—maybe even in past lives; I had to tell him that when I looked in to his eyes, I saw me; I had to get this feeling out of me before I imploded. *But what if it went down like a lead balloon?* I worried. When I thought about it, though, I realised I'd spent the last decade learning lessons the hard way; it seemed neither here nor there whether I learnt one more now.

As I remembered the strange experience I'd had with Tony, it dawned on me that this could be what it felt like to meet your soulmate. I'd read about extraordinary 'soul recognition' and 'twin flame' encounters. *What if he was, in fact, my soulmate and I didn't do anything about it? Would he seek me out? What if we were soulmates but he didn't realise yet? Or what if I had it completely wrong?* We had made friends on Facebook, but I had consciously decided not to make any further contact with him when I came back to the UK, in fear of getting carried away. When Sonia started a message between the three of us, to thank us both for our help with babysitting and shelf-installation, I said a few words but then later left the group chat. *What if he thought I didn't like him?* Never before did I feel so strongly that life was too short to wait or hold your tongue about important things.

I'm generally not someone who needs stimulants or relaxants to get me in the right state of mind, but at that moment I felt the need for something to calm my nerves. I searched for alcohol but Mum rarely drank and all I could find was an old bottle of Malibu at the back of a cupboard full of tins. It was probably ancient; from a time when *Club Tropicana* was still in the charts and George Michael was still wearing *those* white Speedos. He's probably still wearing them in heaven now … (I love you George, RIP. Actually, I hope you're not resting, I hope you're partying with David Bowie…and Prince … in those white speedos.)

The Malibu had turned to syrup with crust forming around the top and I was suspicious that the volume of alcohol may have tripled, with its extra fermenting time while being tucked behind the chicken soup, but it would have to do. I poured the last dregs out in to a glass and drank it down. Sitting upright on the sofabed, I grabbed my laptop. Hands poised over the keypad, in a nervous, coconutty rum haze I found Tony on Facebook and opened a new message tab.

Hi Tony... I wrote, and then paused. *What was I doing? WHAT ON EARTH was I doing? If I was to say these words, I couldn't then, un-say them.*

Fuck it. I concluded. I'd done this with Nancy and amazing things had come out of that message.

'Hi Tony.... I'm not going to beat around the bush...I'm just going to tell you what I want to say – straight up.

In a few gutsy paragraphs, I told him simply that I'd sensed a strong connection when I first met him and that, for whatever reason, I felt we needed to be in contact. I told him I totally respected the fact that he was going through a separation and it needn't be any more than a friendship. I kept it concise; my heart had no energy left for over-explaining. And I kept it honest; my heart had no energy left to hide the truth.

Feeling a huge weight lift from my shoulders as I finished the message, I closed my laptop and curled up under the duvet. Whatever I had done, was done now. Whatever he thought, was out of my control. Whether he responded or not—and whatever he wrote back—was up to him. I breathed deeply and the butterflies in my stomach closed their wings temporarily as I hit the pillow.

An hour later, I woke up. My body remained still as it slowly came out of subconsciousness. My eyes flicked open wide at the sudden memory of what I'd written. An arm shot out of the covers to reach for my phone and check Facebook. I looked to see if I'd just *dreamt* that I had actually sent an email to a man I'd known for a total of about four hours, telling him that I thought he might be my Soulmate—or something to that effect.

No, I hadn't dreamt it. Yes, I had said all that. And… *fuck!* …he'd replied already.

You know when you get a message—an important one—and you can't read it properly because you're so scared and excited at once? You keep reading the same line over and over, and you get glimpses of words on the lines below, but you kind of put off reading further, in some sort of attempt to draw out the joy… or delay the disappointment. That's what I was doing.

I think it took me fifteen minutes to read about ten lines. I needn't have been scared; the reply was a good one. In a well-scripted message, Tony said that he had felt the same. We were on the same page.

He'd assumed I wouldn't be interested for a number of reasons, least of which, I'd told him I was planning on going away again. He had clocked my eyes straight away too, but used his police poker face to stay neutral and calm. He so wanted to say something that day when we said goodbye at Sonia's door, but resisted.

From that night on we began to write to each other. I told him that I had been through so many relationships and so much heartache that I just couldn't deal with anything but absolute honesty. We promised each other to be open about everything, and to tell the truth about who we were, no matter what. If something clashed between us— better we knew now than later. We agreed on a fundamental foundation: that life was too short to hold back or to pretend to be happy. We learnt so much about one another in those emails. For days-on-end we discussed everything from past relationships to our hopes for a future one; from work life to dream projects; from life as a single person to marriage and children; books and films; music and art; religion and spirituality; death and afterlife; sex and loyalty; money and magic; fears and vulnerabilities; hilarious experiences and deepest, darkest secrets. He told me he was a Scorpio. Of course. I told him all there was to know about me, no holds barred.

Who knew what would happen next, but life just got a whole lot more exciting. Before exchanging secrets with Tony, I'd started to wonder if maybe those nay-sayers were right; that I was 'living in a dream world' by thinking I could find someone who shared my unconventional views and my big desires. Now, it actually became a very possible reality that this person *could* exist… and I may have just found him. It felt unbelievably good to show someone *all* of me, not just the socially acceptable bits. There was nothing to hide anymore. Nothing to fear.

Over the next month, when it seemed like we'd written more words than our hands could handle, we picked up the phone. And when it seemed like we'd spoken more words than our mouths could speak, we arranged to meet back on the island. When we finally reunited after weeks of anticipation, our eyes met in the Arrivals Lounge and the nerves melted away. We hugged, held on tight, and it felt like coming home. I could feel the wheels of my life literally changing speed and direction from the moment we joined. I knew that things were taking an extraordinary turn.

That week I stayed at a friend's house. Tony and I met up each day, and each evening we went separate ways. It was a refreshing start a relationship for me. I'd never been with a guy who I hadn't ended up in bed with after the first few dates. He was a gentleman and he wanted to do things right. Everthing was so different already. And I liked it.

I went back to the England with a heart full of sadness to be leaving Tony, and leaving the sea, but also a heart full of joy, knowing that I would be returning. I was on a mission; nothing would keep me from my soulmate now. I spoke to my manager Claire, who was nothing but happy for me to be going off on a new adventure. I organised a room to rent in Jersey, and I put word out to people I knew on the island that I would be taking art commissions again. For a few more weeks I worked at the chocolate shop, I kept myself busy, and I burnt off excited energy by running and cycling along the canal. It wasn't like being by the sea, but it was water and it would suffice.

Nearing my time to fly back—knowing this time I'd be staying—I went out on my bike for one last ride. The canal near mum's flat had seen me through all the good and bad. We moved house a number of times during my childhood but we were never far from one of the many entrances which led to the River Thames. From eleven years old I'd cycled along the canal to school; during my turbulent puberty I'd hang out with my mates under the bridges; when I met my best friend Lara we'd spend the whole summer whizzing to and from each other's houses via that route; every time I had returned from travels around the world; every time my poor mum had taken me back in after relationship break-ups; every time I had come home to share my happy stories and share time with my family, I had always visited that waterway which connected me to London—my beloved city. It drank my tears, felt my pain, soothed my anger, saw my smiles, heard my laughter and listened to my thoughts for years.

On a beautiful spring day, crisp and sunny, I came to one of my favourite spots. A little footbridge over one of the locks where you could stand and admire all the multi-coloured houseboats lining the side. I stopped to take one more look at the familiar view which changed so much with the seasons. I noticed someone was playing a trombone in one of the houses nearby as I rested my bike on the large wooden black and white peg of the lock. As I stood there, water pouring through the dam like an egg timer, birds sung all around as if to call me away. The trombone in the distance played a tune resembling some sort of End Theme, and light shone through the small archway of the bridge onto the water in a semi-sphere, like the moon building her way to fullness—a symbol of completion. The dappled sun on the overhanging trees created nature's own mirror ball. It felt like a magical dance hall at the last song of the night. I knew this was the end of one part of my life... and just the beginning of another.

CHAPTER 22

The Many Facets of Me

Two and a half years later

"Let's pull our crackers," Tony said, just before we were about to tuck into our food. Knife and fork poised over my roast potato which was gleaming with delicious gravy, I stopped regretfully, my mouth watering, and looked up. Everyone glanced at each other for confirmation.

"Yeah, ok…Good idea…Why not? …Sure," was the unanimous family answer. I picked up the cracker at the top of my place mat.

"Shall we cross arms?" Tony's sister Liz asked, suggesting that we did it the traditional way of a cracker in each hand, making a chain around the table.

"NO! ...no," Tony answered abruptly, "Let's just do one each…it's less complicated," he said.

I looked at her and shrugged; *I wasn't sure how complicated crackers could be, but…whatever.* I put his slightly tense mood down to the stress of catering for nine hungry adults. We had decided to invite everyone to our place for Christmas lunch that year. Tony had been perfecting his Sunday roast for some time, and felt that it would be fairly easy to just add a few more mouths to the table. I was happy to help but he insisted on doing the all the cooking while I acted as kitchen porter to keep things flowing smoothly. It turned out that six extra mouths, was actually quite a lot; it's amazing how many pints of gravy and piles of parsnips one family can get through.

Bangs started to go off and the dogs legged it to the safety of the kitchen with ears back and tails down. *Oohs* and *Aahs* and laughter began to fill the room as tiny flimsy toys, paper crowns and crap jokes were revealed. I turned to Tony on my left, but he was busy inspecting his brother-in-law's plastic helicopter. I spun around to Liz on my right, "Would you?" I asked, pushing my cracker her way.

"Of course," she said, grasping the end. *Bang!* "Oh… you won!" she laughed, turning back to face her eldest son as he poured wine into her glass. I tipped my cracker upside down to see what unexciting contents it held. Nothing came out. *What?* I made a double chin, baffled. *Oh great, I got a dud one. Typical,* I thought, I knew I should have spent more money on decent ones instead of buying the cheapest pack from Amazon. I brought it up to my face and peered inside like a telescope. Something *was* in there, but it was stuck. I poked my fingers in and pulled on a piece of card which had wedged itself across the diameter of the tube. When it dislodged I realised it was a brown parcel tag, and as I pulled it, something which was tied to the string, plopped out. I held the tag while the mystery object swung from it like a pendulum. My heart skipped. I looked at the tag which had writing on it.

'Char, will you marry me?!' It read, in Tony's handwriting. I slid my hand down the string and held a ring. My heart skipped. A beautiful gold ring with a cluster of, what looked like, diamonds.

I looked up and everyone was still chatting and laughing and starting to tuck into their full plates. I looked to my left and found Tony, watching me with a smile. *Really?* Was all I could say; my head was spinning.

"Yes," he laughed quietly. Remembering that we were in the middle of a Christmas lunch, I realised that this wasn't going to be an intimate moment; this was something to be shared. He pulled the ring box out of his pocket and pushed it in front of me. I looked around the table again and held up my parcel tag.

"I think I got a different gift in my cracker to everyone else!" I said with a big toothy grin, assuming that they must all have been in on the surprise. But no one heard me properly or could see what I was holding. A few heads turned in my direction. I dangled it higher and raised my voice one level. "I said… I think I got a better gift in my cracker than you lot!" I laughed.

"What?"

"No way!"

"Oh wow!"

The room erupted with happy noises. I looked at my mum who was sitting opposite, across large the table and she put her hands to her cheeks. "Oh my god!" she cried. "I can't believe it!" Tears filled both our eyes.

"You all knew about this, I take it?" I said, thinking how well they had all kept the secret.

"No. No idea. Not at all," they all replied.

"So, will you give me an answer?" Tony said, looking uncharacteristically shy. In all the commotion, I'd forgotten that I was actually supposed to answer.

This explained why he had been so flustered all morning. There he was, trying to organise a perfect lunch, trying not to forget anything, all the while knowing he had a proposal to make too. The poor man was a wreck.

I'd known from the first week were together that I would marry him. I'd never had a doubt in my mind. And we often talked about life in terms of 'when we were married'. It was just a given for us both. But I had sort of forgotten that there would be a proposal. And I hadn't expected it to be now, at Christmas, in front of the family. I suppose if ever I'd thought about it, I imagined it would happen while we were on holiday or something. But this was perfect. Simple. Natural.

"Yes! Of course! Yes, I will marry you". I threw my arms around him and buried my head into his shoulder, tears suddenly flowing without warning. Everyone cheered and laughed and cried while I stayed there, unable to move until Tony prised me off and gave me a small kiss.

"It's Edwardian," he said. "The ring...it's Edwardian. I thought you'd prefer a vintage piece. Something with history...something with a story".

"It's absolutely stunning," I said, barely able to speak without bursting into tears again. I hadn't expected I would be so emotional in this situation.

Since we'd met, life had been extraordinary. Tony was kind, loving and generous without bounds. He had the enthusiasm and energy of a schoolboy, and the excitement and passion of a teenager. He was loyal to everyone and everything he cared about, and reliable without exception. The positive attitude I'd spent years cultivating, nurturing, growing and harvesting, came naturally to him; it was his default. We talked and laughed for hours, we shared our biggest dreams, we worked in the garden and re-decorated parts of the house, we laid in the sun and enjoyed comfortable silence. We escaped the island and had fun-filled weekends in London—a city he adored too, and we went on French road-trips, Tony confidently finding and communicating his way around the country due to years of family trips, boys' holidays and stints over there with the police. I sat in the passenger seat of the two-seater with the roof down and watched him in awe; *how had I found someone so wonderful?* I did know how, but I almost couldn't believe it. I devoured every minute that we spent together.

However, at times, it had been more challenging than I ever could have imagined. Tony's divorce had pulled and pushed me in ways I never expected or experienced. Forgotten fears and old beliefs resurfaced, taking over my mind like weeds. I began to question if it really was possible to trust a man, after all I'd witnessed. While cleaning the house I'd open cupboards which were stacked with another woman's things, left items looking like they'd not long been used. I'd stumble across drawers full of old wedding and baby albums, and happy holiday photos which looked almost present-day. My insecurities went wild. I had no children of my own to love — or love me unconditionally. I had not known the joy of bringing a baby into the world, as Tony had experienced with his ex-wife; we would never have that unique bond that they shared. And even though their daughter was an adult and lived with us, being a good father, he would never fully cut ties with her mother. I had to accept that she would be in our lives some way or other. I could not pretend his past didn't exist.

There were no relatable guidebooks on this stuff; no online forums which answered my questions. I didn't know anyone in my peer group or family who'd experienced the same circumstances as ours. I found myself asking what my role was within this broken — but still so attached — family unit. My head raged, angry that I should feel like an intruder in their house, mortified that I, a free-spirited person who still felt like a teenager herself, might be seen as some evil stepmother stereotype. I hadn't set out to intrude, I didn't want to be a replacement. I'd simply fallen in love with a man who longed to be loved unconditionally.

Usually, I would have been tempted to flee; it was so much easier to leave than to face the discomfort. *Why should I put up with feeling out of place when I could just find a guy who had no past life? Why should I bother with a man who had other priorities, when I could meet someone who would make ME his world?*

But I loved Tony more than anything and I wasn't going to lose him now that I'd found him. Fleeing wasn't an option anymore; I had to make *myself* my world. It wasn't anyone else's job. Maybe, within this kind human, there was more than enough to go around. Maybe, like a child, I needed to learn to share. This had been my problem...my pattern. I was always looking for someone to complete me... make me their queen. When the reality was, I had to complete myself; I had to be my own queen. Tony stood steadfast, never giving in into my doubts about him, never reacting to my unpredictable moods or meltdowns, never fighting back to my pointed finger and accusations. He simply continued to love me and remained unchanged, showing that he was a good man who had nothing to prove or justify. The truth was, I knew little about the complexities of marital separation, or the affect it had on dependants of any age. A dusty old tuxedo and an out-of-date bridal dress were the only black and white things about divorce.

My mind was stubborn though, and wasn't easily persuaded to let go of the old stories that I'd told myself for years about men and my worth. But letting go was crucial if I wanted to keep stepping into a better version of myself. Let go, I must, if I wished to keep rising, be my highest self and fulfil my wildest dreams. I had achieved so much already in my life by pushing myself out of the comfort zone again and again; being alone in the world had taught me to trust in the face of poverty and fear; I found those situations easy now and wasn't challenged by them anymore. But now I needed to learn new lessons; I needed to learn how to stick at something and not just leave when it got tough. I needed to learn to see things from all angles, not just mine.

With time, faith and daily practice of mindfulness, the negative thoughts slowly dropped away bit by bit and new constructive ones replaced them. Like a computer rebooting, reprogramming and upgrading, I saw my body as a machine which needed regular finetuning; and my soul as the battery which needed a constant, steady flow of power. Without either, I would run down, explode or stop functioning.

As always, I had to work the answers out alone, the only way I knew how. My mum always used to say to me, "You don't make anything easy for yourself, do you, poppet?" She was right; something in me always wanted to figure things out the hard way. I guess that's just who I was: curious, philosophising, always digging for the core. In the end, I had to look to myself for the love I sought. I had to call upon those in the Spirit world for support when there was no one in the physical who could clear the confusion. At times, when I was all out of ideas, I'd always go back to the simplest plea to the Universe:

"Please help me to see the truth".

It was my mantra when I became overwhelmed or disillusioned. And somehow, a vision or something or someone would always come along, or happen, or shift. When I had no energy left for positive thought, there was something so magical and beautiful about a simple prayer. An absolute surrender to the thing that is bigger than us. The thing which makes intricate flowers bloom and tiny creatures with brains and hearts run around or fly; and snowflakes with no two the same, and tsunamis, and multicoloured sunsets, and mirror-like lakes and life-taking earthquakes.

I had spent most of my life feeling like I didn't belong; it was time to make *home,* something which was in *me*, not somewhere I only ever visited or borrowed or tagged along to. I didn't *need* a man—or a marriage—but I did want to share my journey with someone. I wanted to join forces with another soul and walk through life together. I wanted a partner in crime to take risks with and watch each other's backs. I wanted a friend to laugh with, a lover to love with. I just didn't want to lose myself in the process.

No wonder then, that I was emotional when Tony proposed. I knew all too well that a ring, an engagement and marriage held absolutely no guarantees of anything. But to me, it symbolised an unbreakable circle of strength and honesty, which flowed round and around, through me, Tony, my stepdaughter-to-be, and the dogs... no matter what. Through good times, hard times and indifference. We may not have been a conventional family, but we were a team, of sorts.

Gathering myself, I looked at my pile of turkey, carrots and roast potatoes. "I suppose we better eat!" I said, my tummy still feeling a little tingly but my appetite slowly coming back.

"A toast!" Tony's brother-in-law shouted, bringing in a bottle of champagne and filling glasses. "To Tony and Char!"

Within two and a half years I'd gone from living a nomadic, single, frugal existence, to living in a seaside home with Tony, his daughter Billie, and the two little Yorkshire Terriers. I then somehow managed to acquire a tattoo apprenticeship, complete it and open my own studio. I was now a business-owning, tax-paying, family-meal-making, dog-walking, Jersey resident. A lot had changed in a short time. It was so different to the day-by-day, place-by-place, eating-on-the-go, walking-around-naked, painting-all-night life that I'd come from.

Although I didn't know what it was as it was happening, I realise now that there was a long and necessary period of adjustment, which often felt very unnerving. It seemed to take an eternity to acclimatise to the massive changes in my life which, in contrast, had occurred in record time. Tony made me so incredibly happy but I needed to find a balance within it all; the cells in my body needed to catch up with external events. I wanted a relationship and loved my extended family, but I still needed freedom too. Writing became a big part of my adjustment process — and my sanctuary. Almost down to the day, it took me the same amount of time to finally find my groove with everything in this new life, as it did to complete my book. It was four years since we first met that day in Sonia's house, and as I worked on my last chapter, Tony's divorce finally came through, and Billie announced that she would be moving out and buying a house with her boyfriend. The year 2020 heralded a new phase for all of us.

~~~

The first time I came to Tony's house, I met the dogs. But as any dog-lover understands, they very quickly became more than just pets. They were like little people; babies that melted your heart and never grew up. Romeo was a senior, yet tiny, pooch with a big personality. It's safe to say that he was closer in size to a kitten. Walks were a never-ending task of keeping him from picking fights with other hounds that were twenty times bigger; he had the classic small-man-syndrome. He was father to the other dog, who was almost double the size of him. She was like an angel: affectionate, obedient, and often looked human in some peculiar way. She'd sit with me while I was writing, come over to me when I was upset and explore with me on the beach. Amidst the challenges of fitting into a new family and a new way of life, she was a constant source of unconditional and unjudgmental love; always excited to see me; happy for this unfamiliar woman to be in her home. Given to Billie when she was just little, she unpredictably chose a name for the puppy which was a word she didn't yet know, but which she'd heard once and loved: 'Maui'.

On the day I moved in, feeling a wet nose nudge my hand as I emptied my modest possessions into the house, I looked at Maui and laughed; *Maui...my secret code word,* I thought, *...turned out to be a dog...of course!* Signs from the Universe so often came with a sense of humour and a nonsensical approach. And my 'Maui code' had led me, not only to my soulmate, but to an even more open mind and a deeper compassion. Tony and Romeo, Billie and Maui; two dads and two daughters, trying their best to navigate unchartered territory. In totally unforeseen circumstances, I fell into their lives—and in love—with all four of them.

Later that evening, once all our guests had gone home and we'd filled and emptied the dishwasher twice, I opened the back door and felt cold air flood in. I grabbed a blanket from the cupboard where we kept beach bags and sun hats and wrapped it around my shoulders before stepping outside. It was dark, but brighter than normal; a full moon shone fiercely and illuminated the garden. I looked out to sea. The moonlight left a mercury-like top layer on the water, mesmerising in the way that it rippled and shimmered continuously.

"Back in a minute," I called to Tony who was still clearing up. "Just going to the seawall".

"Ok mermaid!" he called back, "Don't get washed away, it's a really high tide tonight".

I walked to the end of the garden and pushed the small gate which opened onto the walkway. The glow of string bulbs which lined the path all the way from town to St Aubin, was barely needed with the big white orb in the sky; and despite being Christmas night, I still looked left and right, out of reflex, before crossing the cycle track. Any other time of day, wheels would be whizzing past on the popular promenade. We had to be especially careful with Maui and Romeo that they didn't get mowed down by bikes or skateboards. Arriving safely at the seawall, I leant my elbows on the solid structure which had originally been put in place by the Germans during the Occupation for defence against tanks. The waves lapped right up to the wall; an hour earlier they would have been spraying over the top, but the tide had just begun her retreat.

Apart from the sea, it was quiet. I breathed in deeply and smiled. It had been such a busy, magical and fun day, but it was good to finally stop talking and just listen. On closer inspection, the silver on the water now looked more like millions of little mirrors or crystals moving around. I reached my arms over the wall to stretch my back and a glimmer on my hand caught my eye. I had momentarily forgotten about my new ring. Like the moonlit waves, the diamonds were twinkling, beckoning me to watch them and get lost in their allure.

When I was younger, I never saw the appeal of diamonds. I thought people only wanted them because they were expensive and flashy and proved a level of wealth or relationship status. Thinking back to my engagement on my sixteenth birthday, the diamond chip ring was as much as my boyfriend could afford, and I secretly would have preferred a turquoise stone or lapis lazuli anyway. But now I understood differently. Learning how diamonds formed over billions of years, starting out as carbon, experiencing intense heat and pressure under the earth; and the way in which they were teased out of their exterior which looked like nothing more than dirty old rock, was quite mind-blowing. These little gems had a whole lot of history, had gone through a whole load of tough times to get to where they were, and in the end, only showed their true glorious selves after some serious TLC. I resonated with that. After much cutting back and polishing, the result was a multi-faceted natural beauty; every angle offered a slightly different reflection within her; one face — a million expressions. Moving my hand from side to side to admire the jewellery which felt so special and so precious, I simultaneously stared into the gems and into the water. The sparkles merged into one another.

The diamond had been on an arduous passage into light...to being found... to blossoming into its highest form. I thought about my own journey. All the magic and beauty that had come out of the darkness in my own life. Between the twinkling reflections of the sea and of the ring, I started to see reflections of my past. Every time I had chosen to go somewhere new or do something wild or push my limits to the very edge, like the diamond, I was carving my whole being into a different version of myself. Doing so allowed me to explore yet another one of the many facets of who I was. If I had only experienced one direction, then I would never have seen all those other sides to myself. I would never have discovered just how much I was capable of.

My first boyfriend made a catalytic comment about 'acting above my station,' suggesting that it was a bad thing to think of myself as someone who could do something special or different. But we all have something special and unique within us, and we must let it be seen; it's just a matter of carving it out. When my dad died, I felt the fleetingness and fragility of life and it stayed with me every day. Life is too short — and too long — not to pursue happiness, or to act like a victim when we have so much power. It is never too late to start something or start again. When I left Dan, I thought I'd made a huge mistake. But he went on to have a big family, which he'd always wanted, and I decided not to have children, which turned out to be exactly what I wanted — I just didn't know it back then, I was too busy aiming for what I thought a young woman *should* be aiming for. Bulimia brought me to some of my darkest times but taught me to listen to my body. It was crying out to be listened to and loved for what it was. With Adam, I went through deep pain and was forced to find true self-love; I also found writing which changed my life forever. And with Will, I realised that hiding parts of yourself, only leads to life withholding its magic from you. I didn't need my soldier 'hero'. I was my hero.

I could have done so many things in my life differently and suffered a lot less. But suffering showed me a compassion which I don't think I would have known otherwise. Pain cracked my heart and my mind open, and made me understand other people better. As we hear in so many quotes, fables and stories: the treasure is always hidden in the deepest holes; stars can only shine if there is darkness; no mud no lotus. At each difficult or strange fork in my path, life gave me a chance to take a new tangent and explore a new area.

It's not that I think a woman has to sell her body, or travel with no money, or do anything else involving high risk in order to live; nor do I promote it. I just believe that you must do what *you* feel called to do, to set yourself free. Those are the things that I had to do at those times in my life. Now, other things give me feelings of freedom. And in the future, they will change too. I believe that by following my ever-evolving callings, whatever they are, leads me to joy and purpose. I don't trust that everything will go *my* way. I trust that things will go the way that's *best* for me in the end. I haven't got it all figured out; I'd be worried if I thought I had. I have these clairsentient abilities, but I am easily clouded. Fear, lust, busyness, impatience and a rebellious spirit often take over. Finding a balance between my spirituality and my physical, practical, human existence here on the planet is an ongoing task for me; I can easily get lost in the non-physical realm. As the tree of life symbol shows (roots in the ground, branches reaching skyward), I have to work hard to make solid foundations while reaching for the light, to keep that equilibrium.

I don't expect people to agree with everything I've done. All I know is that everything I've done is a part of who I am, and I refuse to be ashamed of who I am. *We are what we are*, and denying it only ever ends in a kicking and screaming of the soul. 'Good' and 'bad' are mostly just labels… descriptions… judgements, depending on the person doing the judging, their country, background, personal experience, state of happiness, religious beliefs. Nature is not 'good' or 'bad'. It both destroys and builds, nurtures and neglects; it is the ultimate dark and light. And we are nature too. We are dark and light. One cannot exist without the other.

I realise now that I was always at war with parts of myself. Some parts I was proud of, some I was ok with, but some parts I just wouldn't accept or show to others in fear of seeming strange or unaccepted. The part which was too sexual, the part which lost all energy when doing things that didn't make my soul happy. The part which — despite always being offered good jobs — couldn't hold them down because I needed to work for myself. The part which needed to rest a lot, the part which needed plenty of alone and quiet time. The part which I thought was too flabby or disproportioned or ugly. The part which needed to do passion projects and let new ideas form, despite not getting paid for them. The part which turned away from money and possessions so I could appreciate what I already had. The part that needed to dig my hands in plant pots instead of hitting the keypad. The part that needed to process feelings and emotions which came up when I was going through big life transitions, instead of simply 'keeping calm and carrying on'. The part which needed to observe nature, watch the sky change colour, witness a tiny bird making a nest. The part which needed to commune with spirit and listen to the whispers and songs of my heart.

When I finally stopped feeling guilty for needing *inner* adventures over assets, and finally accepted all my 'flaws' and 'imperfections,' I noticed that I made far better… far more fruitful… far more lucrative… far more grounded… far more important… far healthier…far more successful decisions for the long-term, instead of just fighting fires every hour of every day. Over and above money and things and a 'perfect' image, it was always *time* and *self-love* which brought me the most freedom. And freedom brought me happiness.

I gazed at my left hand and wondered about the jewellery's past—and its future. *Who wore it before me? Was she an artist too? Did she love the ocean? Did she have freedom?* I looked up to the stars and prayed that the next girl to wear the ring would have the liberty to be her true self too.

Since being plucked from the bottom of that pool in Ibiza when I was a baby, I seemed to struggle to ever feel at home. But I have learnt to find home in myself and in the illusive thing that is bigger than us. Life *can* be what you wish it to be. If you just dare to do things differently. If you just dare to go deep.

Author Bio

Having always been an artist, Charlene currently runs her one-woman tattoo studio on the tiny Channel Island of Jersey. She has hundreds of female clients who open up to her, as they would a therapist, telling her their fears, fantasies, sorrows and regrets. When she shares her stories with them, she instantly feels their bodies relaxing under the needle. They are comforted and reassured to hear that they are neither strange or alone in what they are thinking, feeling or going through. She tells them that there is much magic to be found when life gets dark.

Growing up in South East England, London has a huge place in her heart, but she always knew she needed to be by the sea. Travelling across the globe and then moving to Jersey, she came and left over and over again, unsure whether to drop anchor or not, never really feeling like just one place was home. However, the island was where she found herself and subsequently, where she found her soulmate. Living with her fiancée, his daughter and two Yorkies, she realised that home is wherever the love is.

Please share your experience of reading
this book, using #imustbeamermaid

Instagram:
Charlene_Hickey_Mermaid

Thank You

———◆———◆———

Thank you for reading about my journey.

I really appreciate your feedback. Please leave me a review on Amazon so I can write more books like this and connect with more kindred spirits.

Love,

Charlene Hickey

xxx

Printed in Great Britain
by Amazon

54548515R00222